Edith Wharton's
The Age of Innocence

Edith Wharton's
The Age of Innocence

New Centenary Essays

Edited by
Arielle Zibrak

BLOOMSBURY ACADEMIC
LONDON • NEW YORK • OXFORD • NEW DELHI • SYDNEY

BLOOMSBURY ACADEMIC
Bloomsbury Publishing Plc
50 Bedford Square, London, WC1B 3DP, UK
1385 Broadway, New York, NY 10018, USA

BLOOMSBURY, BLOOMSBURY ACADEMIC and the Diana logo are trademarks of
Bloomsbury Publishing Plc

First published in Great Britain 2020

A catalogue record for this book is available from the British Library.

Library of Congress Control Number:2019949561

ISBN: HB: 978-1-3500-6554-3
          ePDF: 978-1-3500-6555-0
          eBook: 978-1-3500-6556-7

Typeset by Integra Software Services Pvt. Ltd.
Printed and bound in Great Britain

To find out more about our authors and books visit www.bloomsbury.com
and sign up for our newsletters.

Contents

List of Tables

Acknowledgments

David Avital and Lucy Brown, our editorial team at Bloomsbury, made working on this project a joy. The two anonymous readers of the volume proposal provided invaluable insight and feedback. Sharon Kim, Laura Rattray, Emily Orlando, Donna Campbell, and Meredith Goldsmith were all early supporters of the idea for this volume. We are very grateful to Bradley Stevens for allowing us to use his painting for a cover image (and for his thoughts on realism!) and to Sarah Blackwood for her insights into the occasion of the centenary. Thanks also to Nina McConigley, who connected us with Beth Nguyen. Trevor and Jonah Pederson lent much support to the editorial process. Lastly, we would like to express our gratitude to the Edith Wharton Society, an organization that has worked for almost forty years to keep Wharton scholarship vital, foster the careers of Wharton scholars, and inspire new generations of readers. This book is dedicated to its members past, present, and future.

Contributor Biographies

Shari Goldberg is Assistant Professor of English at Franklin & Marshall College and the author of *Quiet Testimony: A Theory of Witnessing from Nineteenth-Century American Literature* (Fordham University Press, 2013). She researches modes of human receptivity in US literature and culture and her work has been published in journals including *American Literature, Nineteenth-Century Literature, Paragraph,* and the *Henry James Review.* Her current project connects the psychology of suggestion to literary visions of personhood developed in turn of the century novels. In 2018–2019, she held a Boston Medical Library Fellowship in the History of Medicine.

Hildegard Hoeller is Professor of English at the College of Staten Island with an appointment in English and Women's Studies at the Graduate Center of the City University of New York (CUNY). She is the author of *From Gift to Commodity: Capitalism and Sacrifice in Nineteenth Century American Fiction* (University of New Hampshire Press, 2012) and *Edith Wharton's Dialogue with Realism and Sentimental Fiction* (University Press of Florida, 2000), as well as co-author with Rebecca Brittenham of *Keywords for Academic Writers* (Longman, 2004); she is also the editor of the Norton Critical Edition of Horatio Alger's *Ragged Dick* (2007). Her essays have appeared in *PMLA, American Literature, Studies in American Fiction, ESQ, American Literary Realism, African-American Review, Edith Wharton Review,* and other scholarly journals and edited collections. A former president of the Edith Wharton Society, Hoeller is currently editing the *Old New York* volume of the *Collected Works of Edith Wharton* (Oxford University Press) and is slated to be co-editor of the *Translations* volume of the same series.

Margaret Jay Jessee is Assistant Professor of English and Director of English Honors at the University of Alabama at Birmingham. Her work on Edith Wharton has appeared in *JML: A Journal of Modern Literature* and in *Edith Wharton: Critical Insights* (Salem Press, 2017). She is co-director of the

2020 conference sponsored by the Edith Wharton Society. Her other work has appeared in the journals *Arizona Quarterly*, *South Atlantic Review*, and *Nathaniel Hawthorne Review*, as well as in the edited collections *Nathaniel Hawthorne in Context* (Cambridge University Press, 2018) and *Liminality, Hybridity, and American Women's Literature: Thresholds in Women's Writing* (Palgrave-Macmillan, 2018). Her book, *Murderess to Doctress: The Affective Legacy of the Abortionist in Nineteenth-Century American Literature and Culture*, is forthcoming with Routledge Press.

Gabi Kirilloff is Assistant Professor of English at Texas Christian University, where she specializes in digital humanities, twentieth-century American literature, and new media studies. She has worked on several digital projects, including the *Willa Cather Archive*, the *Walt Whitman Archive*, and the Novel TM project. Her research has appeared in journals such as *Digital Scholarship in the Humanities (DSH)* and the *Journal of Cultural Analytics*. Much of Kirilloff's research uses digital tools and computational methods to explore the portrayal of gender in fiction.

Beth (Bich Minh) Nguyen is the author of the memoir *Stealing Buddha's Dinner* and the novels *Short Girls* and *Pioneer Girl*. Her work has received an American Book Award and a PEN/Jerard Award, among other honors, and has been featured in numerous anthologies and university and community reads programs. Nguyen was born in Saigon and grew up in Michigan, where her refugee family was resettled. She is a professor in the MFA Program at the University of Wisconsin, where she teaches fiction and creative nonfiction.

Virginia Ricard teaches American literature at the University of Bordeaux Montaigne in France. For the past ten years, the main focus of her research has been Edith Wharton. In 2012, she edited a special issue of *The Journal of the Short Story in English* on Wharton's short stories. Since then, she has published a number of critical essays on Wharton's work in both English and French: "Walking in Wartime: Edith Wharton's 'The Look of Paris'" (Palgrave, 2016), "La Conviction jubilatoire d'Edith Wharton," (Modernités, 2016), "Reading *The Age of Innocence* in France," and "An Unknown Letter from Edith Wharton to Minnie Bourget," both in the *Edith Wharton Review* (2017). More recently she has contributed chapters to *The New Wharton* (Cambridge University

Press, forthcoming 2019) and *L'Amérique au tournant: La place des États-Unis dans la littérature française entre 1890 et 1920* (Classiques Garnier, forthcoming 2019). In 2018, she published the first English translation of a little-known lecture Wharton had given in Paris ("America at War: Edith Wharton on the National Character in 1918," *Times Literary Supplement*, February 14, 2018).

Carol Singley is Professor of English at Rutgers University-Camden, where she teaches American literature and childhood studies. She is the author of *Edith Wharton: Matters of Mind and Spirit* (Cambridge University Press, 1995); co-author of *House of Mourning, House of Mirth* (Fahrenheit, 2013), and author of *Adopting America: Childhood, Kinship, and National Identity in Literature* (Oxford University Press, 2011). She has edited four books on Wharton: *The House of Mirth Casebook* (2003) and *A Historical Guide* (both Oxford University Press); *The Age of Innocence* (Houghton Mifflin, 2000); and *Ethan Frome* (Broadview, 2013). She is editor or co-editor of *Anxious Power: Reading, Writing, and Ambivalence in Narrative by Women* (SUNY, 1993), *The Calvinist Roots of the Modern Era* (New England, 1997), and *The American Child: A Cultural Studies Reader* (Rutgers University Press, 2003). She is General Editor of the thirty-volume *The Complete Works of Edith Wharton* (Oxford University Press) and past president of The Edith Wharton Society.

Margaret Toth is Professor of English and the director of the film studies minor at Manhattan College. Her research interests include late-nineteenth- and early-twentieth-century US literature, film, and adaptation studies. Her scholarship on Edith Wharton has been published in such journals as *Modern Fiction Studies* and the *Journal of Narrative Theory* and in the collections *Edith Wharton in Context* (ed. Laura Rattray) and *Edith Wharton and Cosmopolitanism* (eds. Meredith Goldsmith and Emily Orlando). She is editing *Hudson River Bracketed* (Volume 25) for the *Complete Works of Edith Wharton* (Oxford University Press). Her current book project, *After Innocence: Edith Wharton and Post-War Writings on Art and Faith,* is an intertextual study that focuses on the figure of the artist and forms of spirituality in Wharton's late works.

Arielle Zibrak is Assistant Professor of English at the University of Wyoming. Her research interests include American women writers, gender and sexuality studies, the *fin de siècle*, aesthetic theory, and the relationship between art and politics. She is currently at work on a monograph about the various ways in which the transatlantic reform realist novel was contested on aesthetic grounds in the late nineteenth and early twentieth centuries, and a book entitled *Guilty Pleasures* about the cultural history of women's genre fiction. Her essays and reviews have appeared in *Arizona Quarterly*, *ESQ*, *Criticism*, *Edith Wharton Review*, *ALH*, *The Baffler*, *The LA Review of Books*, and *The Toast*. She has also served on the Executive Board of the Edith Wharton Society.

Introduction: "Each Time You Happen to Me All Over Again"

Arielle Zibrak
University of Wyoming

This volume marks the centenary of the publication of Edith Wharton's *The Age of Innocence*, a novel that has been almost uniformly praised since its initial serialization in the *Pictorial Review* in 1920 and its receipt of the Pulitzer Prize for fiction the following year. At the time of its publication, William Lyon Phelps—a professor of literature at Yale, which would award Wharton an honorary doctorate of letters in 1923—wrote in his *New York Times* review of the novel: "Edith Wharton is a writer who brings glory on the name America, and this is her best book. After reading so many slipshod diaries called 'novels,' what a pleasure it is to turn the pages of this consummate work of art."[1] In the years since, it has appeared on almost every "Best American Novels" list, has been adapted to film, television, and theater multiple times, has inspired contemporary rewritings, and is regularly cited as a favorite text by present-day authors including Ta-Nehisi Coates, Roxane Gay, and Beth Nguyen, whose essay on reading *The Age of Innocence* as the teenage daughter of refugees concludes this volume.[2]

Though the past 100 years have brought few doubts regarding the merit of the novel as a work of art, they have brought curiously little celebration of what *The Age of Innocence* brings to the table in the form of social critique, literary innovation, or cultural significance. Published in a moment of high modernism—at the same time as works like Joyce's *Ulysses* and Fitzgerald's *This Side of Paradise*, and in the middle of the publication of Proust's epic *In Search of Lost Time*—*The Age of Innocence*, despite its obvious merits, has long been deemed a throw-back text both thematically and stylistically. For this reason, it is perhaps the most underrated highly rated novel in the history of American letters.

Such a paradox began with the controversy surrounding the choice of *The Age of Innocence* for the relatively new and prestigious Pulitzer Prize. The jury's first choice for the fourth recipient of the award in 1921 was Sinclair Lewis's *Main Street*, a work that indulged America's fixation with its own moment and the region of the country that was then known as the Middle West. If New York in the early 1920s seemed to Americans to be a relic of the past, with its connections to the conventions of the hierarchical European culture America was destined to escape, the Middle West was its egalitarian future. Set in Minnesota in the teens, *Main Street* was the epitome of literary cool for Americans at the end of that tumultuous decade. But it was Wharton, not Lewis, who emerged with the 1921 prize after the jury's decision was overturned by the board on the grounds that Wharton's novel did more to "uplift American morals." In a telegram to Lewis, Wharton herself lamented these terms:

> When I discovered that I was being rewarded—by one of our leading Universities—for uplifting American morals, I confess I did despair. Subsequently, when I found the prize shd [*sic*] really have been yours, but was withdrawn because your book (I quote from memory) had "offended a number of prominent persons in the Middle West," disgust was added to despair.[3]

Wharton later satirized this awards drama in the 1929 novel *Hudson River Bracketed*, wherein a "Pulsifer Prize" is awarded to a realist novel entitled "The Corner Grocery." As Meredith Goldsmith demonstrates, Wharton's position in relation to both prize juries and the literary marketplace is one that chafes at faddism—and the novel of "main street" was one such fad that seemed to promise endurance to many of her peers.[4] In her own 1927 essayistic consideration of "The Great American Novel," Wharton rejected the idea that the newly conceived dream of such a comprehensively representative work would have to be about middle America and mounted a convincing case for cosmopolitan fictions that depicted the United States as a new world power following the great war.[5] The international context, the historical setting, and the largely missed irony of the title of *The Age of Innocence* have led many readers—but not all—to assume it is a far tamer and less critically important work than it actually is. The actress Michelle Pfieffer, who starred as Ellen Olenska in the 1993 film adaptation by Martin Scorsese, acknowledged that

Scorsese, who had previously directed *Taxi Driver* (1976), *Raging Bull* (1980), *Goodfellas* (1990), and *Cape Fear* (1991)—films famous for their controversial violence—"described it as his most violent film."[6] The counter-intuitiveness of this claim aligns with many of the critical revelations realized in this volume: *The Age of Innocence* is set in a world where people rarely say what they mean, and what the novel itself appears to say about its greatest themes (history, modernity, internationalism, sexuality, and gender) undergoes, in these pages, a series of startling reversals.

As Hildegard Hoeller reveals in her essay in this volume, from the time of the composition of her first novel *Fast and Loose*, at the tender age of 14, Wharton's career is one that has always been plagued by a thwarted desire to shock. As Hoeller describes, earlier outline drafts of *The Age of Innocence* had the affair between Ellen and Newland explicitly consummated, which would of course have made a far greater splash in this regard than the final version that consigns the realization of the couple's erotic relationship to the subjunctive with the subtle gesture of Ellen returning an unused room key in a sealed envelope. The marketing of the novel in anticipation of its publication traded on this potential allure; Hoeller quotes a racy advertisement that appeared in *Publishers' Weekly* in 1920:

> Why was this American girl forced to leave her brutal Polish husband? Why did Ellen, Countess Alenska [*sic*], return to New York, seeking to forget? Whispers came all too soon that she had been compromised in the artistic continental society from which she had fled. But in the narrow New York society of the 1870s she was welcomed back, and the whispery of far off Europe ignored, until she and Newland Archer are swept together by mutual attraction, and the old, old question is renewed, shall she create a scandal just because she is unhappy?[7]

Despite such tantalizing promises, even readers at the time received the novel as an extraordinarily well-written teacup drama. Margaret Toth writes here of how Hollywood executives, eager to stave off charges of undue licentiousness, sought to adapt Wharton's novel because her name "would lend the film a level of respectability"—"Edith Wharton" was antonymous with scandal and excitement.

On the surface, *The Age of Innocence* is old-fashioned and even tame. Set almost entirely in the 1870s, among the coterie of long-established New

York families that Wharton was and still is most often associated with, it has traditionally seemed to readers more of a capital-V Victorian novel than a capital-M Modern one. Wharton was well aware of this public perception, writing to F. Scott Fitzgerald at the height of his fame: "To your generation, which has taken such a flying leap into the future, I must represent the literary equivalent of tufted furniture and gas chandeliers."[8] It was a formulation she must have particularly enjoyed; she reiterated it almost exactly to a journalist four years later: "[Mrs. Wharton] says that to the greener growths of her day, she must seem like a taffeta sofa under a gas-lit chandelier."[9] The double-voice of this self-critique is apparent, especially given its analogical content. Wharton made her name in publishing in 1897, with the design treatise *The Decoration of Houses,* co-authored with Ogden Codman. It is a work that polemically eschews the tufted-furniture design style of the Victorian age and advocates for its substitution with a return to the clean lines of eighteenth-century furnishings that lack "dust-collecting upholstery and knick-knacks" and a jettisoning of the "habit of lining chintz curtains and of tufting chairs [that] has done away with the chief advantages of a simpler style of treatment."[10] Wharton's redress for her undeserved "old-fashioned" reputation is a subtle reminder of her popular contributions to modern interior design—contributions that themselves engaged two time periods: a call to imagine a different future via a return to the previous century for inspiration. It's a move Wharton makes in *The Age of Innocence* as well. Despite its historical setting, the novel points far more to the future than the past, concluding with a section set twenty-six years after the main events of the plot, in which the protagonist Newland Archer muses on the changes modernity has wrought within his world from the invention of the telephone, to five-day cross-Atlantic voyages, to the laxity of social mores. In the final moments of the novel, Archer decides not to join his son Dallas on a visit to Ellen Olenska, the lost love of his youth that the 1870s plot of the novel chronicles, telling Dallas to relay a simple message to explain his absence: "say I'm old-fashioned: that's enough."[11] The novel's third-person narrator hews closely to Newland's perspective; his is the only consciousness the novel enters. Therefore, there has been a tendency to read Archer's old-fashionedness as the novel's, and to read the novel's as Wharton's. Margaret Jay Jessee, in her essay in this volume, suggests that Newland's consciousness is not to be read through but around. In Jessee's view, the bluntness of his insight is precisely what the novel critiques, though it is frequently mistaken for what the novel performs. In other words, the old-fashioned character at the center of the novel, whose dominant perspective practically makes him its narrator, paradoxically offers a depth of understanding of the novel's second time period (the twenty-six years later section) as well as its third: the future the novel anticipates.

The centenary occasion of this collection of essays itself, then, makes a Whartonian gesture: it asks us to consider both the period of the publication of the novel (1920) and what it has to tell us about our own moment (2020)—a date that seems fantastically removed from the early-twentieth-century modernity of quick steamer travel and landline telephones. Though the novel is largely celebrated for an almost scientific preservation of its past, it brings as much to bear on a consideration of 2020—a year that is only just yet to happen at the time of my writing—as it does on 1920, an age that Wharton was practically alone among major American novelists in examining with some degree of distance at the same moment of its unraveling through her return to the previous century.

In 1920, the nineteenth amendment to the constitution was ratified, ensuring the right of women to vote; the eighteenth amendment (also ratified that year) prohibited the consumption and sale of alcohol. On September 16, the Wall Street bombing of 1920, likely perpetrated by Italian anarchists, became the deadliest terrorist attack on US soil. In November 1920, the first commercially licensed radio station began broadcasting live results of the presidential election, a development Eric Burns identifies as "the birth of mass media."[12] In many ways, these events signal beginnings within a teleological view of history: progress toward gender equality, the growing need for regulation of intoxicating substances, the rise of terrorism, and a media-run political system. It's tempting to connect these developments to their twenty-first-century analogs: the Women's March following the election of President Trump and the birth of social media movements like #timesup and #metoo, the pharmaceutical drug crisis, rampant gun massacres, and the proliferation of Fox News—an outlet Nicole Hemmer calls "the closest we've come to having state TV."[13] As even this cursory list suggests, such historical nodes are related more thematically than sequentially.

Consider two images of women protestors from these two periods separated by a hundred years. In the first, taken on January 10, 1917, a group of women from the National Woman's Party, wearing long black coats and fashionable cloches, stand outside the White House wielding a hand-sewn banner that reads "Mr. President, How Long Must Women Wait for Liberty?" In the second, taken in 2016 at the Czarny protest against proposed abortion legislation, a Polish woman carries a sign made of cardboard on which she has affixed two pieces of 8.5 x 11 inches printer paper that reads: "I can't believe I still have to protest this fucking shit."[14] The Czarny protest image circulated widely on social media, resulting in many such similar signs carried by older protestors in the United States—indeed, in front of the White House—during the Women's March on Washington that took place on January 21, 2017. Such juxtaposed images suggest not a linear path forward but a circling back to the same problems in different guises and materials. Indeed, their very language resists a narrative of progress as the foundation of its protest. Wharton was likewise skeptical of modern utopian notions of progress; *The Age of Innocence* is the novel in which she most clearly performs this skepticism both thematically and formally.[15]

Because of this, *The Age of Innocence* is perhaps best read with its various time periods collapsed into one another as interrelated phenomena rather than distinctly arranged as a causal sequence.[16] Reading the novel in this way, its observations about individual and group psychology and the functioning of complex social systems become equally applicable to aspects of countless periods and settings. For example, 2020 is the year in which the Chinese government plans to enroll all of its citizens into a database that processes its "social credit system," wherein individuals will be given scores that rank them on the basis of their "goodness":

> [T]he score is built upon personal data including social status (education and professional background), credit history, social connections (including the credit score of one's social connections), and behavior patterns … befriending people with high scores while unfriending those with low scores would improve one's rating … [low scorers] would struggle to rent a car, find a job and might be publicly shamed.[17]

Most Western accounts have heralded this new system as the dawning of a dystopic age of communism wherein, in the words of American Vice President Mike Pence: "China's rulers aim to implement an Orwellian system premised on controlling virtually every facet of human life."[18] Bing Song, director of the Berggruen Institute's China Center, takes a more nuanced approach to understanding this system, suggesting that "a more appropriate term to describe the initiative is a 'social trust system,'" with "many measures ... intended to curb official corruption, tackle official dereliction and improve efficiency in enforcing court decisions, as well as punish unethical behaviors of professionals."[19] Such a description might equally apply to the code of conduct to which Newland Archer clings in *The Age of Innocence*. While the code of old New York may keep him from leaving his wife to pursue passion, its restrictive social system is one Archer ultimately embraces for what it prevents more than for what it upholds. The financial scandal occasioned by the dishonesty of Julius Beaufort in the latter part of the novel is in no way unrelated to Archer's decision to eschew sexual desire in favor of the party line; the scandal demonstrates the dire consequences of abandoning those conservative values. Archer is disgusted by the repeated indiscretions of serial adulterer Lawrence Lefferts and sees both sexual and financial probity as key to upholding social order. The stakes of his emotional affair with Ellen Olenska extend far beyond its potential to derail his personal life.[20] In the end of the novel, his decision to adhere to the old ways allows him to celebrate his own "good citizenship," a status he comes to prize above all else:

> He had been, in short, what people were beginning to call "a good citizen."
> In New York, for many years past, every new movement, philanthropic, municipal or artistic, had taken account of his opinion and wanted his name. People said: "Ask Archer" when there was a question of starting the first school for crippled children, reorganising the Museum of Art, founding the Grolier Club, inaugurating the new Library, or getting up a new society of chamber music. His days were full, and they were filled decently. (349)

In 2020 China, Newland Archer would have a high social credit score. Wharton would likely see the 2020 Chinese system as neither wholly "bad" nor "good," nor so different in anything beyond scale from the codes of closed societies within the American past and present. *The Age of Innocence* still has a lot to teach us about tacit systems of ethical conduct in general; Wharton's ironic mode allows her to equally depict their merits and drawbacks. As a contemporary reviewer of the novel observed: "she has described these rites and surfaces and burdens as familiarly as if she loved them and as lucidly as if she hated them."[21] Even Archer himself remarks, at the novel's end and regarding a general dissolution of old New York customs: "Looking about him, he honoured his own past, and mourned for it. After all, there was good in the old ways," while he simultaneously recognizes: "There was good in the new order too" (350).

Archer is a clean-lined, eighteenth-century chaise of a character. His values and decisions simultaneously illuminate the shortcomings and merits of the American past as they gesture toward the problems and solutions of the American future. As Gabi Kirilloff argues here, the novel "draws our attention to the way in which even progressive change becomes traditional when viewed through the hindsight of history." That, in the twenty-first century, we've come to see Archer's version of the "old ways" as so fundamentally un-American we can only associate them with "Orwellian" communism or the faux aristocracy of Wharton's old New York youth speaks to the acceleration of the very trajectory Wharton identifies in *The Age of Innocence*—not one of social progress or decline, but one of epistemology, in which the lessons of the past are in peril of remaining lost to us forever.

What *The Age of Innocence* depicts is a privileged communism, a closed society that pools its resources via carefully negotiated marriages and investments, and polices its borders through strict rules of conduct.[22] Here, again, the connection to modern-day China holds fast, a connection noted by a reviewer of *Crazy Rich Asians* author Kevin Kwan's *China Rich Girlfriend*: "In the same way that Edith Wharton catalogued the Gilded Age via novels like *The Age of Innocence*, Kwan in his novels is doing his bit for a China that now has the second-highest number of millionaires in the world."[23] The popular American television show *Gossip Girl*, which ran on the CW network from 2007 to 2012 and was based on a series of novels by Cecily von Ziegesar, also focuses on a small coterie of privileged elite among whom a prodigal daughter wreaks havoc. Like *The Age of Innocence*, *Gossip Girl* features an arch narrator who functions as both satirist and enforcer—reflective of the dialectical stance each fiction adopts toward critique and homage. In a 2009 *Gossip Girl* episode called "The Age of Dissonance," the show's high-school-age characters even mount a dramatic performance of *The Age of Innocence*. The episode ends with a note from Rachel, the character who plays Ellen, to Dan, who plays Newland:

"I'm going back to Iowa, as you must have known. I'm sorry for everything. As Edith Wharton wrote: 'There is no one as kind as you, no one who gave me reasons I understood for doing what at first seemed so hard.'"[24] The novel's lessons seem to resonate even with the show's disillusioned Upper-East-Side teenagers and their implied audience.

In some ways, these references merely signal Wharton's enduring significance as a novelist of manners, but there is something about how *The Age of Innocence* in particular deploys this literary tradition that stands out. Other notable novelists of manners define its boundaries: Jane Austen lightly satirizes the tendencies of the closed societies she depicts but ultimately treats them with tenderness; Henry James savagely rips them apart. It is the subtlety of Wharton's ambivalence, at the height of its powers in *The Age of Innocence*, that distinguishes her approach and establishes her firmly at the center of the tradition.[25] As Ta-Nehisi Coates writes in an *Atlantic* article that I think is worth quoting at length:

> Wharton presents to us a deeply flawed world. But whereas a lesser writer would have stopped there, Wharton shows us how an honorable person, totally apprised of those flaws, might die for that world nonetheless ... When Newland says to Countess Olenska that he is searching for a world where "categories" like husband, wife and mistress don't exist, the much more worldly, and wiser, Olenska looks at him and says, "Oh my dear— Where is that country?"
>
> Where is that country.
>
> I fucking love that line. It says so much about how we both underestimate, and overestimate, our imagination. I think some of the Old Virginians must have thought much the same when faced with the beast of slavery—Where is that country.[26]

Coates is the rare critic who is able to draw broader historical lessons from the structures of thought Wharton depicts. This is especially notable as Wharton is typically appreciated for the historical particulars of her depictions. Early critics such as Harry Hartwick focused almost exclusively on the material culture of *The Age of Innocence*, a tendency that persists in popular and student readings of the novel—there is even a *Medium* article devoted to cataloging everything Ellen Olenska wears in its pages, as though she were a present-day Instagram "influencer."[27] In her own time and thereafter, Wharton's novels have often been read as *romans à clef* of old New York, a tendency she didn't much admire but saw as inevitable.[28] These kinds of readings distract from the fact that the psychological realities she depicts are so thorough as to be exportable. In Goldberg's reading here, for example, the narrator notes that Ellen's drawing room smells of "Turkish coffee and ambergris and dried roses," not primarily to envelop us in the scents of the period, but to communicate the complex levels of narrative access to Newland's consciousness. Through narrative technique and a mode of portraying history that is thematic rather than plainly documentarian, Wharton is able to teach us not only about 1870s New York, but also, as Coates suggests, about 1850s Virginia, and, as I do, about 2020 China.

More than a chronicle of a rarefied 1870s society consigned to the same fate as their once ubiquitous city-block-sized mansions, *The Age of Innocence* is a novelistic study of competing desires and allegiances: between risk and safety, love and duty, the present and the past. Its exploration of these poles is played out within the context of its love plot: Newland Archer, its stultified protagonist, mired in the traditions of his old New York "tribe" and yet longing for the change he imagines possible when reading romantic literature in his bookcase-lined study, must decide between his young fiancée, May Welland, the most perfect specimen of old New York femininity and innocence, and her cousin the Countess Ellen Olenska, a free spirit fleeing an unhappy European marriage. May is precision: a literal archer, a schemer, a keeper of secrets, a hider of sentiments, and a purchaser of highly appropriate articles. Ellen is chaos; in a representative scene, she runs out of her house "bareheaded" to rescue a neighborhood child with a skinned knee (121). She arranges her flowers against the custom, speaks candidly in public, and is possessed of a magical little charm bracelet from which a gold cigarette case can be detached—she is a woman who smokes. (So, sometimes, was Wharton.)[29]

It could be said that the novel has two kinds of readers: those who admire the unconventional and bohemian Ellen (as Beth Nguyen reveals she did here) and those who side with the calm and steady May (whose defense has been most notably articulated by Gwendolyn Morgan).[30] Or, to put it differently, those who lament the foreclosure of Newland's romance with Ellen and those who applaud his choice to stay with May. Much has been made of Wharton's own troubled and potentially loveless marriage to Boston's Edward "Teddy"

Wharton, which suffered an extra-marital affair on her part in 1908 before ending in divorce in 1913, in connection to the novel and its depiction of a time when divorce was unthinkable—"our legislation favours divorce; our social customs don't," Newland matter-of-factly explains to Ellen (109)—but to draw comparisons between Wharton and Ellen on such grounds has rarely yielded rich insight. The utility or faithfulness of such comparisons breaks down a bit in the context of a critical history that oscillates between assigning Wharton's identification to the characters of Newland, Ellen, and even May.[31]

The system of mutual dependence and control that exists between the three protagonists has, perhaps, more relevance to Wharton's own life than the experience of any individual character. In 1910, Wharton wrote a letter to Teddy in which she referenced his professed unwillingness to be "a passenger for the rest of [his] days."[32] A passenger is exactly what Newland thinks he chooses in May:

> He delighted in the radiant good looks of his betrothed, in her health, her horsemanship, her grace and quickness at games, and the shy interest in books and ideas that she was beginning to develop under his guidance ... she was straightforward, loyal and brave; she had a sense of humour (chiefly proved by her laughing at HIS jokes); and he suspected, in the depths of her innocently-gazing soul, a glow of feeling that it would be a joy to waken. (43)

This fantasy is implied to be a rotten one from the outset. Even Newland realizes

> all this frankness and innocence were only an artificial product ... [a] creation of factitious purity, so cunningly manufactured by a conspiracy of mothers and aunts and grandmothers and long-dead ancestresses, because it was supposed to be what he wanted, what he had a right to, in order that he might exercise his lordly pleasure in smashing it like an image made of snow. (43)

Though Newland can see through the artifice of what should be his "lordly pleasure"—a perfectly innocent and child-like bride—he still desires it. He wants, to use the term Rebecca Solnit coined in the twenty-first century, to "mansplain" the world to her.[33] To do this would require both a bride whose naivety is real (May's is not) and a stable knowledge of the world around him (Newland's is rapidly changing). Like the protagonist of AMC's historical drama *Mad Men* (2007–2015), Don Draper, Newland is only a powerful figure within the context of a culture on the verge of extinction. Both Archer's and Draper's journeys are mapped by their romantic interactions with two women who represent different phases of cultural history: May and Ellen for Archer, and Draper's wives Betty (the paradigmatic mid-century homemaker) and Megan (the sexual-revolution ingénue). While *Mad Men* traces Draper's transformation alongside the culture's, *The Age of Innocence* witnesses the culture's transformation around Archer. The beginning of the novel celebrates the iconoclastic matriarch of May's family, Catherine Mingott, who built her house "in an inaccessible wilderness near the Central Park," with a coy grin (10)—by the time readers would be encountering this passage in 1920, the area was already heavily developed. Newland is like Catherine's house: once vanguard and solitary but quickly lost in a sea of newcomers all around. Gabi Kirilloff's essay in this volume suggests that Newland is not merely "old-fashioned," but rather represents "a historically specific, transitional form of masculinity," evidenced by the fact that the verbs Wharton most often uses to communicate his actions are those—Kirilloff reveals through computational analysis—that have been more frequently used to communicate the actions of women in earlier novels. If, as Kirilloff suggests, "Newland is only 'old-fashioned' by twentieth-century standards," would he be "old-fashioned" by twenty-first-century standards? In some ways, he is the perfect figure of the twenty-first century man just entering adulthood. Virginia Ricard's essay here observes that Wharton "mak[es] fun of Archer's galloping imagination—of his bovarism." In the context of the novel, his tendency toward social isolation and daydreaming makes him feel like an outlier. It is under such assumptions that he, as Margaret Jay Jessee argues, falsely associates his own perceived outsider status with Ellen's real one.

If the twentieth-century version of a modern young man—exemplified by Newland's son Dallas and even Don Draper—is an avuncular go-getter, a salesman, and a thinker of the big; the twenty-first-century modern young man finds himself cloistered much like Newland: not in a "Gothic library with glazed black-walnut bookcases and finial-topped chairs," but in the virtual world of his phone, poring over clever memes and social media apps rather than volumes of romantic poetry (2). The advent of social media not only brings our culture back to the kind of group-regulated social control that allows the

Chinese social credit system to function, it also creates an enveloping sense of social isolation. A recent study in the *American Journal of Preventive Medicine* revealed that, while heavy social media use decreases users' perceived social isolation, it worsens their symptoms of actual social isolation.[34] In both Newland's and Mark Zuckerberg's societies, the representation of sociality often threatens to eclipse its practice.[35] Newland's failed attempt to precisely read his circumstances and the ensuing loneliness that failure creates are the result of his mistaking the avoidance of perceived social isolation for a choice that would ensure a real sense of belonging or fulfillment within the context of an intimate relationship.

In the novel's famous ending, Newland chooses the imaginary over the real Ellen:

> Archer sat down on the bench and continued to gaze at the awninged balcony. He calculated the time it would take his son to be carried up in the lift to the fifth floor, to ring the bell, and be admitted to the hall, and then ushered into the drawing-room. He pictured Dallas entering that room with his quick assured step and his delightful smile, and wondered if the people were right who said that his boy "took after him."
>
> Then he tried to see the persons already in the room—for probably at that sociable hour there would be more than one—and among them a dark lady, pale and dark, who would look up quickly, half rise, and hold out a long thin hand with three rings on it … "It's more real to me here than if I went up," he suddenly heard himself say; and the fear lest that last shadow of reality should lose its edge kept him rooted to his seat as the minutes succeeded each other. (364–365)

This passage is read variously throughout this volume as an "acquiescence to a stultifying existence" (Singley), a masculine appropriation of female-coded behavior that signals Newland's status as a "New Man" (Kirilloff), a connection to the novel's Francophilia (Ricard), a depiction of the momentary crossing of a split Jamesian consciousness (Goldberg), and a disappointing choice of the past rather than the future (Nguyen). It also underscores the emergence of the modern problem of representational desire.[36] Despite Hoeller's compelling argument that the novel is not quite as sexy as Wharton might have imagined, it is still infused with a deep erotic tension that thrives on the suggestive rather than the enacted: "'stay with me a little longer,' Madame Olenska said in a low tone, just touching his knee with her plumed fan. It was the lightest touch, but it thrilled him like a caress" (63). Newland can only experience the *suggestion* of desire. And he can find such suggestions only outside of the structures where he understands himself to be capable of experiencing belonging. "You gave me my first glimpse of a real life," he tells Ellen, "and at the same moment you asked me to go on with a sham one" (244). In the end, he seems to find he prefers the "sham one" himself. But Newland does not really choose between going up or staying down, between sexual passion or familial duty. His paralytic indecision is the fixed point around which the various time periods of the novel—and their modes of understanding such diverse topics as love, society, masculinity, modernity, and representation—revolve.

The painful ambivalence Newland experiences over which woman to choose, which animates the bulk of the novel, is overshadowed by the fact that he never has any actual choice at all. His reluctance to break his engagement with May in order to explore the possibility of a passionate love affair with Ellen can be read not just as a fear of violating the traditions of old New York, but also as a fear of becoming—like Wharton's Teddy—a passenger to Ellen himself. In reality, he is in control of neither woman nor, even, his own fate. As Emily Orlando argues: "Archer is not a close reader, and Wharton's women continually expose him as such. Ellen Olenska and May Welland succeed in collapsing his readings of them and, what is more, they read him more accurately than he reads himself."[37] In other words, as Beth Nguyen writes in her essay in this volume: "In the end, it is the women who all agree, without ever saying so, to uphold the old New York system."[38] Though he avoids the danger of Ellen's unpredictable autonomy, eventually, May steers his ship anyhow, skillfully deploying the news of her pregnancy to send Ellen away and engineer the novel's final, searingly cruel, farewell dinner for her seductive cousin. May's hidden cruelty is one of the most delicious things about the novel—one that was missed by early readers who took Newland's account at face value.[39] In a tense scene in the second half of the novel, when Newland plans a secret rendezvous with Ellen in Washington, May lets on that she knows what he's up to: "'The change will do you good,' she said simply, when he had finished; 'and you must be sure to go and see Ellen,' she added, looking him straight in the eyes with her cloudless smile, and speaking in the tone she might have employed in urging him not to neglect some irksome family duty" (269). In this moment, Newland interprets a "mute message" from May to him:

> [I]t meant: "Of course you understand that I know all that people have been saying about Ellen, and heartily sympathise with my family in their effort to get her to return to her husband. I also know that, for some reason you have not chosen to tell me, you have advised her against this course ... hints have indeed not been wanting; but since you appear unwilling to take them from others, I offer you this one myself, in the only form in which well-bred people of our kind can communicate unpleasant things to each other: by letting you understand that I know you mean to see Ellen when you are in Washington, and are perhaps going there expressly for that purpose; and that, since you are sure to see her, I wish you to do so with my full and explicit approval—and to take the opportunity of letting her know what the course of conduct you have encouraged her in is likely to lead to." (269)

The supposed mute message Newland imagines is much kinder than the message May forcibly communicates immediately after, which the reader can ascertain but Newland seems to miss entirely:

> [May's] hand was still on the key of the lamp when the last word of this mute message reached him. She turned the wick down, lifted off the globe, and breathed on the sulky flame.
> "They smell less if one blows them out," she explained, with her bright housekeeping air. On the threshold she turned and paused for his kiss. (270)

"One blows them out" might be a good title for a novel written from May's, rather than Newland's, perspective—or perhaps a self-help book authored by May on the topic of eradicating the problem of a husband's lovers. Such cruelty does not, however, paint May as vindictive, but rather as sober and responsible. After all, even Newland finally realizes, at that fateful final dinner for Ellen, "the fact that New York believed him to be Madame Olenska's lover. He caught the glitter of victory in his wife's eyes, and for the first time understood that she shared the belief" (342–343). Rereading the novel with the understanding that May definitively knows, or rather that she firmly believes, Ellen and Newland have slept together makes her behavior positively sober and undeniably admirable. Such an appreciation for May's stratagem, however, is rarely arrived at by first-time readers.

Just as there are untranslatable sayings that cannot be exactly explained outside of the language in which they occur, there are certain themes and concepts in *The Age of Innocence* that remain an unmappable province of experience—they can't typically be seen on first readings. If, as I suggested before, two kinds of readers of the love plot of *The Age of Innocence* are those that admire Ellen and those that admire May, another way to divide the readership of the novel is between first-time readers and rereaders. This is not a sensational novel with fantastic and surprising plot revelations per se, but it does have deep revelations of consciousness. Both Carol Singley and Shari Goldberg suggest here that the free indirect discourse Wharton employs to plunge her readers into Newland's mind is its own specific brand of narration, deeply informed by new developments in psychology and the philosophy of the mind. For Goldberg, Newland does not fully evolve over the course of the novel outside this bringing closer together of the two halves of his own split consciousness. Yet, if he himself does not change in some fundamental sense, his views do seem to from the novel's beginning to its end.

Just as it asks us to see the future through a re-examination of the past, *The Age of Innocence* performs many acts of both internal and external second reckonings. Kirilloff notes Wharton's tendency to "filter character action through auxiliary verbs," making the retroactive assessment of action more significant in the novel than action itself. Newland's initial view of marriage, for instance, is at once both hopelessly optimistic and forlornly dull. On a visit to the venerable van der Luydens, he contemplates their long union by way of an observation that:

> Mrs. van der Luyden's attitude said neither yes nor no, but always appeared to incline to clemency till her thin lips, wavering into the shadow of a smile, made the almost invariable reply: "I shall first have to talk this over with my husband." She and Mr. van der Luyden were so exactly alike that Archer often wondered how, after forty years of the closest conjugality, two such merged identities ever separated themselves enough for anything as controversial as a talking-over. (50)

Initially, for Newland, marriage is the complete merging of minds and personalities under the stringent rubric of the cultural laws and values that guide them. From this viewpoint, a couple don't learn to live within or beneath the institution of marriage—they become it. Little by little, he comes to see that "marriage was not the safe anchorage he had been taught to think, but a voyage on uncharted seas" (40) and, after he and May are married, he learns that even "safe" choices are not without their dangers and sacrifices:

> he took refuge in the comforting platitude that the first six months were always the most difficult in marriage. 'After that I suppose we shall have pretty nearly finished rubbing off each other's angles,' he reflected; but the worst of it was that May's pressure was already bearing on the very angles whose sharpness he most wanted to keep. (204)

Singley's essay addresses Newland's failed individualism, of which this desire to maintain one's angles is undeniably a part, arguing that it is an uncharacteristically female and Europeanized character (Ellen) who seems to more accurately reflect those transcendentalist habits and values to which Newland only aspires. Newland finds himself the passenger after all, a passive viewer of the progression of time in which he can only witness the same themes return revised.

Just as Archer is forced to confront the same realities multiple times, so too does the novel itself function on different levels at each subsequent rereading. The oft-quoted romantic dialogue that takes place between Ellen and Newland might be said of the novel itself:

> "Do you know—I hardly remembered you?"
> "Hardly remembered me?"
> "I mean: how shall I explain? I—it's always so. Each time you happen to me all over again." (289)

Like history itself, *The Age of Innocence* teaches the same lessons again and again, but, each time, readers emerge with new insight. All of the critics who have contributed to this volume are consummate rereaders and their essays both acknowledge and unpack what happens to this novel upon repeated encounters. The following essays situate *The Age of Innocence* in evolving notions of nationalism, cosmopolitanism, gender, philosophy, theories of mind and media, and personal history in ways that speak to both Wharton's period and our own.

In the first essay in this volume, Carol Singley reads Wharton as engaging in a tradition of writing on American individualism that is typically consigned to white, male writers who were historically granted an autonomy largely denied to women. Singley reads both Newland and Ellen as characters whose struggles to define themselves by and against the norms of their respective worlds expose the fallacies of individualism within a larger sociohistorical context than the moment in which they arrive. By assigning qualities of American individualism to Ellen rather than Newland, Wharton suggests that American individualism is only possible outside of the confines of America.

Margaret Toth then turns to an under-studied film adaptation of the novel, the 1934 RKO "talkie" made in Wharton's own lifetime, to demonstrate how the novel itself was written with film adaptation in mind as what Toth calls a "prose spectacle," citing "the complex rhetorical and aesthetic impulses— writing, painting, theater, sculpture, and, despite her distaste for it, even film— that motivate her work." Toth's reading illuminates Wharton's burgeoning awareness of entertainment mass markets as well as her contributions to film aesthetics and theory through a reading of both the 1934 film and the text of the novel alongside foundational film theorists such as Sergei Eisenstein, Béla Balázs, and Rudolf Arnheim.

Gabi Kirilloff's essay is the first study of *The Age of Innocence* to use verb-mapping data. Kirilloff collected data with colleague Matt Jockers at the University of Nebraska Center for Digital Research in the Humanities from over 3,000 nineteenth- and twentieth-century novels to examine the gendered meanings of actions performed by the novel's characters. Kirilloff's research demonstrates how such verb uses in the nineteenth- and twentieth-century novel are gendered. Her essay explores the consequences of these results for an interpretation of *The Age of Innocence* to suggest how future Wharton scholarship might build upon these initial findings. Her study of *The Age of Innocence* surprisingly reveals that, judging by the verbs consistently associated with them, May and Newland do not fully comply with old New York's gender ideals. Through linking Newland with emergent—rather than antiquated— forms of masculine behavior, Kirilloff argues that Wharton creates a character who is not simply "old-fashioned," but who represents a historically specific, transitional form of masculinity.

Just as Kirilloff reverses familiar critical assumptions about Archer's "old-fashionedness," Virginia Ricard offers readers a new model for understanding the novel's relationship to the well-worn European vs. American cultural theme with which Wharton and her friend and muse Henry James are so deeply associated. Ricard argues that Wharton inverts the "international theme" through the novel's encounter between a New Yorker with "cosmopolitan views" and a cosmopolitan who returns to a familiar New York. Demonstrating the stodgy conventionality of Americans alongside the social modernity of the French, Ricard complicates familiar binaries, not only of America and Europe, but also of good and bad moralities and notions of conservativism vs. progressivism between the two continents, to argue that the novel has as much, if not more, to say about France under the Second Empire as it does about old New York.

While Wharton emerges as a theorist of individualism, gender, film, and internationalism in the previous essays, Shari Goldberg's essay makes a convincing case for Wharton as theorist of mind and narrational form. Goldberg argues that the "doubled vision" of Newland's consciousness is consonant with contemporary notions of double-consciousness, which, while primarily known through the work of W. E. B. Du Bois, were pioneered by Du Bois's teacher, William James, whose theory held that two streams of consciousness were present within a single body, maintaining their distinction through independent chains of memory. In Goldberg's reading, Wharton creates a unique style of free indirect discourse that both reflects and expands on this theory.

The split in consciousness that Margaret Jay Jessee depicts in her essay is, in turn, between how the novel depicts actual emotion and how it depicts affected emotion. Turning to a more literal rereading through a reconsideration of her own 2012 article, "Trying It On: Narration and Masking in Edith Wharton's *The Age of Innocence*," Jessee examines *The Age of Innocence* anew as a work that deploys literary affect to model how readers ought to "read around Newland in order to understand how other characters feel" rather than merely "trying on" the affects of other characters. Jessee argues that the novel posits intimacy itself as "an act of misreading, rethinking, and recursively considering feeling."

Hildegard Hoeller places *The Age of Innocence* in dialogue with the four novellas that would be published together in book form under the title *Old New York* four years after its publication. Hoeller argues that these novellas, which use the same title Wharton had originally planned for *The Age of Innocence*, function as a sequel to *The Age of Innocence* wherein Wharton finally achieves the depiction of "scandal" that she originally intended for her Pulitzer-Prize-winning work. In so doing, she further complicates the dialectic between innocence and experience that animates the earlier novel. Hoeller's reading demonstrates how Wharton re-imagined the old New York of her youth to deliberately focus on social transgression, giving us a new lens through which to reread the novel—and Wharton's compositional strategy as a whole—as one to which hidden scandals assume centrality.

The volume concludes with a personal essay on her own rereading experience by novelist Beth Nguyen, who recounts how the social codes depicted in the novel occasioned revelations about the code-switching and struggles with American assimilation that Nguyen herself experienced as the child of refugees from Viet Nam who were resettled in the American Midwest. Revisiting that geographic territory about which Wharton herself was so torn, and in which Nguyen found another racially homogenous closed society, she asks: "For people of color, what is the experience of immersion into Wharton's white world—and into worlds of whiteness in general? What is lost and what is learned through such dissonance?" For Nguyen, the experience of rereading Wharton's work is figured as a nostalgic journey: "a fond, somewhat bittersweet retreading of somewhere that is no longer—but it is also a way to go back to my own old self." *The Age of Innocence* is, for the novelist, a place in which to encounter both the other and the self—a visit to a foreign time and place one nonetheless knows intimately.

A recurring theme throughout Wharton's writing is the fantasy of a country free from the social limitations and structures of power that hemmed in her own life and destroyed so many of her best characters. The "Land of Letters" that, she writes in her autobiography, "was henceforth to be [her] country" is not dissimilar to Lawrence Selden's "Republic of the Spirit" where one would experience freedom "from money, from poverty, from ease and anxiety, from all the material accidents" in *The House of Mirth* (1905).[40] Both imagined places seem to be versions of an answer to Ellen Olenska's desperate question in *The Age of Innocence*, which Ta-Nehisi Coates so admires: "where is that country?" In rereading *The Age of Innocence* myself, this time through the rich ideas presented in the following essays, I've come to see that these places exist, not beyond the shapes of a map, but outside the lines of a chronology. It is only by Wharton's virtuosic ability to inhabit multiple moments at once that they fleetingly come into vision before receding again, just out of reach—a shadow of recognition from the past, a glimmer of possibility from the future.

1

Edith Wharton, *The Age of Innocence*, and American Individualism

Carol J. Singley
Rutgers University-Camden

After decades of disparagement by critics who viewed her as either a disciple of Henry James or a grande dame of literature out of touch with American life, Edith Wharton has been elevated, notably through the efforts of biographers and feminist and cultural critics from the 1970s onward, to the stature she deserves. She is now widely hailed as a major American writer, not only of manners but also of morals, not only of the upper class but also of class dynamics, and not only of women's lives but also of gender relations. The growing body of critical work on Wharton addresses the broad range of her writings—poems, plays, and nonfiction as well as novels and short stories— and notes her contributions to modernism as well as to realism and naturalism. This criticism is also increasingly comparative, further signaling Wharton's significant, secure place in the American literary canon. Despite this critical attention, however, Wharton's work remains curiously outside one traditional line of inquiry that would instantiate her in a conversation routinely associated with American literature: that related to myths of American individualism and to qualities of American heroism. Indeed, explorations of selfhood have been so pervasive in discussions of American writing as to be hallmarks of American literature itself.

American individualism evokes the myth of the solitary white male hero, exemplified in literary texts that pre-date and surround Wharton's writing. Readers may think, for example, of the opening line: "Call me Ishmael," in Herman Melville's *Moby Dick* (1851); of the bardic yelp: "I sing and celebrate myself," in Walt Whitman's "Song of Myself" (1855); and of Huckleberry Finn's solitary plan "to light out for the Territory ahead of the rest" in Mark Twain's *Adventures of Huckleberry Finn* (1884). Contemporary with Newland Archer's yearning for Ellen Olenska in *The Age of Innocence* is Jay Gatsby's hopeless reach toward Daisy Buchanan and the green light on Long Island Sound in F. Scott Fitzgerald's *The Great Gatsby* (1925). Also in conversation with Wharton's figure of a deflated hero is Hemingway's wounded protagonist in *The Sun Also Rises* (1926), who resigns himself to making do with the materials at hand. Indeed, a grasp toward elusive ideals frames Wharton's work, even as her engagement with literary naturalism, in many ways the antithesis of heroic American individualism, directs attention away from it. Wharton's 1920 Pulitzer Prize-winning novel of failed aspiration and a thwarted relationship owes as much to this romantic tradition as to a naturalistic one. Indeed, Newland Archer's very name—"new land"—signals his immersion in the myth of the American Adam, codified by R. W. B. Lewis in a book by that name.[1]

This essay explores the cultural myths of American individualism in *The Age of Innocence*. It proceeds with awareness that doing so not only runs the risk of presuming a monolithic ideology to describe "American" literature but also positions Wharton in a tradition dominated by white male writers who were largely at liberty to take for granted the social, political, and geographic mobility that was often denied to women; and it acknowledges that, for Wharton, who enjoyed the privileges of wealth and class, such freedoms were nonetheless hard-won. Indeed, the achievement of autonomy associated with individualism is as important for the author of *The Age of Innocence* as it is for its protagonist. Although one might cautiously argue for biographical connections in the novel, the correspondence between author and protagonist Archer is significant. Wharton was 57 when she wrote the novel, the same age as Archer when he sits on a park bench outside Ellen's Parisian apartment and decides whether or not to see her. Archer's trajectory parallels Wharton's journey as she left New York, first for Paris, and then for the south of France, and as she reflected, through the construction of the novel, upon the old New York society that had nurtured her but from which she needed to flee in order to pursue her passions: writing, art, travel, and friendships.

The differences between Wharton and her hero are also significant. Wharton, unlike Archer, who marries and settles into family life, seized the chance for romance, engaging in an extramarital affair with Morton Fullerton in 1908 and divorcing her husband of twenty-eight years, Edward (Teddy) Wharton, in 1913. Wharton associates the embrace of European culture not with Archer, but with Ellen, in whom she inscribes many attributes typically associated with male individualism, including retreat from the encumbrances of society, a motif that dates to James Fenimore Cooper's *Leatherstocking Tales* of the early 1800s. Wharton's old New York represents cultural restriction and the blind following of convention; Europe, in contrast, offers privacy and artistic expression. In this respect, Wharton reverses the usual pattern of westward expansion found in American literature and follows in the tradition of Nathaniel Hawthorne, who, at the end of *The Scarlet Letter* (1850), portrays Hester Prynne leaving Puritan strictures in Salem for relative freedom in Europe. Ellen, the reader infers, lives a more fulfilled life by returning to Europe than she would have lived in New York. Wharton thus inserts herself both in the form of Archer's quest for romantic fulfillment within society's confines and in the form of Ellen's more reasoned choice to flee these constrictions.

When analyzed with awareness that the traits of American individualism are distributed between Archer and Ellen, Archer's failure to attain these ideals becomes evident. Lacking initiative and averse to risk, he often hesitates, misses opportunity, and suffers the consequences of indecision. Life seems to happen to him rather than the reverse, as Archer himself realizes at the end of the novel: "Something he knew he had missed: the flower of life."[2] He can only assess his life with ambivalence: "there was good in the old ways" (347) and "there was good in the new order too" (349). Circumstances and the organized will of others run counter to his gestures toward creative freedom, such that he becomes a master of compromise, a portrait of benign resignation. One can view Archer's lackluster achievement as exemplary of Wharton's recurrent fictional theme of conflict between the individual and society, inflected by her deterministic outlook; however, his situation involves more than the workings of literary naturalism. Archer's dilemmas take place within a cultural discourse about the changing definitions of the individual, one that complicates and challenges notions of autonomous selfhood that previous writers of the nineteenth century took for granted. *The Age of Innocence* reflects a social movement at the turn of the twentieth century in which individualism, while touted, was also channeled and constrained. Viewing Archer in this light reveals Wharton to be an astute realist with a keen sense of cultural context.

I.

The literary history of American individualism dates to the mid-twentieth century, when a profusion of critics celebrated the strength of the American character, touted democracy, and expressed an optimism born of the post-World War II era and ensuing Cold War against the Soviet Union and communism. Sacvan Bercovitch, observing that among these critics' achievements was their ability to conflate notions of American history with those of American literature, points as one example to Robert Spiller et al.'s *Literary History of the United States* (1948).[3] Spiller's influential volume, Bercovitch notes, proceeds teleologically from sections entitled "The Colonies" through "The Democracy" and "Expansion" to "A World Literature." As the editors write in the opening "Address to the Reader": "increasing power and vitality are extraordinarily characteristic of [our nation]. ... Never has nature been so rapidly and so extensively altered by the efforts of man in so brief a time. Never has conquest resulted in a more vigorous development of initiative, individualism, self-reliance, and demands for freedom."[4]

Spiller proceeds to connect these heroic qualities to the literature produced by major American authors. Ours has been a literature "profoundly influenced by ideals and by practices developed in democratic living. It has been intensely conscious of the needs of the common man, and equally conscious of the aspirations of the individual. ... It has been humanitarian. It has been, on the whole an optimistic literature, made virile by criticism of the actual in comparison with the ideal."[5] Also voicing this sentiment was F. O. Matthiessen's landmark *American Renaissance* (1941), which identified five writers from the period 1850–1855 who, in "an extraordinarily concentrated moment of literary expression," helped to form a national identity and a literature equal in quality, as Matthiessen's title suggests, to the work produced by writers of the European Renaissance.[6] Ralph Waldo Emerson, Henry David Thoreau, Nathaniel Hawthorne, Walt Whitman, and Herman Melville are the writers Matthiessen celebrates for exhibiting robust ideals that further American democracy and spur a national exploration of its geographic and political potential.

More studies of American individualism, which can be said to originate with Matthiessen's formalist approach, were published into the 1950s. R. W. B. Lewis, who would go on to write a prize-winning biography of Wharton in

1975, posited the myth of the American Adam (1955), advancing an over-arching concept that Richard Chase's study of the "American romance-novel" in *The American Novel and Its Tradition* had anticipated (1933).[7] This myth-and-symbol school of criticism continued with Richard Poirier's description, in *A World Elsewhere* (1985), of the "American obsession with inventing environments that permit unhampered freedom of consciousness."[8] Poirier's hero, reflecting Matthiessen's and Lewis's focus on an idealized, aesthetically contained figure, is comfortably located beyond space and time. This work was complicated, however, by a temporally grounded study by Carolyn Porter that identified the figure of the "participant observer." In her 1981 historicized analysis, *Seeing and Being*, Porter moves the timeline of American writers forward to the end of the nineteenth century by addressing Henry James's *The Golden Bowl* (1904) and by situating the narrative action of the novel within the context of capitalistic expansion and its ensuing commodification of others in service to self-gain. Porter does not mention Wharton in her book, but even a cursory reading of *The Age of Innocence* reveals connections with her thesis. Wharton, keenly sensitive to social context, presents in her portrait of Newland Archer a man who is as immersed in his world as he fancies himself detached from it. Porter's aim, to "reconnect Emerson to the society he manifestly did not transcend" because "no writer transcends his or her historical and social context,"[9] also speaks to Wharton's project: to present a "dilettante" (4) who samples life but cannot immerse himself fully in it.

Using these mid-twentieth-century myth-making critics as a touchstone, readers can appreciate from the first chapter of *The Age of Innocence* that Archer is a poor candidate for the kind of American self-sufficiency and individualism that Matthiessen and others tout. By many measures, he fails to achieve the sought-after independence associated with this myth, as Wharton makes clear in her rehearsal of his shortcomings throughout the novel. A slave to convention, he predictably performs social roles. He arrives at the opera fashionably late, habitually displays a gardenia in his lapel, and grooms his hair with not one but two brushes. As Wharton writes: "what was or was not 'the thing' played a part as important in Newland Archer's New York as the inscrutable totem terrors that had ruled the destinies of his forefathers thousands of years ago" (4). He repeatedly conforms to others' expectations, neglecting his own desires.

Nor do Archer's material circumstances lend themselves to originality or innovation. The principle of American individualism has always been tied to economic mobility. As former Federal Reserve chair Ben Bernanke has phrased it: "A bedrock American principle is the idea that all individuals should have the opportunity to succeed on the basis of their own effort, skill, and ingenuity."[10] Similarly, John Cawelti, writing about the early nineteenth century, notes that "faith in America made it commonplace that a man could become rich if he worked at it."[11] Archer's comfortable class and family position would seem to obviate the need for assumption of risk that usually accompanies an individual's bid for a more rewarding and lucrative life. Already wealthy, he has little motivation to rise on his own merits or to negotiate his identity in relation to mobility—qualities fundamental to the formation of American character since Benjamin Franklin. Archer's class privilege does come at a cost, however. Membership in an American aristocracy allows the individual to be part of the group but implicitly forbids his departure from it in quest of goals of his own choosing. It conceives of steps taken away as detrimental to the individual as well as to the community. Archer's membership in old New York society thus forms a stasis from which he cannot move.

II.

The romantic pursuit of individualism has its basis in nineteenth-century American literature, as Matthiessen and others point out. In particular, Ralph Waldo Emerson's essays serve as a touchstone for Wharton's novel, with his ideas informing Archer's successes as well as his failures. Emerson's writings make it clear that being a member of the upper class does not preclude striving for individualistic ideals. On the contrary, as Emerson observes in "Manners": one can be a gentleman in society and also possess originality and courage, values essential to American individualism. In this essay Emerson writes that the word "gentleman" is useful to describe "the heroic character"; however, he distinguishes "gentleman" from the word "fashion," which has "a narrow and often sinister meaning." "The gentleman," Emerson continues, "is a man of truth, lord of his own actions, and expressing that lordship in his behavior, not in any manner dependent and servile either on persons, or opinions, or possessions. … [P]ersonal force never goes out of fashion."[12] Rather than meet these Emersonian standards, Archer lets fashion and habit dictate the terms of his New York life.

It would be overreaching to call Wharton an Emersonian romantic. A realist, she resisted unwarranted claims of optimism found in her time, such as those espoused by proponents of New Thought, who held that, as Richard Weiss explains, mere "states of mind can affect objective reality."[13] She subjects her characters to the forces of social law and seldom allows them to reach their goals merely by wishing for success. Throughout the novel, Archer is given to wishful thinking and romantic flights of fantasy. His desire to escape with Ellen to a land where society's rules do not apply to them epitomizes this kind of idle dreaming, as does his being uncontrollably moved by the ribbon scene in the production of the sentimental play, *The Shaughraun*, and his mistaking the pink parasol belonging to the Blenker girl for Ellen's umbrella. Still, Wharton endows Archer with agency and the ability to imagine his future and take steps toward it. This potential for self-fulfillment is reflected in Emerson's notion that "in the moving crowd of good society, the men of valor and reality are known, and rise to their natural place."[14]

Archer forgoes the chance for personal happiness with Ellen, but Wharton gives him the opportunity to rise, as Emerson writes, to his "natural place" "in the moving crowd of good society" through public service. Enmeshed in conventional family life, he is thrilled when the governor of New York, Theodore Roosevelt, urges him to run for office with the rousing words: "You're the kind of man the country wants, Archer. If the stable's ever to be cleaned out, men like you have got to lend a hand in the cleaning" (346). Archer "eagerly" answers "the call" and wins the election, but he serves only one term in the State Assembly. He loses reelection and wonders, before sinking "back thankfully into obscure if useful municipal work," whether "men like himself were what his country needed" (346). He reviews his brief career in public service with ambivalence, as he does most everything in his life: "He had done little in public life; he would always be by nature a contemplative and a dilettante. … He had been, in short, what people were beginning to call 'a good citizen'. … His days were full, and they were filled decently. He supposed it was all a man ought to ask" (346–347). Emerson makes it clear that one should indeed ask for more. In "Manners," he reinterprets traditional displays of heroic valor, such as those found in strife-ridden medieval days, to the realities of the modern age. He writes that today "the competition is transferred from war to politics and trade, but the personal force appears readily enough in these new arenas."[15] Although Archer fulfills his role of "good citizen" by serving on boards and charities, he lacks the "personal force" that Emerson advocates. His record is one of accommodation rather than achievement, let alone transcendence.

Using Emerson as a touchstone, one can chart a path that Archer might have taken. His choices contrast with those of a minor character, Emerson Sillerton, whose name pays homage to the transcendentalist. Through her depiction of Sillerton, Wharton hints at what individualism amidst New York's social constraints might look like. Professor Emerson Sillerton has the audacity to pursue a vocation as an archeologist with a vigor that Archer never shows toward his own career as an attorney. Both Sillerton and Archer were born into old New York society, with its attendant privileges and obligations, but Sillerton displays resistance and originality that Archer refuses to claim for himself. Sillerton's "personal force," to use Ralph Waldo Emerson's term, is such that society, even if disapproving, has no choice but to mold itself to his unconventional ways. Old New York may think Sillerton odd or even pity him, but Wharton shows with characteristic wit that society, not Sillerton, misses the mark. She writes that, despite Sillerton's impeccable social standing, he was a "thorn in the side of Newport society; and a thorn that could not be plucked out, for it grew on a venerable and venerated family tree. He was, as people said, a man who had had 'every advantage'" (219).

Emerson Sillerton not only dares to engage in serious work ("Nothing— as Mrs. Welland had often remarked—nothing on earth obliged Emerson Sillerton to be an archeologist, or indeed a professor of any sort"), but he also defies New York customs by living in Newport in the winter rather than in the summer, as do his peers, and by doing other "revolutionary things" such as filling his house with "long-haired men and short-haired women," giving a party for an African American, and exploring "tombs in Yucatan instead of going to Paris or Italy" (219–220). Apropos of Archer's romantic predicament, Sillerton pursues these pleasures with a wife who dumbfounds old New York because she "submitted so tamely to [his] eccentricities" (220). Society members feel sympathy for Amy Sillerton, whom they judge as having been deprived both socially and financially by her husband: "But at least, if he was going to break with tradition and flout society in the face, he need not have married poor Amy Dagonet, who had a right to expect 'something different,' and money enough to keep her own carriage" (220). But Wharton makes it clear that the Sillertons enjoy their unconventional patterns, "apparently unaware that they were different from other people," and oblivious to the fact that surrounding families attend their "dreary annual garden-parties" only out of a sense of obligation (220). Emerson Sillerton dares to "hitch [his] wagon to a star," as Emerson advises in his 1870 essay, "Civilization,"[16] and this act of nonconformity not only goes unpunished but is also rewarded with freedom to go wherever intellect and imagination lead him.

Archer's shortcomings are also evident in the transcendental imagery Wharton uses in the novel. The dominant metaphor in Emerson's writings is that of sight, focalized in the image of the "transparent eyeball," which Emerson introduces in his essay, "Nature."[17] The transparent eyeball sees all and embraces all, absorbing what the world has to offer and elevating the spirit. Numerous references to sight appear in *The Age of Innocence*. In the first scene, Archer looks out at the sea of faces in the opera house, measuring his social worth and that of his soon-to-be-fiancée, May Welland. These socialites, in turn, gaze upon the newly arrived Ellen Olenska. Archer's vision is restricted. He sees only what others see: a scandal created by Ellen's return to New York after a failed marriage to a European count. Far from achieving the liberating wholeness promised by Emerson's transparent eyeball, he settles for codependence rather than independence. His first and lasting alliance is with old New York and May: "As he entered the box his eyes met Miss Welland's, and he saw that she had instantly understood his motive. ... Her eyes said: 'You see why Mamma brought me,' and his answered" (17). Although Archer is sparked by curiosity and immediately attracted to Ellen, he joins the group in dismissing her as a faded beauty and rallies with them to offset this intruder's impact. He measures Ellen's import as others do, negating the source and depth of his feelings.

III.

Given Archer's susceptibility to others' opinions, it is no small irony that he prides himself on standing apart from others even as he relies on society's rules.

Gazing at his peers, he thinks he is "the superior of these chosen specimens of old New York gentility; he had probably read more, thought more, and even seen a good deal more of the world than any other man of the number" (8); however, "at heart a dilettante" (4), he only dabbles at individualism. Embracing this conformist notion of "masculine solidarity," he "instinctively felt that … it would be troublesome—and also rather bad form—to strike out for himself" (8). A misalignment of sight and insight fuels Archer's fantasies about being the man who will liberate May sexually and emotionally, and it leads him eventually to realize that her vision is a form of blindness:

> It would presently be his task to take the bandage from this young woman's eyes, and bid her look forth on the world. But how many generations of the women who had gone to her making had descended bandaged to the family vault? He shivered a little, remembering some of the new ideas in his scientific books, and the much-cited instance of the Kentucky cave-fish, which had ceased to develop eyes because they had no use for them. What if, when he had bidden May Welland to open hers, they could only look out blankly at blankness? (83)

In this much-cited passage, which evokes Plato's allegory of the cave in *The Republic*, Wharton also mines the American romantic tradition; she evokes not the expansive, enlightened metaphor of the transparent eyeball, as found in Emerson's writings, but its opposite.

Wharton's descriptions of sight resonate with those found in the underbelly of literary transcendentalism, a dark romanticism in which eyes and insight debilitate and haunt, as they do in Edgar Allan Poe's fiction. For example, in Poe's gothic tale, "The Tell-Tale Heart" (1843), the narrator's description of the old man with "the eye of a vulture—a pale blue eye, with a film over it,"[18] parallels Wharton's portrayal of Sillerton Jackson, the society gossip who, upon returning Lawrence Lefferts's opera-glass, "scrutinized the attentive group out of his filmy blue eyes overhung by old veined lids" (11). Wharton similarly evokes Poe, a writer she admired and was forbidden to read as a child,[19] in her depiction of Archer on a course of self-destruction similar to the downward spirals found in Poe's tales, when, at every turn, as Archer becomes enamored of Ellen, he binds himself more tightly to May.

The operations of the perverse, for which Poe is famous, find their way into Wharton's novel. For example, Archer suggests that he and May announce their engagement on the very night that Ellen rivets his attention at the opera house. He follows his boss's and family's lead in advising Ellen against divorce when her freedom would make his own possible. And he rushes to St. Augustine to press May to advance their wedding date after an intimate meeting with Ellen at Skuytercliff. When Archer meets with May in Florida, she accurately senses that his affections lie elsewhere, although she mistakenly targets Mrs. Theodore Worley, with whom Archer was once involved. When she offers to release him, Archer feels "dizzy with the glimpse of the precipice they had skirted" (150), but he declines to claim his freedom. Rather, his will is sabotaged by an uncontrollable force such as the one Poe popularizes in his 1845 short story, "The Imp of the Perverse." Poe explains the meaning of such an "imp" through the story's narrator, who relates what the mind might do at the edge of a cliff, in the same language that Wharton uses to describe Archer's dilemma: "We stand upon the brink of a precipice. We peer into the abyss—we grow sick and dizzy. Our first impulse is to shrink from the danger, and yet, unaccountably, we remain."[20]

IV.

Poe's unstable narrators—with their tortured egos and divided psyches—presage what would become by the early twentieth century a familiar challenge to the concepts of selfhood and American individualism as a whole. As Daniel Borus notes, the growth of cities, markets, and corporations made it hard for individuals to declare their independence from increasingly intertwined networks of social and economic forces that pressed and shaped them.[21] The fragmenting mechanics of modern life created new understandings of the self that previous romantic theories of individualism had taken for granted. These modern pressures of social and psychic interdependence did not escape Edith Wharton's attention; indeed, much of her fiction is concerned with ongoing tensions between the individual and the social group to the extent that the integrity of the self is threatened.

Without being overtly psychological, *The Age of Innocence* describes the growing sense of multiply constructed selfhoods, introduced by Sigmund Freud and made popular by social psychologists at the end of the nineteenth century.

These new understandings of identity complicated and even contradicted Emerson's philosophy, which had its basis in the Scottish Common Sense understanding of the self as a complete and immutable soul, responsive to right reason. Emerson posited an autonomy and authenticity that turn-of-the-century realities seemed to refute. Increasingly, society shaped and even seemed to create the individual. As Borus writes: "A mass politics in which the 'crowd' took on a life of its own undercut the republican politics in which autonomous, rational and self-aware individuals made informed decisions. ... A unified, self-determining, transparent and disembodied self was inconsistent with practices of modern life."[22]

Wharton depicts the strength of collective identity in several ways, chiefly through Archer's New York family, which functions seamlessly to create its own culture. This constellation of friends and relatives, described not as a "crowd" but as a "tribe" (15), has its own shared values, practices, and expectations. Family, as Barlow writes, works to define the self by providing it with cultural and financial support,[23] but it also constrains. In the beginning, Archer seems at one with family. For example, he sits in the opera box "of old Mrs. Manson Mingott, whose monstrous obesity had long since made it impossible for her to attend the Opera, but who was always represented on fashionable nights by some of the younger members of the family" (5). He agrees with the ruling about Ellen's unseemly appearance by Sillerton Jackson, who "was as great an authority on 'family' as Lawrence Lefferts was on 'form'" (9). Enmeshed in "this forest of family trees," he "approved of family solidarity" (10, 12). He is gratified that his engagement to May "had been carefully passed upon in family council" (29), and he concurs when the van der Luydens sanction Ellen's inclusion in New York society: "As long as a member of a well-known family is backed up by that family it should be considered—final" (56–57). By the end of the novel, however, Archer comes to see this consensus as alienating and imprisoning: May's "incapacity to recognize change" strikes him as "a kind of innocent family hypocrisy, in which father and children had unconsciously collaborated" (348).

Through these and other references, Wharton demonstrates a modern sensibility and points out epistemic flaws in the myth of individuality as it faces pressure on the concept of selfhood. The multiple time frames—the 1870s when Archer is a young man; the early 1900s when he is 57; and the

1920s when Wharton writes the novel—are themselves evidence of change in the early twentieth century, "of a world in flux, where the boundaries of the self have indeed dissolved."[24] Emerson, in "Nature," called for "an original relation to the universe,"[25] but the idea of a single American character was in conflict with apparent multiplicities and potential splitting of the self into parts.

The Age of Innocence thus demonstrates Wharton's awareness of two sides of American individualism: (1) the notion, advanced as early as St. John de Crèvecoeur in 1782 in his *Letters from an American Farmer*, and expanded upon by Emerson and Walt Whitman that "the American [is a] new man";[26] and (2) the reality that every American "carried with him or her the culture of the homeland,"[27] which inspires emulation if not imitation, especially among the upper classes, who have "a tenacious cultural allegiance to the mother country [England]."[28] The first myth holds, idealistically, that one can leave the past behind; the second emphasizes, more realistically, that "[n]o person is immune to the past; no one makes an independent fresh start."[29] These states— of being self-made and tradition-bound—coexist in Wharton's novel, with Archer simultaneously resisting and depending upon old New York, a culture which is itself derived from European traditions.

No scene more vividly reflects this turn-of-the-century experience of fragmented and dissociated selfhood than the one describing the farewell dinner that Archer and May host for Ellen. The event is choreographed to banish Ellen permanently from old New York society, but it is celebrated, for appearance's sake, as the merry occasion of a young couple's first formal party. This disingenuousness contributes to the scene's sense of unreality, in which Archer has the dizzying sensation of leaving his body. He sees himself as if from above, but this feeling of ascension lacks the transcendental elevation of spirit that Emerson envisions in his essays. It has only a quality of self-consciousness: "Archer, who seemed to be assisting at the scene in a state of odd imponderability, as if he floated somewhere between chandelier and ceiling, wondered at nothing so much as his own share in the proceedings" (335). Preoccupied to this point with his personal crisis, Archer is now shocked to contemplate his identity as it has been constructed by others, and he painfully sees himself as others do: he has a "vast flash made up of many broken gleans" that all of New York believe he and Ellen are lovers, and understanding this, he "guessed himself to have been, for months, the center of countless silently observing eyes and patiently listening ears" (335). No longer the hero in his own drama, he is instead the participant-observer such as the one Porter identifies in Henry James's novels. The strength of collective rather than individual identity is further reinforced when the guests turn the topic of conversation to the scandal of Julius Beaufort's financial dealings, and Archer realizes: "It's to show me ... what would happen to *me*" (335, original emphasis). Family now becomes not benignly hypocritical but malevolently so, as the strength of innuendo "closed in on him like the doors of the family vault" (336).

V.

The image of the closing vault suggests stasis and imprisonment, making it possible to read Archer's disappointing end as a fait accompli. But the issue is not that Archer lacks options, rather, it is that he fails to exercise them. Membership in New York society appears to be permanent and inflexible, but Wharton does present opportunities for individualistic ventures. Archer suspects as much when he fantasizes about reading Faust with May on their honeymoon in the Italian lakes, and when he utters unexpected platitudes such as: "Women ought to be as free as we are" (83). He is predisposed, as few of his peers are, toward the arts and letters, and accordingly enjoys conversing with Ned Winsett, an aspiring writer, and with M. Rivière, an intellectual. He is also captivated by new paintings in Ellen's apartment and regularly receives shipments of books to keep abreast of the latest ideas; however, although he fancies himself innovative, he lacks the originality and courage that Emerson espouses. The American scholar, Emerson writes, possesses abundant "self-trust": "Free should the scholar be—free and brave ... without any hindrance that does not arise out of his own constitution."[30] Archer only gestures toward self-direction.

Because he responds to some cultural signs and ignores others, Archer concludes that change is not possible. In fact, change is possible; moreover, the social boundaries separating insiders and outsiders have always been more fluid than he realizes. Wharton says as much in her depiction of another minor character, the free-spirited Duke of Austrey, whom old New Yorkers take pains to entertain. A European aristocrat, the Duke represents everything that elite society seeks to emulate. Yet, when abroad, the Duke eschews convention and simply goes, in romantic fashion, "where he's amused" (90). In fact, Wharton shows that society is not a static monolith, but a fluctuating wave. This point is driven home when, at the end of the novel, Fanny, the daughter of once-scandalous Julius Beaufort, is engaged with no social impunity to Archer's son, Dallas.

Wharton demonstrates through other characters that there are creative solutions to personal dilemmas. Mrs. Manson Mingott's story is relayed in the first chapter of the novel, as if to serve as a blueprint for Archer's journey. Her father, Bob Spicer, scandalized New York when, not more than a year after his marriage, he left his wife and children after falling in love with a Spanish dancer. He and his lover escaped "mysteriously (with a large sum of trust money)" on a ship to Cuba and were never heard from again (10). Wharton writes within the main plot of the novel a subplot about a man who does manage to break away from the restrictions of old New York society. In contrast to Spicer, Archer is slavishly devoted to formalities.

A few details in the novel suggest that Archer may have contemplated an exotic escape with Ellen like the one Bob Spicer made with his dancer. When he meets Ellen in Boston, he is carrying a newspaper, *The Commercial Advertiser*. Since Boston published no newspapers by this name, Archer may be carrying a New York paper, possibly the daily *New York Commercial Advertiser*. More likely, the publication is a weekly publication originally called the *New York Spectator and Weekly Commercial Advertiser*, which changed its name in 1876 to the *Weekly Commercial Advertiser*. Mainly concerned with mercantile issues, the paper included information about the availability of commodities. Importantly for Wharton's plot, it also published lists of arrivals and departures of freight and passenger steamships. Was Archer hoping to leave with Ellen on a passenger ship? If so, he settles instead for a day's excursion with her in the Boston bay, which returns him to his point of departure.

Wharton also suggests the importance of place in shaping opportunity. Bob Spicer met his Spanish dancer not at the staid Academy of Music, where Archer first sees Ellen, but at Castle Garden, a site of popular entertainment from the 1820s through the 1850s. Best known for P. T. Barnum's presentation of singer Jenny Lind in 1850, Castle Garden appealed to the masses just as the

Academy of Music appealed to the elite. Whereas Bob Spicer boldly ventured outside the confines of old New York to pursue his heart's desire, Archer is tied to the Academy of Music and its conventional ways. "Held fast by habit" (351), he escapes with Ellen only in his mind. Wharton further emphasizes the narrowness of Archer's world—and its fear of outsiders—with the reference to Castle Garden. By the 1870s, when most events in the novel take place, Castle Garden, no longer a theater, was used by the US government as the east coast federal immigration center, a precursor to Ellis Island. It processed nearly eight million immigrants between 1855 and 1890. Literally a site of national diversity, Castle Garden became an entry point for the same immigrant interlopers who alarm old New York families like the Archers, Lovells, and Wellands.

Bob Spicer's colorful story also sheds light on Archer's relationship to Mrs. Manson Mingott. Like her namesake, Catherine the Great, Empress of Russia, Mrs. Mingott wields power in New York society as its reigning matriarch. Bearing the legacy of her nonconformist father, she rules without relinquishing the sense of independence that her father's example taught her. She "fearlessly" married her daughters to Europeans "in heaven knew what corrupt and fashionable circles, hobnobbed with Dukes and Ambassadors, associated familiarly with Papists, [and] entertained Opera singers" (14). She has the audacity to construct a mansion near Central Park—"an inaccessible wilderness" to old New Yorkers (13)—and keep a first-floor boudoir. The fact that she employs a "mulatto maid-servant" (213) at a time when the number of domestic positions available to African Americans was shrinking due to competition from groups of Irish, German, and Italian immigrants, further illustrates her willingness to depart from social norms. Although *The Age of Innocence* seems predicated on the assumption that social class is fixed and that breaches bring peril, Catherine Mingott's life story testifies to the permeability of social class boundaries—and the myriad ways in which power relations constantly reconfigure themselves. This is a lesson Archer fails to learn.

Catherine Mingott speaks her mind with a commanding presence associated with American principles of individualism and provokes others to do the same. For example, she challenges her family to exceed the limits of conventionality, pronouncing them too "scared" to venture north of Fortieth Street. She confronts Archer specifically, and as the daughter of a rebel provides a model for his own insurrection. Every bit a Spicer, she laments lack of initiative in the Mingott line and poses the novel's central question:

> Ah, these Mingotts—all alike! Born in a rut, and you can't root 'em out of it. ... Ah, my dear Mr. Archer, I thank my stars I'm nothing but a vulgar Spicer; but there's not one of my own children that takes after me but my little Ellen. ... Now, why in the world didn't you marry my little Ellen? (153–154)

With a twinkle in her eye, Mrs. Mingott encourages Archer to flaunt convention, but she never simply grants freedom to others. They must want it badly enough to claim it for themselves. Archer proves ambivalent.

VI.

The ambiguous status of the self can be seen in the work of Wharton's contemporaries. William James, in *Principles of Psychology* (1890), contended that the self was not only an autonomous identity but also the result of recognition that one garnered from others. Such acknowledgment created the social self and made self-respect possible: "Properly speaking, a man has as many social selves as there are individuals who recognize him and carry an image of him in their mind."[31] Clergyman and essayist Gerald Stanley Lee constructed a career as an expert on crowds and mass behavior, arguing that imitation and suggestion were at the root of behavior. Mixing reformist and manipulative impulses, he created a bestseller with his book, *Crowds: A Moving-Picture of Democracy* (1913). As people united under ethical leadership, he maintained, they would through the dynamism of the crowd move closer to the ideals of democracy. He praised Walt Whitman for sounding this cry. As Borus notes, these writers and others, such as W. I. Thomas, Franklin Giddings, William McDougall, and Robert Park, used imitation-suggestion "to account for social solidarities and broad similarities in behavior among homogeneous population ... [and also] to present a notion of how consensus might be achieved in times of ethnic and class conflicts."[32]

Wharton knew the value of expertise and leadership. She also understood their necessity in times of threat. In *The Age of Innocence*, she ascribes these group-saving qualities to May and her tribeswomen. They are an indomitable force with the authority and vision to create as well as regulate family and society. Amidst a growing awareness of consumer culture and the social self that emerged from it, then, Wharton invests power in the machinery of this female-dominated New York clan. Their world is at odds with the integrity of the self, such as Emerson and Whitman espoused, a fact that Wharton also realized when she wrote in 1923: "there is no Whitman singing in this generation."[33] Nothing illustrates the notion that the self is formed in social interaction more than Archer's marriage to May. Old New York principles, customs, and rituals subsume him; when he fancies he will travel to escape their stultifying effect, May ensures his presence with her duplicitously announced pregnancy. Archer capitulates and compromises until, by the novel's end, he has "lost the habit of travel," which is Wharton's metaphor for the journey of soul:

> Since [May's] death, nearly two years before, there had been no reason for his continuing in the same routine. His children had urged him to travel. ... But Archer had found himself held fast by habit, by memories, by a sudden startled shrinking from new things.
>
> Now, as he reviewed his past, he saw into what a deep rut he had sunk. The worst of doing one's duty was that it apparently unfitted one for doing anything else. (350–351)

Wharton invests qualities of American individualism not in Archer, but in Ellen, who inherits Catherine Mingott's intrepid independence. Ostensibly fulfilled by art, history, and culture in Europe, and eschewing traditional, domestic roles for women, Ellen embodies Emersonian ideals. Much of her story takes place outside the frame of the novel, as if Wharton found American literary discourse insufficient to limn the dimensions of a female individualist. Ellen is single and child-free, an artist not a mother, and a free spirit so powerful that she cannot be bound by American standards of nineteenth-century womanhood. Archer can only imagine her life in France as he gazes upward at the light in her window. American individualism, Wharton suggests, is possible, but not in America. Ellen's life is similar to the one that Wharton chose when she made her home in France. Aware of the possibilities for Archer's escape, readers feel pity for his acquiescence to a stultifying existence. But mindful of the pressures that family and culture exert on him, they also understand why he does no better.

Edith Wharton's Prose Spectacle in the Age of Cinema

Margaret A. Toth
Manhattan College

On July 20, 1933, Edith Wharton sent an indignant note to Appleton, her publisher, about an offer the company was handling for the film rights to *The Age of Innocence*. In her characteristically acerbic tone, she writes:

> I received from you two days ago a cable asking if I would accept an offer of approximately nineteen hundred dollars for my share of the picture rights taken from the stage version of "The Age of Innocence." I have cabled in reply: "Offer ridiculous. Am writing," but I have since reflected that perhaps a figure has been left out of the cable, for I cannot believe that you would seriously consider such a proposal on my behalf.[1]

While it is unclear whether or not Appleton's original cable contained an error, Wharton would go on to accept an offer of $10,000 from RKO the next month. Wharton scholarship frequently rehearses the author's personal distaste for film—as Scott Marshall states in his foundational essay on Wharton and cinema, she viewed film-going as "trendy, mindless experiences to be avoided by serious, intelligent people"[2]—but it has given less attention to documents like this letter, which reveal her savvy negotiations in Hollywood markets. In the last two decades of her career, Wharton actively courted studio contracts for many of her novels and profited considerably from her works' adaptation to the silver screen. Indeed, according to Parley Ann Boswell, Wharton "earned more money by selling her fiction to Hollywood than any other American writer of her time."[3]

The Age of Innocence was adapted to film twice during Wharton's lifetime, first as a silent film in 1924 by Warner Bros. and then as a talkie in 1934 by

RKO. (It would be adapted yet again over fifty years after Wharton's death in 1993 by Martin Scorsese.) During increasingly fraught arrangements for a stage adaptation of the novel in 1921—plans that ultimately fell through and were not realized until 1928—Wharton wrote to Rutger B. Jewett at Appleton to urge for a film adaptation instead: "I have always much preferred the idea of a cinema, which might, I think, have a success; and I am cabling you today in that sense."[4] While Wharton doesn't elaborate on her logic here, the highly visual nature of the novel might have shaped her reasoning. The novel's keen pictorial sensibilities, something that original reviewers of the novel emphasized, made it a natural choice for adaptation to an optical medium. In a review for the *New York Times*, William Lyon Phelps, for example, claims: "I do not remember when I have read a work of fiction that gives the reader so vivid an idea of the furnishing and illuminating of rooms in fashionable houses as one will find in *The Age of Innocence*."[5] Scriptwriters, whether for stage or screen, would discover not only convincing dialogue and a moving plot in the novel but also an intrinsic, ready-made *mise-en-scène*—sets, settings, lighting, costuming, hair and makeup, and even blocking—in Wharton's rich descriptions.

The novel also, and perhaps primarily, lends itself to cinematic adaptation. Indeed, it functions as what I refer to throughout this essay as a "prose spectacle." In a review for *Publisher's Weekly*, Katherine Perry uses visual metaphors to describe the novel's power in a way that recalls early cinema of attraction, stating that it radiates an "almost metallic brilliance": like *The House of Mirth*, it "dazzle[s] the reading public, hypnotizes the eager eye which would not lose one significant word."[6] Here Perry intuitively recognizes what modern critics have referred to as the different "representational systems" available within Wharton's writing. As Brigitte Peucker argues, film—by nature a multi-modal form of art in which various forms of expression "collide"—is "particularly congenial to the artistic concerns of Wharton, whose work not only manifests a pronounced interest in the visual, but whose mode of allusion so frequently involves the multiple layering of painterly and writerly references."[7] In other words, it is not just Wharton's "settings and her clean linear narratives with well-constructed story lines and rounded differentiated characters" that make her writing suitable for adaptation.[8] It is also the complex rhetorical and aesthetic impulses—writing, painting, theater, sculpture, and, despite her distaste for it, even film—that motivate her work and ultimately produce a prose spectacle.

The 1924 adaptation is considered lost, so unless a print is discovered, we will never know if it lived up to its promise as a prose spectacle captured on film. The 1934 adaptation, the focus of this essay, is extant, but it has not fared well in the eyes of contemporary or modern critics.[9] Co-written by Sarah Y. Mason and her husband Victor Heerman—a screenwriting team that won an Oscar for their adaptation of *Little Women* the year before in 1933—and directed by seasoned theater director Philip Moeller, the film starred two fashionable actors in the main roles: Irene Dunne (Ellen Olenska) and John Boles (Newland Archer). The on-screen pair had, two years prior, won over audiences in a similar story about forbidden desire and longing, the adaptation of Fannie Hurst's *Back Street* (Universal, 1932). According to Boswell, however, "for all of its impressive credentials, *The Age of Innocence* is an unremarkable film that best fits into the Hollywood subgenre of the 'teacup drama.'"[10] Similarly, Linda Costanzo Cahir calls the film "thin, spiritless, and aseptic,"[11] echoing early reviews that praised the fine acting and beautiful staging but quibbled with the film's airless quality. As the reviewer for the *New York Times* stated: "the photoplay ... leaves the spectator curiously cold and detached from the raging emotions of the story. It seems to have everything but the ability to quicken the pulse and mist the eye."[12] Margaret McDowell usefully identifies some of the challenges faced by scriptwriters seeking to adapt *The Age of Innocence*. While the novel is highly pictorial—making a shift to a visual medium relatively painless—other aspects of Wharton's writing resist translation, particularly narrative voice and pacing.[13] The adaptation also suffered from the historical conditions under which it was made, including both the Production Code, to which it had to adhere, and Hollywood's difficult transition from silent to sound film.

These criticisms of the 1934 film adaptation are not unwarranted. In the first section of this essay, I look at how Wharton's novel was "Hollywoodized" for the silver screen. More specifically, I examine the ways in which the novel got sucked into a mass-market machine that stripped many adapted novels in this era of their rich and complex textures; however, I also argue that the 1934 version is more compelling than it might appear at first glance. While he doesn't analyze it in detail, Marshall states that the 1934 *The Age of*

Innocence, though not a great film, is "a highly interesting one" that makes several "surprising choices."[14] I agree with his assessment and contend that the film deserves serious examination; it emerged out of a transitional moment in Hollywood, which also coincided with the era in which European intellectuals such as Sergei Eisenstein, Béla Balázs, Rudolf Arnheim, and others were beginning to theorize about the art of film. In the second part of this essay, I bring this school of thought—early film theory that went on to shape how we currently understand film aesthetics and philosophy—to bear on the 1934 adaptation. Boswell observes that "whatever *The Age of Innocence* [1934 film] does not tell us about Wharton's novel, the film does suggest that Hollywood movies were becoming more complicated, with their own discourse and a faint but undeniable integrity."[15] I build on this claim, asking what we can learn by applying early film theorists' ideas about such issues as cinematography, montage, and sound to the 1934 adaptation. Ultimately, I demonstrate that such an approach provides insight not only into the film and the Hollywood industry but also into Wharton's novel itself, particularly its status as prose spectacle.

By situating the 1934 film within these two historical frameworks—mass markets and burgeoning film theory—I am shifting away from what is arguably the most common methodology in adaptation studies, one that prioritizes, and sometimes even fetishizes, the question of an adaptation's fidelity to the original work's "integral meaning."[16] Along with Robert Stam, I contend that there is no such thing as a singular or sanctioned integral meaning or, as he puts it, "transferable core."[17] For example, the 1934 film version emphasizes Wharton's commentary on generational differences and social change under modernization, while Martin Scorsese, in his 1993 adaptation, focuses on Wharton's treatment of society as spectacle and the ritualistic, institutionalized nature of old New York. Both of these meanings are embedded in the novel and extricated by the scriptwriters and filmmakers, and neither is "right" or "wrong."[18] Stam proposes replacing the fidelity model with "a more satisfying formulation [that] would emphasize not ontological essence, but rather diacritical specificity."[19] In the second part of this essay, I adopt this approach, analyzing what, precisely, happens when we move from one mode of discourse to another, namely, from prose spectacle to cinematic expression.

The Age of Innocence and the Hollywood machine

Describing the fate of Wharton's novels on screen, Cahir claims that the works' complex range of emotions and internal struggles often get erased, with the films instead relying on simplistic plot devices such as the love triangle. "Edith Wharton's writing has the disturbing power of art," Cahir states, but "far too often, when translated to film, Wharton's capacity to disturb is muted by filmmakers, whose talents are not up to the complexities of the task, or by the industry's money-making motive, which overwhelms all other concerns."[20] The adaptations of Wharton's novels made in the 1920s and 1930s in particular underwent the process of Hollywoodization, that is, a simplification of intricate plots and complex characterization in order to appeal to the broadest audience possible and therefore increase studio revenue. In this historical moment, studio personnel would scour the pages of popular magazines, looking for potentially profitable material and frequently bidding on option rights the week the stories or novel installments appeared in print (and occasionally before they appeared). This method became particularly advantageous as hysteria about Hollywood's licentiousness reached a fever pitch; the industry had earned, "by the early 1920s," a "reputation as a wild place where scandal and sin were rampant."[21] Studio executives reasoned that attaching well-established authorial names to their projects—particularly a name like Wharton's, which evoked old New York values and elegance—would lend the films a level of respectability and, as Boswell puts it, "prestige."[22]

In her article on the various adaptations of Anita Loos's *Gentlemen Prefer Blondes* (1925), Bethany Wood describes the machinery of magazine publications and adaptations, both stage and film, in this period. Wood is interested in the practicalities of how print stories moved into different media formats in the 1920s and 1930s, but she also explores how gender ideologies were woven into and expressed through them:

> [W]omen's periodicals served as a trove of material for producers and screen writers seeking well-developed narratives and characters to adapt for the stage and screen. Several narratives, including *Gentlemen Prefer Blondes*, *Show Boat*, *The Old Maid*, *Old Man Minick*, and *The Age of Innocence*, followed this path from women's magazine serial, to novel, to stage, to

screen during this period, mapping a significant route for concerns and representations of femininity through mainstream entertainment.[23]

While Wood focuses on Loos in the piece, her observations also are applicable to Wharton's writing in this period. Wharton's elaborate exploration of gender and power often gets undermined by the medium, such as the advertisements for homemaking products or high fashion surrounding the works serialized in magazines like *Pictorial Review*. When scriptwriters adapted works like *The Glimpses of the Moon* (1922) or *The Children* (1928) for the screen, they reduced them to titillating love-triangle stories while removing far more titillating aspects, such as the pedophilic overtones of *The Children*. Indeed, as Boswell claims, the "Hollywood factory ... mutilate[d] the work of writers in unprecedented ways" in the 1920s:

> They routinely bought a property with a famous author's name attached and then put it through the machinery of a production assembly line of story writers, screenwriters, and scenario specialists. When the final product came off the assembly line ... it was of a standardized size, shape, and texture. As such, to anyone who had either written or read the original work, the film was, more often than not, almost unrecognizable.[24]

The works, in other words, were Hollywoodized, pushed through a highly regulated process that yielded homogenous, sterile end products, ones that frequently distorted the authors' artistic objectives.

The 1934 version of *The Age of Innocence*, while Hollywoodized, is not unrecognizable. In fact, it is fairly faithful in terms of plot, with some minor changes and necessary excisions made to keep within the standard feature running time. It even, and perhaps surprisingly, maintains significant plot points that push the boundaries of the Production Code. For example, in a scene in which Ellen and Newland engage in intimate conversation about Ellen's failed marriage and her need for autonomy, Ellen states to Newland that, even though she is separated from her husband, she "must have love."[25] This line, which passed under the radar of the censors, breaks the Production Code's explicit rules about representations of infidelity[26] and implicit rules about women laying claim to sexual desire and agency. Interestingly, the adaptation also maintains the plot line about May's pregnancy scheme, a narrative move that lends more depth and complexity to May's character in both the novel and the film. Occasionally the dialogue is lifted word for word, including May's lines about how she wasn't sure she was pregnant—even though she told Ellen she was—and her triumphant, "And you see I was right!"[27]

The adaptation is also visually recognizable. The various elements of *mise-en-scène*, including the set design, costumes, hair and makeup, properties, and blocking, are in place and on point. In a representative scene early in the film—the equivalent of Chapter Four in the novel—Newland visits Granny Mingott with May and her parents to discuss the young couple's engagement. Granny's wealth gets conveyed through the elaborate furnishings of her parlor—the interior of her home is described as "stately" in the novel—while her eccentricity emerges through her costuming, hairstyle, jewelry, and props, such as her flamboyant cane (19). More subtly, Newland's affinity with the unconventional Granny—an affinity that foreshadows the bond he will go on to form with Ellen—is reinforced through the blocking of the scene. He immediately sits next to Granny on a small sofa and puts his arm around her while the Wellands keep a polite distance. When Granny and the Wellands begin discussing Ellen's unseemly outings with Beaufort, Newland swiftly gets up and walks out of frame, uncomfortable with the gossip. Then, when Beaufort and Ellen arrive, Beaufort claims Newland's vacated seat on the sofa, while Ellen takes the spot on the other side of Granny, thus signaling the rivalry that will emerge between the two men. The adaptation, then, translates all the rich visual descriptions packed within Wharton's novel about what the characters wear and the spaces they occupy, but it also makes a more adventurous effort to capture the underlying dynamics and tensions among the characters in visual terms through blocking and gestural movement.

Despite such attempts, however, the intensity of feeling in the novel is indeed flattened out in the translation process. The major obstacle the screenwriters face is how to convey the central force that drives the narrative forward: Newland's interiority, namely, the fact that he is seething with repressed desires and entertaining complex ideas about conformity and rebellion within a constrained, conventional, and hierarchical society. Even in the hands of a gifted actor—one with supreme control over facial expression and body language—such internal struggles are difficult to express on screen unless the film resorts to voiceover, as the Scorsese version does. The scene in which Newland, concerned about his growing attachment to Ellen, travels to Florida to see May and try to convince her to change their wedding date provides a good example of how the film falls short in this respect. In the novel, Newland and May have their first candid conversation about their feelings, and readers also get their first glimpse of May's own complicated interiority, which is largely withheld throughout the novel. When Newland hotly urges that they forgo a long engagement and marry sooner—"Why should we dream away another year? ... Don't you understand how I want you for my wife?"—May shrewdly responds: "I'm not sure if I do understand ... Is it—is it because you're not certain of continuing to care for me?" (104). This is not the response Newland expects from his ostensibly naive fiancée, and it prompts him to unprecedented honesty. He admits that he isn't sure, and May boldly states that she will cede any rights she has over him: "I couldn't have my happiness made out of a wrong—an unfairness to somebody else" (105). Newland is moved both by her generosity and by his relief that she hasn't suspected his feelings for Ellen, and he responds by reassuring her of his devotion.

While this exchange offers a momentary sense of closure in the novel—the couple embrace, with May's eyes "full of happy tears"—the chapter ends on a note of uneasiness. Wharton devotes two final paragraphs to the undisclosed emotions and judgments still churning below the surface within each character (106). Newland, for his part, "understood that her courage and initiative were for others, and that she had none for herself. It was evident that the effort of speaking had been much greater than her studied composure betrayed, and that at his first word of reassurance she had dropped back into the usual, as a too-adventurous child takes refuge in its mother's arms" (106). Wharton also provides an intimation of how May interprets the incident: "May seemed to be aware of his disappointment, but without knowing how to alleviate it; and they stood and walked silently home" (107). This is a key scene in the novel, establishing patterns that will go on to structure the couple's life for decades: Newland will continue to infantilize May and underestimate her own psychological struggles, while May will continue to choose the path of passivity or passive aggression over direct assertiveness. Indeed, this dynamic informs every interaction we witness between the two in the remaining pages of the novel, including the scenes in which May holds the farewell dinner for Ellen and in which she reveals her pregnancy to Newland. And yet, as essential as this pattern is, Wharton unfolds it delicately and subtly.

The adaptation does not capture the nuance of this scene, though it does adopt the visual logic at work in the novel. For example, at the beginning of their conversation, the couple stroll through "an old orange-garden beyond the town," which the film translates into a long tracking shot, the camera keeping its distance (100). As their conversation moves from small talk to more intimate discussion about their engagement, the camera cuts to a medium shot to underscore Newland's emotion. Similarly, when May expresses her concern that Newland's affections might lie elsewhere, we get the first medium close-up of the scene, with the camera registering in detail the worry on her face. From here, the editing pattern shifts to a series of reverse shots as the couple converse, until Newland finally joins May, seated on a bench. As in the novel, this shift to a two-shot provides a sense of resolution—the couple, now sharing the frame, embrace, with May smiling and teary—but, beyond the skeptical look on Newland's face, we have little sense of how he is interpreting this moment and no insight into May's misgivings. That is, we remain on the surface of the image, where the novel can dive below, into the characters' psychological states.

This shortcoming is present in many of the scenes, particularly the ones in which Wharton, in the novel, documents Newland's thoughts in a proto-stream-of-consciousness manner. For example, in the novel's wedding scene, Newland becomes almost catatonic, even as complicated ideas and wild emotions rage within him; the reader gets just as lost in these thoughts as Newland does, and we, too, are startled when his best man brings him back to reality with a stage whisper: "Newland—I say: she's here!" (129). The film's only attempt at capturing Newland's conflicted feelings at the wedding is a moving point-of-view shot from his perspective as he walks up the aisle with his new wife while looking at Ellen seated in a pew. This scene, the Florida episode, and other moments in the film justify the *New York Times* reviewer's assessment that the film is "a painstaking but emotionally flaccid photoplay."[28] They also demonstrate the ways in which the novel has been Hollywoodized. The original work is stripped of its intricacy and replaced with a straightforward love triangle, as in the wedding scene, when Newland is literally on the arm of one woman while gazing upon another.

There is no question, then, that the film faces limitations when it comes to translating Wharton's rich language. But what happens when we shift our focus to look more intently at the cinematic language of the film, that is, the different tools of cinematography, editing, and sound that it employs? How does the film experiment with these devices—many of which were fairly innovative at the time—to attempt to grasp the deeper meanings available within the novel? In this context, that moving point-of-view shot in the wedding scene holds weight and significance. It is one of only a handful of subjective shots in the film, so it registers differently with the viewer, taking on a charged valence. In other words, it might not be able to convey Newland's inner monologue, but it nevertheless performs important narrative work. In the following section, I look more closely at such cinematic language in the 1934 adaptation, couching my reading within the scholarship of early film theorists. This language— occasionally quite sophisticated—sits in stark tension with the Hollywoodized aspects of the film. In other words, the film might reduce Wharton's language through Hollywoodization, but it frequently replaces it with a language of its own, one that interacts dialogically with the original work.

The Age of Innocence and early film theory

While there are many seminal studies in early film theory, I draw in this section upon ones that coincided with Wharton's career and the production of the 1934 film adaptation. The earliest work I use is Hugo Münsterberg's *The Photoplay: A Psychological Study*, which was put out by Wharton's publisher, Appleton, in 1916. The latest texts I consider are Rudolf Arnheim's *Film as Art* (1932) and various essays by Sergei Eisenstein that span from the year the film was released into the early 1940s. I also engage influential works by Béla Balázs, including *Visible Man* (1924) and *The Spirit of Film* (1930). These thinkers pursued various overlapping objectives: to defend cinema against those who claimed it was mere "mechanical reproduction" of reality;[29] to engage in a debate about presentation versus representation; to distinguish film from its closest sister art, the theater, by focusing on cinema's distinctive spatial and temporal faculties; and to develop what Eisenstein called a "cinematic diction,"[30] a complex language that is unique to film alone. Combined, these aims undergirded a more primal, urgent goal: to overturn the accusation that film was a "half art,"[31] "a spoilt and dissolute child of theatre."[32]

These intellectuals also occasionally discuss adaptation, with varying perspectives on film's capabilities and deficiencies when it comes to translating the written word to the screen. Balázs, for instance, is pessimistic about cinema's power in this respect, anticipating some of the concerns both contemporary and modern critics voice about the 1934 adaptation of *The Age of Innocence*: "A writer's success depends on the power and subtlety of his writing. The artistic nature of film resides in the power and subtlety of its images and its gestural language. This explains why film has nothing in common with literature."[33] In one of his more poetic moments, he describes the attenuation inherent in the process of adapting great works to the screen:

> What survives on screen is the bare bones of the original storyline. What vanishes is the lovely flesh of profound ideas, the tender skin of lyrical tones. Of these beautiful charms, nothing remains but a naked skeleton, something that is no longer literature and not yet film, but simply a "content" that does not yet embody the "essence" of either art form. A skeleton like this needs a completely different covering of flesh, a different epidermis, if it is to acquire a visible, living shape in film.[34]

While theorists like Münsterberg are equally skeptical—"the novel on screen … must be lifeless and uninspiring"[35]—Eisenstein is more optimistic. In his groundbreaking essay on Charles Dickens and D. W. Griffith, "Dickens, Griffith, and the Film Today," he attempts to identify and interrogate the elements that make up the figurative "epidermis" that Balázs mentions. Specifically, he looks at different narrative practices at work in Dickens's writing and demonstrates how Griffith's films deploy them in transmuted fashion. He, too, relies on a biological—and, more specifically, evolutionary—metaphor to describe this process, stating that "this relationship [between Dickens's novels and US cinema, of which Griffith is representative] is organic, and the 'genetic' line of descent is quite consistent."[36]

While Eisenstein and others don't use the term prose spectacle to describe Dickens's writing, they do acknowledge its pictorial qualities. Balázs, for instance, states that "there are writers who have a particularly visual imagination, and whose books seem to be made for film. Dickens, for example. Every page, when read, provides a visual image."[37] Eisenstein moves beyond imagery to identify the ways in which Dickens's manipulation of space and time anticipates such filmic devices as cross-cutting, flashbacks, and flash-forwards—or, depending on our perspective, the ways in which these filmic devices were inspired by writers like Dickens. Cinematographic techniques like distance (particularly the close-up), framing, and shot composition, as well as various editing techniques, such as the dissolve cut or montage, are also key in Eisenstein's view, as they hold the power to accentuate particular objects or draw forth emotional or intellectual responses from an audience. Comparing Dickens's cinematic writing to Griffith's filmic practices, for instance, Eisenstein claims that "Griffith has all this in as much a Dickens-esque sharpness and clarity as Dickens, on his part, had cinematic 'optical quality,' 'frame composition,' 'close-up,' and the alteration of emphasis by special lenses."[38] Eisenstein instinctively grasps the complex aesthetic impulses motivating Dickens's writing, including not just painterly or theatrical rhetorical devices but also proto-cinematic ones.

I argue that the 1934 film *The Age of Innocence* makes use of cinematic language in order to tap into a similarly complicated artistic discourse at work in Wharton's novel. The film doesn't always succeed in bringing Wharton's prose spectacle to life, but analyzing it alongside early film theory allows us to see why the tools of cinema might be more effective when adapting Wharton's work than, for instance, the conventions of theater. The screenwriters' and Moeller's primary goal in the adaptation is to convey how the generation Newland and Ellen occupy imprisons them and thwarts their relationship, which is presented as an authentically intimate and sensually charged bond, as opposed to the proper and somewhat antiseptic legal union Newland and May form. As in the novel, the film suggests that if Newland and Ellen had been born even one generation later their story would have concluded differently—and likely more happily.

Wharton, for her part, begins to set up these ideas in the first two chapters, which borrow, in a sophisticated manner, from various modes of art. The novel opens with a description of "Christine Nilsson ... singing in Faust at the Academy of Music in New York" and Newland's arrival at his opera box (3). While not quite ekphrastic, the descriptions of Nilsson's performance put the reader in the role of the diegetic audience. We, too, look at the stage and admire the elements of *mise-en-scène*, such as the performers' costumes and props (4) or the elaborate pastoral setting—"no expense had been spared"—all expertly lit by strategically placed footlights (5). And we, too, hear the Daisy Song Nilsson sings. In other words, Wharton's theatrical discourse is evident in the opening chapters, making it immediately apparent why the early reviewers would claim that readers are "dazzled" by her descriptions.

But Wharton also emphasizes the function of vision in ways that push beyond mere description of a theatrical performance and into prose spectacle. She carefully describes the staging of the operatic performance, to be sure, but she also situates it within her own narrative staging. That is, the ocular language is layered and overdetermined, as we gaze upon characters who also gaze upon both the legitimate performance and other characters' social performances. We also frequently look through characters' eyes. For example, we don't merely see May in our readerly minds. We see her, the "warm pink mount[ing] to [her] cheek, mantl[ing] her brow to the roots of her fair braids" (5), through Newland's mediated gaze. Even more complexly, we sometimes see through others' eyes as they attempt to approximate another character's visual perspective, as when Newland, "following Lefferts's glance," sees Ellen enter Mrs. Mingott's opera box (7). Moreover, characters also suspect they are being watched and on display (11)—and they are, by and for both other characters and us as readers. And finally, the chapter mobilizes devices that, as in Eisenstein's assessment of Dickens, accord with film. Some of these are temporal and therefore related to editing, as in the mini-flashback to Newland's dinner with his family and his after-dinner cigar in the library prior to the opera. Others are cinematographic, such as the multiple point-of-view descriptions or the figurative close-ups—some achieved through Lefferts's opera glasses—on May and Ellen's faces. The chapter even feels filmic in its sonic qualities, as the muffled tones of Nilsson singing the Daisy Song burst onto the page in full tonal clarity when Newland opens the door to his opera box.

This prose spectacle informs several of Wharton's goals in the novel, including her thematic treatment of generational differences and the wave of modernization that is about to sweep through old New York. Wharton overtly announces the time period in the opening sentence—it is "the early seventies" (3)—and, through the use of prolepsis in the second sentence, suggests the ways in which Newland's society will change: "Though there was already talk of the erection, in remote metropolitan distances 'above the Forties,' of a new

Opera House which should compete in costliness and splendor with those of the great European capitals, the world of fashion was still content to reassemble every winter in the shabby red and gold boxes of the old Academy" (3). While this line directly refers to imminent changes to the physical landscape of New York, others in the opening chapters allude to social change. For instance, the narrator states that "the persons of their [Newland and May's] world lived in an atmosphere of faint implications and pale delicacies," indicating that this is a time long past and even exotic (12).

Significantly, the 1934 film version does not include this scene at the opera. Originally, the screenwriters planned to open with Newland visiting the Wellands on a "wintry and bitter day."[39] According to the estimating script currently housed at the Lilly Library, this opening would have emphasized not generational but rather class differences. Mason and Heerman envisioned an opening tracking shot that registered the gap between the haves, the Wellands and their guests, and the have nots, the workers employed in various tasks upon the Wellands' street: "CAMERA IS MOVING up to house from across street and an impression of social extremes is got as it passes street-cleaners … at work pushing snow down manhole in centre of street; others loading dump wagon."[40] As a driver tries to stay warm in the unforgiving elements, he engages in a brief conversation—the opening dialogue of the script—with the foreman overseeing work on the Wellands' home in preparation for an event they are hosting:

> FOREMAN (watching activity of canopy being put up at mansion)
> It's funny how little they can put up with, when they live in this neighborhood.
> DRIVER
> Yeah, I guess they think it's colder than over on the river where I live.[41]

Again, this opening prioritizes class differences, casting the Wellands and their peers as a privileged set that profits off the labor, here performed in hazardous conditions, of others. Ultimately, however, these images and the dialogue were discarded, with Mason and Heerman instead determining to focus on questions of generational change and technological transformation.[42]

The more traditional and staid opening of this estimating script was instead replaced with a daring opening sequence in the style of Soviet montage, that is, the editing together of discrete images that, when combined, work to elicit an intellectual or psychological response in the viewer rather than to facilitate the storyline.[43] Arnheim describes this more philosophical tradition of montage as follows: "if strips of film are joined one to another, it is observed … that they do not simply stand 'additively' beside one another but take on quite different shades of meaning through juxtaposition."[44] The opening of *The Age of Innocence*, quite original for its time in Hollywood, follows this principle.

The opening montage is only one minute long, and yet it is composed of over forty-five different shots, meaning that, on average, most shots appear on screen for only a fraction over a second. This chaotic editing pace is matched by the unsettling quality of the images themselves. The first ones, many of which are aerial shots, are devoted to New York City's skyscrapers and busy streets. Each frame is highly mobile, with the camera sweeping quickly and shakily into the depth of the frame or across the images—many of which appear to be still photographs of the city—so that, as viewers, we get unnervingly immersed into the images. Just as we are about to grasp what we are seeing, however, one shot dissolves into the next, making it impossible to gain our spatial bearings. From here, the montage moves into images that represent the city's nightlife, including exterior shots of Times Square at night and interior ones of brilliantly lit nightclubs, featuring close-ups of champagne being poured, white flappers drinking and twirling, and black performers dancing and playing instruments. While the first images evoke anxiety about urban sprawl, these ones—equally kinetic and fast-paced—produce discomfort about white women's sexuality and racial mixing. The next set of images displays headlines, all of which are devoted to moral and social decay, on electronic marquees and newspapers. For instance, we see a headline about murder interspersed with shots of gangster violence and multiple front-page stories about divorces and sex scandals. The last newspaper, with the headline "ARMSTRONGS TELL ALL TO JUDGE," dissolves into a shot of the aged Newland and the young Dallas—the latter of whom is reading that particular article to learn about what is happening with his lover, Mrs. Armstrong—and viewers at last enter the film's proper diegesis. This bold montage immediately announces the film's interest in modernity and the consequences of social change.[45]

The following brief scene, set in the backseat of a moving automobile—another indicator of modern technology—deepens this theme, as Newland and Dallas engage in a brief conversation about the differences between their generations, a disparity underscored by the decision to make Dallas Newland's grandson, whereas in the book Dallas is his son. Dallas responds to Newland's statements about the sanctity of marriage and its function in stable societies with a flippant: "Past generation stuff." But then he asks his grandfather about his own personal history with a married woman—he has heard rumors— and Newland begins to narrate his past: "It was later in the year than this. I remember, there was snow on the ground."[46] The camera cuts from the backseat to a close-up of the moving car's wheel, which dissolves into the turning wheel of a horse carriage traveling across a snow-lined street. The opening montage and brief first scene, then, function to set up the film's flashback structure; the film is almost entirely one long flashback, though we do return to the present of the 1920s—or, as Wood argues, the 1930s[47]—at the end. They also highlight generational gaps, an idea further reinforced in the first scene set in the past. As Newland visits the Wellands, Mrs. Welland complains about how courting etiquette was different in her day; in other words, each generation differs from the one before and after it, though the film suggests that the leap into modernity is more radical than previous incremental changes.

With this concept of generational difference established, the film turns to focus on Newland and Ellen's illicit desire and their moral struggle against it. Their dilemma in some ways serves as a substitute for generational conflict, with the film suggesting that the two are figuratively out of time, that is, occupying the wrong era. This gets conveyed primarily through various cinematographic choices—especially framing, distance, and movement—as well as the non-diegetic score, all devices that are used to distinguish Newland and May's attachment, which belongs in this time period, from Newland and Ellen's attachment, which does not. For example, the camera tends to maintain a polite distance from May and Newland when they are on screen together. Even in two-shots, which are generally more intimate, the camera often sits far away, objectively recording their interactions. By contrast, when Newland and Ellen first encounter one another at the post-opera ball, they are each shot in individual medium close-ups; and, once they are left alone together on the ballroom floor, the camera dollies in on a two-shot of the couple on two separate occasions, reducing the frame around them and creating the sense that they are alone together in the crowd. A clear spark of energy exists between the two, and while this is partially achieved through the acting—

particularly Dunne's magnetic performance—it is also achieved through the medium itself. The film follows this particular pattern—static and distanced when May is on screen and expressive and intimate when Ellen is presented—throughout. Balázs referred to close-ups as "film's true terrain,"[48] since forced perspective isn't something that can be achieved in the theater. *The Age of Innocence* makes judicious use of this terrain, reserving the close-up—often paired with a soft filter—for Dunne in order to show both how Ellen differs from the rest of the women in her generation and why Newland is so attracted to that difference.

The film's non-diegetic music also, quite literally, underscores these ideas about the romance—and tragedy—of living in the wrong time period. *The Age of Innocence*'s musical score was directed by the legendary Max Steiner, who composed over 300 film scores in his lifetime and would go on to acquire fame for his work on such films as *Gone With the Wind* (MGM, 1939) and *Casablanca* (Warner Bros., 1942). In his 1933 score for *King Kong* (RKO), Steiner began developing codified practices about when and how music should be used in films, rules that still largely govern cinematic music today.[49] He continued to refine these practices the following year in his work for *The Age of Innocence*, adopting various principles—such as using non-diegetic music to signify emotion or provide narrative cues[50]—in order to approximate the music of Wharton's language. While the written word and classical music are markedly different media, the two interact dialectically in provocative and effective ways.

After the sweeping orchestral arrangement that accompanies the opening credits, the first third of the film is curiously and resoundingly silent. This part of the film contains only a mono-track—the dialogue—with just one scene, the post-opera ball, making use of music: a diegetic waltz played by musicians at the Wellands' home. The non-diegetic score doesn't enter the film until the flower shop scene, the moment in which Newland's growing feelings for Ellen, as well as his awareness of her difference from May, are revealed to both himself and the audience, arguably for the first time. Wharton describes this moment as follows:

> As he wrote a word on his card [for May] and waited for an envelope he glanced about the embowered shop, and his eye lit on a cluster of yellow roses. He had never seen any as sun-golden before, and his first impulse was

to send them to May instead of the lilies. But they did not look like her—there was something too rich, too strong, in their fiery beauty. In a sudden revulsion of mood, and almost without knowing what he did, he signed to the florist to lay the roses in another long box, and slipped his card into a second envelope, on which he wrote the name of the Countess Olenska; then, just as he was turning away, he drew the card out again, and left the empty envelope on the box. (56)

This is a crucial turning point in the novel, as it is the first of many times that Newland acts impulsively on his infatuation with Ellen.

Quite significantly, this is the moment at which the film begins making use of a non-diegetic score, not the earlier courting scenes between Newland and May or even the emotional Florida scene, which is almost eerily silent when compared to similar scenes from Hollywood films of this era. Newland walks through the door to the flower shop, and the score subtly enters the film with him. As he spots the yellow roses that remind him of Ellen's warmth and vibrancy and sits down to compose a message to send to her, the romantic score—a variation of the opening credits music, but stripped down to strings alone—swells in volume and intensity. The music intensifies even more as the camera provides a cut-in shot of the note he is writing—"Dear Ellen These few roses which as you know are called the 'Richness of Life' I—I"—and then cuts back to a Newland overcome and at a loss to find the appropriate words. He ultimately discards the note, and the music decrescendos as he departs the shop, fading into silence.

The scene, then, makes use of the written word—the note Newland begins to write—but it conveys more meaning, at the level of emotional and narrative cueing, through the score, in other words through the film's musical language. From this scene forward, Steiner makes liberal use of non-diegetic music. This particular musical theme, what we might think of as the "forbidden desire" variation, appears at multiple points over the course of the film, primarily in the scenes in which Newland and Ellen appear on screen together—at the winter cottage, in the museum, as Ellen departs for Europe—appropriately waxing and waning to convey their intimacy, passion, and longing. It even occasionally plays when they aren't on screen together, as when Ellen reads May's honeymoon letter out loud to Granny; here the music subtly, but significantly, suggests that Newland and Ellen's love transcends physical and temporal boundaries. Moreover, Steiner makes use of a different piece during a montage that shows images from Newland and May's honeymoon, the only scene that sets the married couple's interactions to music. The tonal qualities of the music differ sharply from the forbidden desire variation, as the montage images are set against a jaunty, almost patriotic, piece written in a major key.

The score, then, gets strategically employed to capture the dynamics and themes embedded in the novel. Even the climactic scene between Newland and May, in which she reveals her pregnancy and seals Newland's fate, is set to a resonant silence—again, quite an unusual choice on Steiner's part. But the absence of the score helps to convey the contrast between Newland's views toward May and Ellen—one detached, sterile, and even cold, the other rich, textured, and pregnant with desires both articulated and unspoken. Most early film theorists lamented the introduction of sound to cinema—"sound film," Balázs wrote, "burst upon the scene, with catastrophic force … attach[ing] itself to a highly developed cinematic art" and "throw[ing] it back to the most primitive stage"[51]—but here we see that, when used or withheld selectively and deliberately, it can bring Wharton's language to life in a powerful, though of course transposed, manner.

***

Long after the publication of *The Age of Innocence*—and well into the late-twentieth and twenty-first century—artists working in various media continue seeking out ways to dialectically converse with the novel. For instance, Scorsese's 1993 film version, with the advantage of more evolved cinematic technologies—including the lenses used to capture the fractured images seen through the opera glasses in the opening scene or the zoom lens employed in select scenes—enacts an even more sophisticated dialectical relationship to the original. Sabine Haenni notes Scorsese's "zooms, close-ups, long shots, quick cuts, and pans,"[52] while Peucker praises the film's cinematographic movement, much more kinetic in 1993 as cameras became lighter and easier to maneuver over time: "The ostentatious movement of the camera in *The Age of Innocence* … calls attention to itself, underlining the way in which the camera virtually generates space and gestures toward the three-dimensionality of that cinematic space in the process."[53]

Interestingly, the most recent stage production at the Hartford Stage, which premiered in the spring of 2018 and was adapted by the writer and filmmaker Douglas McGrath, also makes several adventurous and occasionally cinematic choices, ones perhaps inspired by the two film adaptations. For example, McGrath introduces a narrator referred to as The Old Gentleman, thereby shifting parts of the novel from "third-person narrative into a single first-person voice" and approximating the filmic voiceover.[54] He also commissioned an original musical number by Stephen Foster, "Beautiful Dreamer," hearkening back to the musical strategies of both Steiner in the 1934 film and Elmer Bernstein, who composed a magnificently haunting score for the Scorsese adaptation. McGrath, in a description of his adaptation methodology, indirectly points to how Wharton's prose spectacle will continue to inspire artists working in visual media a century after the novel's publication date: "In a book, everything looks wonderful. But in a play or movie, you have to compress it. You have to look for the emotional center of it. You can't really have a fidelity to the text. You identify the heart of the story, and find what is relevant to human life now."[55]

The 1934 adaptation of *The Age of Innocence* followed this methodology, identifying generational change and modernization as "the heart of the story." It also used the tools of cinematic language available at the time—ones that were continuously evolving—to dialogically interact with Wharton's original prose spectacle. Therefore, while perhaps appearing modest or even crude to the twenty-first-century viewer, such devices as movement, framing, distance, editing, and non-diegetic sound all work together to communicate the themes and interpersonal dynamics that structure the original work.

Acknowledgments

Much of the research for this piece was conducted at the Lilly Library at Indiana University under the sponsorship of an Everett Helm Visiting Fellowship. I thank the institution for this opportunity and the librarians at the Lilly for their generous assistance during my time there.

"You Must Tell Me Just What to Do": Action and Characterization in Wharton's *The Age of Innocence*

Gabi Kirilloff
Texas Christian University

When we reflect on literary characters, we often associate them with their actions: Edna Pontellier walking into the sea, Jane Eyre fleeing across the moor, Ahab thrusting his harpoon into Moby Dick. Along with other forms of characterization, including physical description and dialogue, character behavior shapes our understanding of character identity. As Henry James concisely notes: "What is character but the determination of incident? What is incident but the illustration of character?"[1] When we reflect on a character's actions, we tend to concentrate on those that are integral to the plot's movement, actions that, if left out of the story, would drastically alter the shape of the narrative; however, these actions represent only a small portion of the sitting, walking, going, sighing, and looking that major and minor characters perform. The ways in which authors choose to frame these types of actions do not always overtly contribute to characterization; whether an author chooses to describe a minor character as "muttering" or "murmuring" may not seem significant within the context of a single sentence, nor perhaps even within a single novel. But, in examining such choices across a large corpus, patterns in the depiction of actions, and the types of characters associated with these actions, begin to emerge.

Wharton's *The Age of Innocence* is filled with seemingly mundane actions that shape our perception of character and plot: Ellen Olenska's decision to "get up and walk away from one gentleman in order to seek the company of another" contributes to her unconventional status among New York's social milieu, while the fact that Newland Archer "dawdled over his cigar" pegs him as a dilettante.[2] As Donald Pizer observes, Wharton's New York "exerts a web of compulsion which powerfully shapes and controls individual belief and behavior."[3] Key to interpreting this "web" is the link between turn-of-the-century gender norms and notions of propriety; as Janet Beer and Avril Horner concisely note, the novel's characters are "fettered by their perceptions of what it means to be a man or a woman."[4] Recent work on novelistic action suggests that many of the behaviors Wharton describes as either gender normative or transgressive (such as Ellen's "walking away") are closely tied to the depiction of character gender throughout nineteenth- and early-twentieth-century novels. In my previous computational work with Matthew Jockers on nineteenth-century action and gender, we argue that there is a strong correlation between a character's gender and the actions that character performs.[5] In a corpus of 3,329 novels, certain verbs (such as "murmur" and "sit") are strongly associated with female characters, while others (such as "mutter" and "walk") are strongly associated with male characters.

In what follows, I use computational tools to compare Wharton's use of verbs in fifteen of her novels with over 3,000 nineteenth- and twentieth-century novels. Despite May's assertion that she and Newland cannot "behave like people in novels," characters in *The Age of Innocence* do behave in ways consistent with the majority of male and female characters in nineteenth- and early-twentieth-century novels (68). The same is not true of several of Wharton's other novels; for example, characters in *The Marne* perform actions more typically associated with the opposite gender. I argue that, in *The Age of Innocence*, Wharton creates a baseline of "typical" behavior that underscores moments in which characters behave unexpectedly. For example, May's ineptitude at needlework is surprising and unsettling precisely because Wharton persistently links May with conventional, domestic behavior. I posit that the minute actions performed by specific characters in *The Age of Innocence* provide further insight into Wharton's depiction of gender propriety: in reading the small, but deviant, actions that Newland and May perform, I argue Newland and May do not fully comply with old New York's conception of gender propriety.

Though seemingly antithetical characters, May and Ellen perform similar actions throughout the novel. This result supports interpretations by Margaret Jessee, Evelyn Fracasso, and William Cain, among others, who view the differences between May and Ellen as products of Newland's focalization.[6]

As Jessee argues, May and Ellen are "not oppositional; instead, they are two halves of a whole";[7] however, I argue that May is not simply more powerful than appearances suggest, but also more "masculine." Similarly, while male characters in *The Age of Innocence* perform verbs (such as "took" and "come") typical of male characters more broadly, Newland repeatedly performs verbs (such as "felt" and "knew") that are associated with female characters in the nineteenth, but not twentieth, century. This distinction is significant; Wharton aligns Newland with actions and behaviors "conventional" for twentieth-century men, but "unconventional" for nineteenth-century men. In linking Newland with these behaviors, Wharton creates a character who is not, as Jean Witherow writes, "locked in the old order."[8] Nor is Newland what Mark Nicholls refers to as a "loyal member of his tribe."[9] Rather, through linking Newland with emerging forms of masculine behavior, Wharton creates a character who represents a historically specific, transitional form of masculinity. Though Newland and May appear to be "imprisoned in the conventional," a close examination of their seemingly mundane actions highlights the way in which both characters deviate from novelistic and societal norms (59).

***

In order to closely examine Newland's and May's unconventional actions, it is first necessary to establish patterns in the depiction of character, action, and gender in *The Age of Innocence* and to compare these patterns to broader novelistic trends. I use computational tools to extract gendered pronouns ("she" and "he") and the verbs these pronouns perform. This method does not measure all of the ways in which character action can be portrayed (it does not, for example, look at adverbs), however, it does offer one metric for tracking and comparing character behavior. Influenced by the work of Franco Moretti, Ted Underwood, and Matthew Jockers, among others, this work is grounded in observations about frequency, trends, and outliers;[10] however, I do use the results from the computational study to guide my reading of specific moments in Wharton's work. In this sense, the following examination utilizes both analytically driven computational methods and interpretation driven by humanities research methods. Therefore, this is both a distant and close reading study.[11]

Employing a computational approach allows me to compare Wharton's verb usage with broader trends in the nineteenth- and twentieth-century novel:

I compare the use of verbs in *The Age of Innocence* with 100 novels written between 1900 and 1940.[12] To better understand how *The Age of Innocence* fits into Wharton's body of work, I included fifteen of her published novels in this corpus.[13] In addition, I compare Wharton's novels with the results from my previous study with Jockers, in which we extracted and examined the relationships between gendered pronouns and verbs in 3,329 nineteenth-century novels.[14] It is important to note that these dates reflect publication dates, not the time periods in which the novels are set. Because *The Age of Innocence* was written in 1920, but is primarily set in the 1870s (with the last chapter of the novel occurring at the dawn of the twentieth century), it is useful to compare the text to both nineteenth- and twentieth-century trends. As I will argue, the way in which Wharton's novel engages differences between nineteenth- and twentieth-century trends is significant.

In order to extract all of the gendered pronouns and the verbs these pronouns perform, I use the Stanford Dependency Parser, a tool that labels parts of speech and grammatical relationships. For example, parsing the sentence "She quickly ran away" produces the subject verb pair "She ran." By collecting the subject verb pairings in which the subject was a female or male pronoun, I am able to record all of the actions performed by female and male pronouns. Rather than count and compare the number of times each verb was associated with a female or male pronoun, I reproduce the classification experiments I performed with Jockers. This type of experiment determines whether there is a strong correlation among the data (in this case, the gender of the pronoun and the verb being performed).[15]

The strength of the correlation is striking among novels from both the nineteenth and twentieth centuries. Consider the following:

> … understood what to do.
> … walked up the hill.
> At the end of the day … went out.

The verbs in these sentences do not appear to be explicitly gendered; however, the machine model is able to correctly "guess" the gender of the subject 81 percent of the time in the nineteenth-century corpus and 83 percent of the time in the twentieth-century corpus based solely on the verb being performed. The difference between these accuracy rates is somewhat surprising. Though

Victorian notions of gender propriety were prevalent at the turn of the century, the advent of liberal feminism and the emergence of the "New Woman" figure would suggest that, during this period, the link between gender and action would become less rigid.[16] Recent work by Ted Underwood, David Bamman, and Sabrina Lee also suggests that the accuracy rate should fall; using computational tools to model character gender in nineteenth- and twentieth-century fiction, they conclude that "[beginning in the middle of the nineteenth century] gender divisions between characters have become less sharply marked."[17] Consequently, it is important to treat the slight rise in the above results with caution, as it may be a misleading product of small corpus size.

Regardless of whether the novelistic portrayal of gender difference becomes more or less "fuzzy" at the turn of the century, the computational research thus far supports two important conclusions. The first is that, in both the nineteenth- and early-twentieth-century novel, there is a striking distinction between the actions male and female characters perform. This result underscores the pervasiveness of gender as a concept. The intentions and rhetorical effect of this correlation vary; however, the strength of the trend (regardless of genre or author gender) suggests that the link between gender and action at times reflects a literary habit rather than an intentional commentary on gender roles. We might read these results as contributing to gender as process, an idea stemming from Judith Butler's observation that "the very injunction to be a given gender takes place through discursive routes: to be a good mother, to be a heterosexually desirable object, to be a fit worker."[18] The correlation between character gender and verbs highlights the way in which individual, seemingly insignificant actions (to murmur rather than to mutter) contribute to a cultural conception of "female" and "male." These results draw our attention to verbs we might not typically consider from this perspective. As Paula Rothenberg notes: "If stereotypes, ideology, and language are truly effective, they go beyond rationalizing inequality to rendering it invisible."[19] The fact that many of these actions are seemingly universal, rather than obviously gendered, points to the extent to which gender is embedded in both practice and language.

The second significant observation is that the verbs associated with each gender shift between the nineteenth and twentieth centuries. This result underscores the historical specificity of gender. The work performed by Underwood et al. supports this claim, as they note that "fictional characters are implicitly gendered in ways that can be quite volatile. Tears and sighs matter in one period, chuckling and grinning in another."[20] Table 3.1 and Table 3.2 show the ten verbs that are most strongly correlated with female pronouns and the ten verbs that are most correlated with male pronouns, in the nineteenth- and twentieth-century corpora, respectively. While there is a high degree of overlap, some of the differences here are suggestive. For example, the introduction of "ran" as a female verb in the twentieth-century corpus seems to go against the nineteenth-century alignment of physical action with male pronouns.

Table 3.1 Ten verbs most strongly correlated with gender in the nineteenth-century corpus.

Female	Male
sat	took
wept	found
looked	rode
felt	walked
heard	come
cried	muttered
loved	left
knew	paid
burst	made
answered	get

Table 3.2 Ten verbs most strongly correlated with gender in the twentieth-century corpus.

Female	Male
cried	come
whispered	called
laughed	got
murmured	took
gave	walked
looked	found
smiled	shouted
sighed	reached
sat	seen
ran	muttered

Though the link between action and gender is pervasive, it is important to note that there are many outliers. In order to examine which novels do not adhere to the overall trends in the corpus, I conducted a hold-one-out validation for each novel. Each novel was successively "held out" while a new classification model was trained on the other novels. The model was then run on the held-out novel, determining whether the aggregation of female and male pronoun/verb pairings for that novel adhered to or departed from the model. This essentially determined which novels, either in their use of female pronouns or male pronouns, did not adhere to the general patterns in verb usage found throughout the corpus.[21] In both the nineteenth- and twentieth-century novels, it was more common for female pronouns to behave "unconventionally" than for male pronouns to act outside of the trends observed. The lack of misclassified male pronouns speaks to the fact that gender stereotypes delineate "appropriate" male, as well as female, behavior. But it is also worth considering that this discrepancy may point to the way in which, in Western societies, the gender binary has traditionally been predicated on an understanding of "male" as primary and "female" as secondary. Nancy Jay articulates this difference: "That which is defined, separated out, isolated from all else is A and pure. Not-A is necessarily impure, a random catchall, to which nothing is external except A and the principle of order that separates it from Not-A."[22] If male identity is the "touchstone" of the Western gender binary, and female identity is the "catchall," it follows that the verbs associated with female behavior may, in a sense, be less narrowly conscripted than those associated with male behavior.

***

Edith Wharton's novels exhibit both typical and atypical behavior in their distribution of gendered pronouns and verbs. Table 3.3 indicates which of Wharton's novels exhibit typical and atypical behavior for male and female characters. For example, in *The Valley of Decision*, characters behave in ways consistent with the general trends observed; however, in *The House of Mirth*, female pronouns in general perform verbs more typical of male characters in the corpus.

Table 3.3 Classification of Edith Wharton's novels.

Novel	Year	Female Pronouns	Male Pronouns
The Valley of Decision	1902	Correct	Correct
The House of Mirth	1905	Incorrect	Correct
The Fruit of the Tree	1907	Correct	Correct
The Reef	1912	Correct	Correct
The Custom of the Country	1913	Incorrect	Correct
Summer	1917	Incorrect	Correct
The Marne	1918	Incorrect	Incorrect
The Age of Innocence	1920	Correct	Correct
The Glimpses of the Moon	1922	Correct	Correct
A Son at the Front	1923	Correct	Correct
The Mother's Recompense	1925	Incorrect	Correct
Twilight Sleep	1927	Incorrect	Correct
The Children	1928	Correct	Correct
Hudson River Bracketed	1929	Correct	Correct
The Gods Arrive	1932	Correct	Correct

Most of Edith Wharton's novels feature female and male pronouns that act in accordance with the trends observed. But, in six of Wharton's fifteen novels, female pronouns perform verbs more typical of male pronouns: the machine model guessed that most of the female pronouns were male pronouns based on the verbs performed. This is a substantial number of outliers for a single author.[23] The fact that some of Wharton's novels adhere to the general trends in the corpus, while others are outliers, indicates that Wharton's usage of verbs is not a consistent element of her authorial voice or novelistic style. Rather, these results suggest that Wharton's verb usage, and its relationship to character gender, is a function of characterization and reflects the themes and issues present in each individual novel.

The frequent misclassification of Wharton's female pronouns is not entirely surprising given Wharton's characterization of many of her female protagonists. In *The House of Mirth*, Lily Bart, independent and confident, struggles to conform to society's expectations and, as a result, loses her economic and social power. Whether Lily's downfall is read as a moralistic warning against excess, or as a critique of the limited options afforded to women, her behavior throughout the novel is consistently unconventional. While Lily's gambling and smoking are obviously coded as "unfeminine," her unconventionality is also reflected in the distribution of commonplace, frequently occurring verbs; female characters in *The House of Mirth* "come," "called," "walked," "got," and "reached" (all verbs typically associated with male characters) far more often than the majority of female characters in the corpus. The protagonist in *The Custom of the Country*, Undine Spragg, is an ambitious social climber who abandons her son and husband for personal gain. In *Summer*, Charity Royall ignores contemporary moral and social mores, becoming pregnant outside of marriage. It is important to note that, while the use of verbs in these novels speaks to the unconventionality of the female characters, it does not speak to the effect or meaning of Wharton's characterization, an issue hotly debated by critics.[24] A typically "masculine" behaving female pronoun is not the same as a feminist, or progressive, female heroine.[25]

The Marne is Wharton's only novel that features predominantly misclassified male pronouns; interestingly, it is one of only four novels in the twentieth-century corpus that features both misclassified female and male pronouns.[26] Given that this outlier has received relatively little critical attention, it is worth considering the way in which this atypical use of verbs reflects the novel's engagement with gender. *The Marne* follows Troy Belknap, an American boy who longs to join the soldiers fighting in France during World War I. While the novel does end with Troy participating in a battle, the majority of the novel focuses on Troy's feelings of frustration. When a passing soldier urges him to join the fight, Troy contemplates "risking the adventure," but, Wharton writes, "he was too visibly only a schoolboy still; and with tears of envy in his smarting eyes he stood, small and useless, on the pavement, and watched the heterogeneous band under the beloved flag disappearing."[27] To "cry" is, as one would expect, strongly associated with female characters in both the nineteenth- and twentieth-century corpora, an association that Wharton seems aware of, since the narrative voice in *The Marne* observes that there is nothing Troy can do for France "not even cry, as a girl might!"[28] Though Troy does not "cry," he frequently sheds tears. In fact, Troy's eyes repeatedly "fill with tears" over the course of the novel.[29] William Blazek links Troy's feelings with a sense of inadequacy, observing that "Troy's frustrated role as a distant observer of the war contains elements of sexual impotence."[30] Though Blazek interprets Troy's *inaction* as a reflection of ineffectual masculinity, the misclassification of male pronouns in *The Marne* also indicates that many of the actions Troy performs are more typical of female characters: "caught," "exclaimed," and "sat" are a few of the verbs Troy performs that are typically associated with female pronouns.

Wharton's characterization of Troy shares similarities with her characterization of her other male protagonists, including Newland Archer. Like Troy, Newland is an observer who longs for direct action. For both characters, the struggle between inaction and action is linked to issues of power and gender. Wharton highlights the way in which Troy's and Newland's sense of masculinity is tied to their complex relationships with seemingly unconventional women. Wharton describes Troy's feelings for Sophy Wicks early in the novel: "Troy Belknap, tall and shy and awkward, lay at her feet and blushed and groaned inwardly at her wrong-headedness ... In spite of everything, he found her more interesting [than other girls]."[31] "Precocious" and filled with "self-confidence," Sophy's unusual qualities inspire Troy's devotion (much as Ellen Olenska's seemingly unconventional opinions and behavior captivate Newland). Troy often blushes at Sophy's "wrong-headedness," while Newland blushes at Ellen's impropriety: "The allusion brought the colour to her cheek, and it reflected itself in Archer's vivid blush" (191). While Troy lays at Sophy's feet, Newland, overpowered by his feelings, "bowed over ... knelt down and kissed the [Ellen's] shoe" (140).

Wharton's portrayal of Troy draws attention to his discomfort when female opinions differ from his own. As *The Marne* progresses and Troy matures, he becomes increasingly disgusted by female characters with whom he disagrees. On encountering female war volunteers, Troy is revolted by their self-assured conception of American superiority: "The women were even more sure of their mission ... Troy, sickened by their blatancy ... during the last days he had been drawn into talk by a girl who reminded him of Miss Wicks."[32] The girl Troy encounters is Hinda Warlick, whose naive confidence sparks Troy's dislike: "He hated all that Miss Warlick personified."[33] Encounters with Miss Warlick continue to remind Troy of Sophy. After Troy encounters a reformed Miss Warlick whose opinions on French culture are now in line with his own, Troy reflects that:

> The sight of Miss Warlick had made Sophy Wicks's presence singularly vivid
> to him ... He wondered that he had not suspected, under her mocking

indifference, an ardour as deep as his own, and he was ashamed of having judged her as others had, when, for so long, the thought of her had been his torment and his joy. Where was she now, he wondered? Probably in some hospital in the south or the centre: the authorities did not let beginners get near the front, though, of course, it was what all the girls were made for … Well, Sophy would do her work wherever it was assigned to her: he did not see her intriguing for a showy post.[34]

What is particularly striking about this passage is Wharton's clear emphasis on Troy's perception of Sophy—this passage is filled with speculation that is not supported by any evidence provided by the narration. As Dianne Chambers observes, many of Wharton's novels focus on the "controlling power of male narrative" by featuring male characters who "observe, judge, and speak for women."[35] Other than a childhood encounter between Troy and Sophy that occurs early in the novel, we never actually see or hear Sophy directly. She is always filtered through Troy's perceptions, much as Ellen and May are filtered through Newland's point of view. Wharton directly highlights the degree to which Troy's impression of Sophy is shaped, not by any actions performed by Sophy, but rather by Troy's tendency to interchangeably link two women: Hinda Warlick and Sophy. Wharton indicates that, for Troy, these two women almost function as the same figure, since, upon seeing a "reformed" Hinda Warlick, Troy assumes that Sophy's opinions have shifted in the same way.

***

According to the hold-one-out validation experiment, *The Age of Innocence* is not an outlier. In the novel, female characters perform verbs widely typical of female pronouns (such as "sat," "wept," and "looked") more often than their male counterparts. Conversely, male characters perform verbs widely typical of male pronouns (such as "walked," "took," and "found") more often than their female counterparts. This is not entirely unexpected; Wharton frequently draws our attention to the ways in which notions of gender propriety inform and restrict action. For example, the narrator notes: "Etiquette required that she [a lady] should wait, immovable as an idol, while the men who wished to converse with her succeeded each other at her side" (51). Wharton links "appropriate" male behavior with motion and female behavior with passivity and stasis, an observation reflected in the computational study; in the nineteenth-century corpus many of the verbs linked to female pronouns are associated with emotion (e.g., "wept"), while many of the verbs linked to male pronouns are associated with physical action (e.g., "walked"). But we might expect to see certain non-gender-conforming behaviors (such as Ellen "walking" up Fifth Avenue with Beaufort or Newland "blushing" in response to Ellen) reflected in these results. It is important to note that what is being measured for each novel is the aggregation of actions performed by female and male pronouns—e.g., the classification of *The Age of Innocence* aggregates the pronouns referring to Ellen Olenska, May Welland, Mrs. Mingott, and other female characters. In order to better understand whether specific characters in *The Age of Innocence* are acting unconventionally, I disambiguated the gendered pronouns referring to the novel's three main characters: Newland, Ellen, and May. I also included instances in which they are named. Thus, Table 3.4 includes the top actions performed by Newland (when he is referred to using the words "Newland," "Archer," and "he"), Ellen (when she is referred to using the words "Ellen," "Countess," "Olenska," and "she"), and May (when she is referred to using the words "May," "Welland," and "she").

These verb distributions engage pre-existing debates about Wharton's characterization of Newland, Ellen, and May. Of the top seven verbs performed by May and Ellen, six are the same. It is tempting to conclude that perhaps this similarity stems from the general use of these common verbs: if all female characters in the novel are performing these verbs, it would not be surprising to find May and Ellen performing them as well. But the top seven verbs performed by other female pronouns in the novel (pronouns not referring

Table 3.4 Most frequently performed verbs for each character.

Newland Archer	May Welland	Ellen Olenska
said	said	said
felt	looked	looked
saw	asked	had
knew	went	sat
looked	had	asked
had	turned	made
thought	sat	turned

to May or Ellen), are different: said, added, had, asked, glanced, seemed, throned.[36] In addition to performing similar verbs, May and Ellen perform verbs that are typical of female characters in the twentieth-century corpus. The only "male" verb in the top seven most frequently occurring verbs for May and Ellen is "went."

Given the established link between gender, propriety, and verb usage, it seems strange that "the young girl who knew nothing" performs similar verbs to the "wayward" and experienced Ellen (35, 118). This result suggests that it is not action, but rather the space in which action occurs, and the objects that are acted upon, that denote unconventionality. As Nancy Bentley observes, Wharton concerns herself with "manners, the imprint of history and locality on the individual, the social signatures of clothing, speech, posture, gestures."[37] By describing May and Ellen as performing similar actions, Wharton focuses on the power of locality and social signatures. What separates socially sanctioned action from transgressive action is material circumstance—buying the wrong house ("It was certainly a strange quarter to have settled in" [52]), wearing the wrong dress ("her dress ... shocked and troubled him" [12]), marrying the wrong man ("to make a wretched marriage" [33]). These results also support the claim that the distinction between May and Ellen is a product of Newland's bias.[38] Following Gwendolyn Morgan's observation that May functions as an "unsung heroine," many critics have focused on how May and Ellen are filtered through Newland's perspective.[39] As Jessee notes, the seeming dichotomy between May and Ellen does not speak to an absolute difference between these characters, but rather highlights Newland's "misperception."[40] Similarly, Fracasso argues that May is "strong[er]-willed" than "Newland could ever have imagined."[41] Cain observes that May is a woman of complexity who "must endure the limits of Newland's lack of knowledge."[42]

Wharton's use of language supports the notion that Newland's perception presents a skewed view of the novel's female characters. When describing her characters' actions, Wharton often denotes not just what action is performed, but how this action appears. Wharton frequently uses the verb "seemed" to underscore the subjective effect of behavior: "She said the words 'my husband' as if no sinister associations were connected with them, and in a tone that seemed almost to sigh over the lost delights of her married life" (86). May does not "grow in womanly stature," she "seemed to grow in womanly stature"

(120). Wharton also filters character action through auxiliary verbs: characters in *The Age of Innocence* do not act, rather, they "had acted," "should act," "would act," and "could act." Such verbs do not simply portray action, they assess action. The high-level usage of auxiliary verbs is not unique to *The Age of Innocence*, but is consistently frequent among Wharton's novels.[43] The use of auxiliary verbs may illuminate one of Wharton's stylistic peculiarities, and yet, more deeply, it also speaks to her ideological engagement with action and the way action is filtered through social discourse.[44]

The critical focus on Newland's perception highlights the way in which May is not the "innocent" that Newland imagines her to be (and is consequently not the antithesis of Ellen's worldliness). Yet, both Ellen and May perform verbs typical of nineteenth-century female characters. This result should not be read as suggesting that May and Ellen are model depictions of nineteenth-century female propriety—rather, in creating characters that mostly behave conventionally, Wharton underscores moments in which characters deviate from the norm. For example, May sits quite frequently throughout the novel (an action strongly associated with female characters in the nineteenth-century corpus); however, Wharton changes May's body posture and physical actions in key moments. An interesting progression in the usage of the verb "sit" occurs in the scenes in which May enters Newland's library. Typically, May is seated. During an interaction between the couple in the library, May performs needlework while Newland reads:

> She fetched her workbasket, drew up an arm-chair to the green-shaded student lamp, and uncovered a cushion she was embroidering ... And suddenly the play of the word flashed up a wild suggestion. What if it were SHE who was dead! If she were going to die—to die soon—and leave him free! The sensation of *standing there, in that warm familiar room, and looking at her,* and wishing her dead, was so strange, so fascinating and overmastering. [italics added] (244)

Newland stands over May, observing her; the unsettling nature of this moment is conveyed through the body postures of both characters. Even though they are in the home, May is positioned within a male space, with Newland standing over her. The threatening aspect of Newland's train of thought, and his desire to exert control, are prompted by her exertion of domestic authority within this physical space: "Newland! Do shut the window" (244). But, in the following scene in which Newland and May converse in the library, their postures shift, reflecting a change in agency as May reveals that Ellen is leaving for Europe. Though "calmly seated" May's words disrupt Newland's posture, threatening his stability: "Archer walked to his usual place by the fire ... She broke off, and Archer, grasping the corner of the mantelpiece in one convulsed hand, and steadying himself against it" (261).

The last scene in which Newland and May are both in the library occurs after Ellen's farewell party. May begins in her usual seated position, however, once Newland attempts to discuss his feelings for Ellen their positions shift:

> She stood up, and as he sat with bent head, his chin propped on his hands, he felt her warmly and fragrantly hovering over him. He looked up at her with a sick stare, and she sank down, all dew and roses, and hid her face against his knee. "Oh, my dear," he said, holding her to him while his cold hand stroked her hair. There was a long pause, which the inner devils filled with strident laughter; then May *freed herself from his arms and stood up.* [italics added] (282)

Scholars have noted the way in which this scene speaks to May's authority; however, May's agency is often linked with a distinctly "feminine" power. Morgan notes that May is motivated by her "respect for convention" and that "instinct and intuition" are the source of her strength.[45] Though Parley Ann Boswell reads May as a "hustler," she views May's power as linked to the "legitimate claim to pregnancy."[46] In addition, scholars have interpreted May's agency as evolving out of her social dependence: Katherine Joslin-Jeske notes that "the social community of economically subjugated women [such as May] generates a power of its own."[47] Though May is all "dew and roses," she does not silently exert authority, nor does she sit "immovable as an idol," rather, she speaks in an "evenly-pitched" tone and moves through the space, "frees" herself and stands up—an unusual series of actions for May (282). Hovering over Newland as she reveals her pregnancy, May's posture offers a direct visual parallel to Newland standing over her, contemplating her death.

In exerting her authority, May adopts a posture that is not, by nineteenth-century novelistic standards, entirely "feminine." This suggests that May's agency is also not entirely "feminine." It may appear tentative to base this observation solely on her posture, however, Wharton continues to complicate May's "femininity" throughout the novel. Wharton repeatedly describes May as "boyish."[48] Though the majority of verbs that May performs are typical of female characters, it is worth noting that Wharton's attention to May's athleticism contrasts with this trend. May performs the verbs "ride," "walked," and "ran," actions strongly associated with male characters in the computational study of nineteenth-century novels. Wharton juxtaposes these activities with conventionally domestic behavior: "She was not a clever needle-woman; her large capable hands were made for riding, rowing and open-air activities" (243).[49] Though, as John Dudley argues, outdoor activities were becoming acceptable for women in the 1870s, Wharton makes it clear that these activities are part of an emerging form of femininity.[50] Wharton links May's participation in these "modern" sports with the masculinization of her body: Mrs. Mingott observes that "[May's] hand is large—it's these modern sports that spread the joints—but the skin is white" (24). Though it is usually Ellen who is critically discussed in connection to the "New Woman" figure, the contrast between the largeness and whiteness of May's hands suggests a distinctly modern, and transitional, form of femininity.[51]

Similarly, Newland's actions link him with changing turn of the century gender roles. In general, Wharton's male characters "felt" more often than the majority of male characters in the nineteenth- and twentieth-century corpora; however, Newland (like Troy) "felt" even more often than most of Wharton's male characters. Newland's propensity to feel brings to mind Edmund Wilson's description of Wharton's male characters: "a man set apart from his neighbours by education, intellect, and feeling, but lacking the force or the courage either to impose himself or to get away."[52] Similarly, Beer and Horner link Newland's sensitivity with powerlessness: "Newland is a sensitive, passionate, imaginative, and generous young man, but … [he is] paralysed by the etiquette and manners of 'old-fashioned Episcopalian New York."[53] John Dudley goes a step further, seeing in these qualities "something less than the 'redblooded' men of action who served as exemplars of American manhood."[54] Wilson's and Beer and Horner's readings suggest that Newland's failure primarily stems from an inability to break free of tradition; however, Dudley's observation differs in that he reads Newland as failing to conform to "accepted standards of masculinity."[55]

According to the computational research, Newland does not entirely "conform" to nineteenth-century standards of male novelistic behavior. Four of Newland's most frequently performed verbs, "said," "felt," "knew," and "looked," are strongly correlated with female characters in the nineteenth-century novel; however, only one of these verbs, "looked," remains correlated with female characters in the twentieth-century corpus. This distinction is significant; it not only points toward the way in which gender roles were changing at the turn of the century, but also suggests that Newland embodies these changes. This correlation speaks to Newland's role in the novel as a "New Man," a figure less discussed, though no less significant, than the New Woman.[56] As Tara McDonald notes, the New Man figure was the ally of the New Woman, "supporting and aiding her attempts at social and political liberation … his gentleness at odds with the definitions of manliness based on professional competitiveness or physical strength."[57] Like the New Man, Newland shows little interest in May's account of her "swimming, sailing and riding" and is bored by her interest in "walking, riding, swimming," instead preferring aesthetic forms of pleasure.

The figure of the New Man was heralded in novels by New Women writers and mocked in the popular press. Wharton's depiction of Newland as a New Man is suggestive in that it is not the utopian imaginings of feminist fiction nor a parody; Wharton's characterization of Newland offers a more nuanced examination of this figure. Newland's propensity to "feel" aligns him with a shifting masculinity that no longer links emotion with femininity. Yet, despite attempting to align himself with female social and political liberation— "Women ought to be free—as free as we are"—Wharton underscores the extent to which he cannot escape his own position of power and privilege: "nor could he, for all his anxious cogitations, see any honest reason (any, that is, unconnected with his own momentary pleasure, and the passion of masculine vanity) why his bride should not have been allowed the same freedom of experience as himself" (38). Wharton's portrayal of Newland as a "feeling," "knowing," and "thinking" man aligns him with a new form of masculinity, but her emphasis on his limitations questions the efficacy and reality of the New Man figure.

This is not to say, however, that Newland ultimately fails to become a "New Man." Many critics view Newland's decision to stay with May as an example of his paralysis and conventional mindset. Witherow sums up this view, noting that, while early in the novel "Newland challenges society's codes," he ultimately "slips easily into the same codes."[58] But it is important to consider the ways in which Newland's actions after May's denouement are not typical of the "old New York" that Wharton describes. Lawrence Lefferts presents a more complete model of the husband who "had most completely realized" old New York's "enviable ideal" (36). Engaging in frequent "love-affairs with other men's wives" Lefferts maintains "another establishment" (36). Yet, during his entire marriage with May, Newland "had been what was called a faithful husband," a rarity in old New York society (286).

Much like his frequent "feeling," "looking," and "sitting," Newland's fidelity is somewhat out of keeping with the nineteenth-century standards of masculinity that Wharton portrays. Instead, Newland's monogamy more closely resembles expected female behavior. Newland's fidelity further links him with the image of the New Man. As McDonald observes, though the New Woman was commonly interpreted as desiring sexual "free unions" or the abolition of marriage, most New Women "did not simply equate women's liberation with sexual liberation ... [they] demanded that husbands refrain from extramarital sex and wives be treated equally ... they thus encouraged men to adapt to the sexual modes of women."[59] The decision to remain faithful to May does not necessarily equate to Newland abandoning his personal desires in order to maintain traditional values. His fidelity also signals his position as a transitional figure. It is telling that, at the very end of the novel, Wharton describes Newland as sitting in a manner that mirrors her earlier comment on female physical stasis:

> Archer sat down on the bench and continued to gaze at the awninged balcony ... and the fear lest that last shadow of reality should lose its edge kept him rooted to his seat as the minutes succeeded each other ... He sat for a long time on the bench in the thickening dusk, his eyes never turning from the balcony. (297–298)

Like the ideal lady who sits, waiting "immovable as an idol" for male companions to move toward her, Newland sits "rooted to his seat," waiting for a "signal." Sitting alone, gazing up at Ellen's window, Newland may appear passive to Dallas. Yet, this behavior is equally out of place among the standards of masculine behavior set by old New York society, in which male desire is granted primacy. Though Newland is certainly not part of the "new generation" that Wharton describes in the novel's last chapter, Newland is only "old-fashioned" by twentieth-century standards.[60]

***

Despite their seeming conventionality, both Newland and May perform actions that are out of place: they depart from their own individual patterns of behavior and from societal expectations about appropriate behavior. As Rick Altman notes: "narrative depends on the simultaneous and coordinated presence of action and character. Narratives are not made of characters here and actions there but of characters acting. Indeed, it is the very fact that a character acts that permits us to recognize successive images as representing the same character."[61] Altman suggests we perceive consistency of action, both in fiction and perhaps in real life, as speaking to character, to selfhood. This point applies to character types, and it applies across multiple novels. The fact that female and male characters persistently act differently in the nineteenth- and early-twentieth-century novel does not explain why authors adhere to or depart from this trend, but it does indicate that even small, almost invisible actions, are correlated with important assumptions about identity.

The computational study of Wharton's verb usage underscores the way in which Wharton's language choices create a baseline of conventionality. Characters in *The Age of Innocence*, for the most part, do what they are told. Moments in which characters deviate from this baseline are both meaningful and startling. May's physical assertion of agency during her denouement seems out of place compared to her normal behavior and posture. Newland's propensity to "feel" does not align with the majority of male characters in the nineteenth-century novel. These results suggest that neither May nor Newland are entirely at home among old New York's tribal order. This interpretation of May and Newland challenges multiple assumptions about the novel: in aligning May with "masculine" behavior, Wharton does not simply show us a powerful woman working from within the confines of Victorian gender roles, but rather a transitional figure with an evolving form of agency. Viewing Newland's actions, including his decision to remain faithful to May, as those of a "New Man" complicates the assumption that Newland fails to embrace a changing world. In this interpretation, the novel does not tell the tragic story of individuals who choose to cling to societal traditions at the expense of personal happiness. Rather, Wharton draws our attention to the way in which even progressive change becomes traditional when viewed through the hindsight of history.

In illuminating the link between language and conceptual issues (such as gender identity), this work also suggests additional avenues for the computational study of Wharton's novels and for the productive use of computational methods in literary studies more broadly. A more thorough examination of Wharton's outlying female characters (such as Lily Bart and Undine Spragg) is necessary in order to better understand how Wharton uses unconventional female behavior to engage issues of gender and propriety. One might also use computational tools to examine Wharton's style in relation to her contemporaries. For example, using stylistic metrics (e.g., sentence length, adjective usage, vocabulary richness, etc.) to compare Wharton to James and Cather could create a unique entry point into conversations about stylistic influence.

Wharton's characterization also suggests a future modification for the computational study of verbs and gender: the fact that May and Ellen perform similar actions, yet are described as antithetical characters, hints at the variety of ways in which character difference can be articulated. Differences in action may point toward more "absolute" differences in the portrayal of character. Characters who perform similar actions but are described using radically different adjectives may point toward unreliable narrators or focalizers. As Wharton is not alone in using an unreliable male perspective to critique male privilege (Willa Cather makes a similar move in her novel, *A Lost Lady*), it would be productive to closely compare the various methods of portraying character difference. The fact that *The Age of Innocence* subverts, without departing from, novelistic trends in character gender and action raises an important point about the computational examination of literary trends: while we often think of outliers as "bucking" convention, works can simultaneously participate in and question dominant trends. As computational models for studying character and gender become increasingly complex, it is important to bear in mind that the mere presence or absence of specific terms does not account for the way in which authors may focus and manipulate readers' attention. The fact that characters in *The Age of Innocence* adhere to persistent patterns of behavior makes room for moments of striking departure. As human readers, we often notice and respond to such moments. When focusing exclusively on trends and patterns, computational work runs the risk of ignoring the way in which unusual and unexpected deviations, however slight, radically alter our perception of character.

Acknowledgments

I would like to thank Matthew Jockers for his assistance in running the code for this project. I would also like to thank the staff of the Holland Computing Center at the University of Nebraska for allowing me to use their services. Finally, I would like to thank the members of the Nebraska Literary Lab.; their feedback, questions, and suggestions contributed greatly to the initial inception of this work.

"Isn't That French?": Edith Wharton Revisits the "International Theme"

Virginia Ricard
Bordeaux Montaigne University

An inattentive reader might be forgiven for thinking that *The Age of Innocence* is a novel about New York, about the city before it became a modern metropolis—when its denizens still huddled in lower Manhattan, followed parochial customs, engaged in small-town gossip, and generally indulged in what Freud later called "the narcissism of small differences."[1] Yet, although it is usually thought of as belonging to Wharton's "New York trilogy," *The Age of Innocence* is in fact almost entirely dedicated to cultural comparison. Between the lines of the novel, a complex portrait of France slowly emerges—complex because the terms of the comparison often run counter to expectation. The novel's ostensible subject is New York—in its quaint 1870s incarnation—but, as I will argue, its real subject is France under the Second Empire. Wharton clearly sets out to challenge American notions of French life and, in particular, French attitudes to modernity, the relations between men and women, and the place of art and literature in everyday life. *The Age of Innocence* is also an object lesson for French readers, calling into question their assumptions about Americans.

It is through Newland Archer's eyes that the reader perceives places, events, and the other characters in the novel. He is—to borrow a Nabokovian term—the author's sifting agent, the character "who sifts the story through his-her own emotions and notions."[2] Archer, as has often been noted, is a divided character, a New Yorker who behaves in accordance with prevailing standards—an insider—but also, in his own view at least, something more: he has a foot outside the "tight little citadel of New York."[3] He "belongs" (62) and, when faced with the unknown, he is even glad to belong—indeed, "he hated to think of May Welland's being exposed to the influence of a young woman so careless of the dictates of Taste" as Ellen Olenska (11). But, as he sits among his peers at the opera, we learn that "in matters intellectual and artistic Newland Archer felt himself distinctly the superior of these chosen specimens of old New York gentility; he had probably read more, thought more, and even seen a good deal more of the world, than any other man of the number" (6). And, because he knows more, Archer understands that the New York rituals and standards that he and his contemporaries live by are merely arbitrary, that is, there is no reason why a specific rite should have been adopted: "they all lived in a kind of hieroglyphic world, where the real thing was never said or done or even thought, but only represented by a set of arbitrary signs" (32).[4] Yet, when he sees May Welland in St. Augustine, he realizes that "he, who fancied himself so scornful of arbitrary restraints, had been afraid to break away from his desk because of what people might think of his stealing a holiday" (99). Archer's ambivalence is summed up at the end of chapter IV: "in spite of the cosmopolitan views on which he prided himself, he thanked heaven that he was a New Yorker, and about to ally himself with one of his own kind" (23). Endogamy is the safer bet.

Archer is not the only divided character. The novel chronicles his encounter with another ambivalent figure: Ellen Olenska. An American by birth, she too, in a sense, "belongs." But she has been away far too long to instinctively understand the intricate rules that regulate life in that particular milieu.[5] Everything about her is foreign, and indeed French. Her behavior and her clothes are "unusual" (7). Everyone remembers the black satin dress she wore to her coming-out ball, and now, equally "heedless of tradition," she wears "bold" sheath robes of red velvet "bordered about the chin and down the front with glossy black fur" that seem to Archer "perverse and provocative" (7). He mentally compares her to a painting he has seen in Paris by Carolus Durand (74). She does not know that "it was not the custom in New York drawing-rooms for a lady to get up and walk away from one gentleman in order to seek the company of another. Etiquette required that she should wait." So, after dinner at the van der Luydens, "unaware of having broken any rule," she rises and, "walking alone across the wide drawing-room," sits down "at Newland Archer's side" (45). Ellen speaks English with a "trailing slightly foreign accent" (13), and often expresses herself "as if she were translating from the French" (90). Once, Archer is even entirely misled by her English, which he only understands by translating it back into French: when she writes "I ran away" (90), he realizes, too late, that what she means is far less dramatic—"Je me suis évadée" means "I slipped quietly away" and there had been no need for him to race to her defense.

The meeting between these two—the insider with "cosmopolitan views" and a woman who has spent most of her life abroad, a cosmopolitan for whom "New York simply meant ... coming home" (122)—calls for a close examination in the novel of the relation between Europe (and more particularly France) and America (and more particularly New York), and of what Stephen Fender calls "the social, emotional, aesthetic and moral responses" of American and European characters to each other.[6] This is the "international theme" that usually marshals a series of antitheses enumerated by Fender in his recent introduction to Henry James's *Daisy Miller and Other Stories*: "(American) innocence and (European) experience ... American local democracy as against European centralized oligarchy; the American egalitarian impulse versus the European love of hierarchy; American spontaneity and European respect for convention; the Americans' imagination fired by the future as against the European's by the past, and so on."[7] Not only is this list incomplete, however, but in *The Age of Innocence* many of these oppositions are reversed. Innocence, democracy, egalitarianism, spontaneity, and "imagination fired by the future": all these are subtly redistributed between New York and Paris and, more often than not, attributed to the "wrong" camp, as it were. In *The Age of Innocence*, rather than reiterating what was, by 1920, received wisdom as to American and French traits, Wharton seems intent on puncturing prejudices on both sides of the Atlantic. The novel, according to one French critic reviewing the French translation, "will give many of our own people a more accurate idea ... of Americans," an idea that "will surprise them." The people they thought were "uncouth, gay, practical and ruthless" are represented here as "serious, thoughtful, austere, almost pathologically reserved, almost painfully bashful, and almost self-effacing in their diffidence."[8] In the same way, the novel calls into question—and sometimes ridicules—blinkered American views of France and what it means to be French.

In the first chapters of *The Age of Innocence*, there is a network of allusions to things French: to places—all of them grand—the "great European capitals"

(3), "the Paris Opera house" (5), the "private hotels of the Parisian aristocracy" (10); to some of the more glamorous moments in French history, with "the 'Josephine look'" (7) and Ellen Olenska's "Empire dress" (9), both of which refer to the First Empire, and with the "Tuileries of Louis Napoleon" (10, 14), which refers to the Second Empire; Mrs. Mingott's "pre-Revolutionary furniture" (10) is emblematic of the monarchy and the eighteenth century;[9] and "a much discussed nude of Bouguereau" (16) or "Monsieur de Camors" (20) allude to the literary and artistic life of France again under the Second Empire. There are, too, French words, some in italics, scattered throughout the text but more numerous in the early chapters than in the rest of the novel. Some pertain to food ("chef" [10], "tepid Veuve Clicquot" [15], "menu" [19], "embonpoint" [24], "filet" and "cuisine" [27]) or clothes and hair ("aigrettes," "glacé gloves," "coiffures" [16], "coiffées" [5]), or to means of transport ("coupé" [36]); others to interior architecture ("portière" [20], "bouton d'or" [15, 16]); still others describe attitudes ("aplomb" [11]) or language ("nuances" [25]), or refer to society and politics ("droit de cité" [14], "esprit de corps" [26]). A few look like French words but are not ("double entendre" [12]). All stand metonymically for France and Frenchness and loudly proclaim that there is a world elsewhere, a world beyond New York. Most evoke the glamour and luxury, the pleasure and frivolity of life in bygone eras. They also signal a sort of Francomania: like the Parisian *anglomanie* that influenced many of the rituals of French upper-class social behavior, there is among old New Yorkers a love of things French that affects their taste and manners.[10] Here, Wharton is tapping into the phenomenon described by Paul Bourget in his book about the United States during the gilded age, *Outre-Mer: Notes sur l'Amérique* (1895).[11] But, as she makes clear in her novel, she is concerned with a time before the arrival of the "new people" (and so before the gilded age), a time when Americans were already going to France for its art and architecture, its landscapes and literature, its fashion and food and wine, but were perhaps spending less, or less ostentatiously. Certainly, most old New Yorkers in the novel seem to have visited France, and the women, when they can, order their clothes from Empress Eugénie's favorite couturier, Worth, and buy their jewelry in rue de la Paix. Both tribes—the Mingotts and Mansons on the one hand and the Archer/Newland/van der Luyden clan on the other—are attracted to France for different reasons. But, as the official visit to May's grandmother shows at the very beginning of the novel, no characters have been more influenced by France than old Mrs. Mingott and Newland Archer himself. Her France is that of the 1850s and the early years of the Second Empire; his is that of the 1860s and the Empire in its grand final moment, just before its sudden end after the defeat at Sedan in 1870. There is, as a result of their common attraction to France, an understanding—later even a secret alliance—between the old lady and the young man. The reader, prepared by the many allusions in the preceding pages, becomes aware, in the space of just three paragraphs, of the effect of France on two very different imaginations. The passage produces a disparate and surprising picture of the country where both Mrs. Mingott and Madame Olenska had once shone. France is represented as both a boon and a bane: a beacon of modernity but also a monster of impropriety.

Mrs. Mingott's "stately" house is, we are told, "an historic document" (19)—an archive to be interpreted. It reveals (as houses so often do in Wharton's work) the life of its principal inhabitant, but also the inner working of our sifting agent's mind, nourished as it is by his reading. Mrs. Mingott is, as we already know, "bold" and fearless and once "mingled freely in foreign society" (10). She has "hobnobbed with Dukes and Ambassadors," "associated familiarly with Papists, entertained Opera singers" (10), and filled her house with souvenirs of that high point in her existence, the "days of her triumph at the Tuileries" (72). After becoming a widow, she "had bodily cast out the massive furniture of her prime"—the furniture that could be seen in other even more venerable "old family houses in University Place and lower Fifth Avenue"—and introduced instead "the frivolous upholstery of the Second Empire" (19). In spite of her great age, she is forward-looking: she has had her house built uptown, well beyond the pale, amid tumble-down greenhouses, "ragged gardens," and the remains of agricultural endeavors that readers, when the novel was published, knew had long since disappeared to be replaced by houses and then by skyscrapers. She likes "all novelties" (21) and refuses to be thought of as old-fashioned. She is, in fact, remarkably modern, dramatically discarding the old and creating a sensation by redesigning her interior, guided by considerations of practicality and pleasure rather than custom. More surprisingly, the source of her modernity is French: it is the spectacular transformations of Paris commissioned by Napoleon III that have convinced her that, in her own neighborhood, "the old clattering omnibuses" would soon no longer bump over cobblestones because they "would be replaced by smooth asphalt, such as people reported having seen in Paris" (19). Her model seems to be the great public works organized by Georges Eugène Haussmann who, between 1853 and 1870, oversaw the much criticized, but always practical, renovation of the French capital. Modern technology, in other words, comes from France, where asphalt, or bitumen, was used at least from the 1850s onwards to pave the streets of the capital (and even a century earlier to make the royal fountains at Versailles waterproof).[12] Mrs. Mingott is nevertheless an exception among her peers. Her fellow New Yorkers, including her own family, seem almost riveted to the past. Only Beaufort, an outsider, expresses any interest in "this new dodge for talking along a wire" (96)—the telephone— or even seems at all familiar with the speculative fiction of Jules Verne or Edgar Allan Poe. As Edmond Jaloux puts it, most of the Americans in the novel seem to live in "blind obedience to the will of their ancestors."[13] The novel's imagery is consistent with that idea: Archer thinks of the van der Luydens, the custodians of old New York, as having been "rather gruesomely preserved in the airless atmosphere of a perfectly irreproachable existence, as bodies caught in glaciers keep for years a rosy life-in-death" (37). Clearly, in *The Age of Innocence*, American imaginations are not all "fired by the future" just as European imaginations are not energized only by the past.

For Archer, Mrs. Mingott's living arrangements conjure up something rather different. He does not think about the material culture of France—its furniture and upholstery, its cities and streets, or even "the whole harmonious running of the vast national machine" admired by Wharton in *French Ways and Their Meaning*.[14] What interests Archer is French literature. And everything, including the layout—"in flagrant violation of all the New York proprieties"—of May's grandmother's house reminds him of the racy French novels he has read. Or rather, he sees everything through the prism of those novels—in this particular case a novel of the Second Empire, *Monsieur de Camors* (1867).[15] "Frivolous" is used twice in the passage (for upholstery and lace flounces) as an almost natural attribute of the French, and is opposed to American "grim harmony" (10)—but in Archer's mind the meaning becomes more specific. For an instant he ludicrously imagines Mrs. Mingott, aged over 70 and drowning in her own superfluous flesh, as a *cocotte*: Archer "had secretly situated the love-scenes of 'Monsieur de Camors' in Mrs. Mingott's bedroom," with its "huge low bed upholstered like a sofa, and a toilet table with frivolous lace flounces and a gilt-framed mirror" (20), unexpectedly visible through the "always open" door of the ground-floor sitting-room. Like her other visitors, he is "startled and fascinated by the foreignness of this arrangement, which recalled scenes in French fiction, and architectural incentives to immorality such as the simple American had never dreamed of" (20). Wharton is, of course, mocking the prudery of "the simple American" here, and "frivolity" is a euphemism for illicit sex, about which, at this point in time, Newland can still laugh: "It amused Newland Archer ... to picture [Mrs. Mingott's] blameless life led in the stage-setting of adultery" (20). "That was how women with lovers lived in the wicked old societies, in apartments with all the rooms on one floor, and all the indecent propinquities that their novels described" (20). The knowing reader has been prepared for Archer's conceit by the earlier allusion to a painting owned by Beaufort, William Bouguereau's "L'Amour vainqueur" (1886)—"Love Victorious"—which represents Cupid carrying away Psyche, both figures naked babes.[16] But Wharton is also making fun of Archer's galloping imagination—of his bovarism.[17] His perceptions have clearly been altered by the books he has read.[18]

Sometimes Archer's daydreaming actually modifies his fate. In a classic scene of cross-cultural misunderstanding that precipitates his wedding, Archer is so full of his reading that he entirely misinterprets the signs that Ellen Olenska attempts to hold out to him. She has gone to Skuytercliff without explaining why. He goes and finds her there, walking home from church through the snow. Together, they enter the "homely little" old Patroon's house. A fire has been lit: "a big bed of embers still gleamed in the kitchen chimney" (95). With its iron pot and its Delft china, the place is both a remnant of the past and a "magically created," fairy-tale-like setting for a profession of love. The conversation is full of pauses and unanswered questions and Archer begins to imagine that Ellen is about to declare her passion for him. He places himself in his preferred position, with his back to her: "Archer imagined her, almost heard her, stealing up behind him to throw her light arms about his neck."[19] He wonders: "What if it were from him that she had been running away, and if she had waited to tell him so till they were here alone together in this secret room?" (95). But his daydream is rudely interrupted: "While he waited, soul and body throbbing with the miracle to come, his eyes mechanically received the image of a heavily-coated man with his fur collar turned up who was advancing along the path to the house" (95). Poignantly, and hilariously, Archer wakes up to the reality of the situation, and sees what Ellen has been trying to tell him all along: she has been running away from Julius Beaufort.

As well as Octave Feuillet's *Monsieur de Camors*, we learn that Prosper Mérimée's posthumously published *Lettres à une inconnue* (1874) is one of Archer's favorite books (73).[20] Written over a period of over thirty years (the last being composed just hours before he died), these letters are also a tale of "Love Victorious," of unexpected love for a mysterious woman in a man who, in Arthur Symons's words, "thought himself secure against the outbreak of an unconditional passion."[21] One of the principal concerns of *The Age of Innocence* is—and here again the imagery (May's Diana-like build, her gift for archery, the arrowless wooden cupid, Dr. Agathon Carver's "Valley of Love," as well as our hero's surname) repeatedly reminds the reader that this is so—the various ways in which societies respond to the disturbances of Eros. In New York, Lawrence Lefferts has repeated affairs, which his wife pretends to ignore; Julius Beaufort, "as became a 'foreigner' of doubtful origin," has "another establishment" (31); and Newland Archer himself has gone through "a season of wild oats" (214), which ruffles no one's sensibilities, as long as it is just that, a season, and he ends up marrying "among the nice" (142). Archer is aware that "in the complicated old European communities, love-problems might be less simple and less easily classified" (68). Indeed, in France, things are done differently. No one is surprised that a member of the Academy and a Senator like Mérimée should have had an almost life-long love affair and friendship with a highly educated, learned woman—the *inconnue* of the title of the correspondence, whose name, Jenny Dacquin, was soon common knowledge. "At the Court of the Tuileries," says Sillerton Jackson … "such things were pretty openly tolerated" (222). But when Archer declares that "women ought to be free—as free as we are" (30), he immediately realizes that these are merely "verbal generosities" (31). In New York, "frivolity" in women is never condoned.

In these passages, Wharton quietly redistributes roles. Not only are Americans in *The Age of Innocence* not modern—apart from one exception—they are not innocent. To be sure, Mrs. Mingott's life has been "blameless" in spite of her connection with France, and her energy is emphatically not sexual. Still, she has been vitalized by France—she is "carnivorous" and likes "new blood" (22)—by its glamour, its fashion, and its modernity. Archer, on the other hand, is far from innocent and the main reason why he and Ellen do not understand each other—"I don't speak your language," Ellen says—is that he is able to see her only in terms of the (mainly French) literature he has read. He is obsessed by Ellen's sexual past: has she or has she not been the mistress of the Count's secretary? It is because of his knowledge of French novels that he is "shocked and troubled" (11) by the arrival of Ellen Olenska. Later, he self-consciously remembers the codes and conventions of adultery in French literature and this constantly interferes with his enjoyment of the moment, even when he is alone with Ellen. When he asks for a private room in an inn after he and Ellen leave Boston harbor, for example, he thinks that "no more guileless-looking cabinet particulier ever offered its shelter to a clandestine couple" (167). Indeed, adultery, the stuff of French novels, which he mechanically associates with Ellen's French past, has its own "hackneyed vocabulary" (216), its codes and conventions, and these are "hateful to him" (216). Later, Archer decides not to draw Ellen into its "familiar trap" (219), and refuses to interpret the return of a key as a "classic move in a familiar game" (231). For Archer, in other words, life imitates art and his reading nourishes, but also distorts, his perception of the world around him. He is far from guileless, often suspicious in fact. By contrast, the European Ellen is more straightforward and more frank. But another character soon further complicates the "international theme" and troubles the France–America polarity introduced in the early pages of the novel.

At the beginning of Book II, during their honeymoon, Newland and May meet a young Frenchman whose conversation fascinates Archer. M. Rivière is explicitly shown to be the counterpart of Archer's journalist friend: his situation, we are told, "seemed, materially speaking, no more brilliant than Ned Winsett's," but while the "eager impecunious" Frenchman has "fared richly," "poor Winsett" has been "starving to death" in New York (140). This entire passage was plainly designed as a comparison between French and American attitudes to art and literature. We learn that the outwardly unremarkable M. Rivière "was a man of about thirty, with a thin ugly face ... to which the play of his ideas gave an intense expressiveness" (139). He is unaffected and speaks with "simplicity" (139), telling Archer about himself: "an insatiable taste for letters had thrown the young man into journalism, then into authorship (apparently unsuccessful)" (140); he had "frequented the Goncourt grenier, been advised by Maupassant not to attempt to write" (140); he "had often talked with Mérimée in his mother's house" (140); and "he had lived in a world in which, as he said, no one who loved ideas need hunger mentally" (140). M. Rivière is proud of his independence, his moral freedom, his *quant à soi*. Nothing about him suggests European wickedness. When he says that he might look for work in New York, Archer is perplexed: "New York for a young man who had frequented the Goncourts and Flaubert, and who thought the life of ideas the only one worth living!" (140–141). Rivière is also a double of Archer himself: a man with literary tastes, although not a writer—a dilettante of sorts. On the way home, Archer realizes that this episode, on which he "ponder[s] deeply," has put "new air into his lungs" (141). May's remarks, when her husband tells her how interesting he finds Rivière, hammer the point home: "The little Frenchman? Wasn't he dreadfully common?" she asks (141). "Clever" and "common" are almost synonymous in May's dictionary—the life of ideas clearly has no place in her world. The thought of going anywhere "chiefly to enjoy good conversation," makes her laugh: "Oh, Newland, how funny! Isn't that French?" (142).

M. Rivière's story is thrown into sharp relief by comparison with an earlier, in a sense parallel, passage set in New York. In chapter XX, Rivière tells Archer that he must provide for his mother and unmarried sister, but adds that it is in his mother's house that he has met and talked to Mérimée. It is there, in other words, that he does what he thinks makes life worth living: "Ah, good conversation—there's nothing like it, is there?" (142). In France, his remarks imply, literature and art have a place in the everyday life of all—old and young, poor and wealthy. By contrast, the sketch of old New York society in chapter XII reveals the atomization of society: "artists, musicians and 'people who wrote' … had never shown any desire to be amalgamated with the social structure" (72). The likes of Winsett, even when they have the opportunity to take part in the "literary salon" once organized by Medora Manson, are reluctant to do so. The better established too are reticent. We already know that there are two competing groups of old New Yorkers, those "who cared about eating and clothes and money, and the Archer-Newland-van-der-Luyden tribe, who were devoted to travel, horticulture and the best fiction, and looked down on the grosser forms of pleasure" (23). But here we learn that, although "literature and art were deeply respected in the Archer set," Mrs. Archer felt that writers and artists "were odd, they were uncertain, they had things one didn't know about in the background of their lives and minds" (72). She is fond of good literature, but does not care to frequent those who write it—much in the same way as she is interested in horticulture but would not care to frequent gardeners. Mrs. Mingott might have been able to make New York more like Paris, but she is, at heart, a philistine:

> Only old Catherine Mingott, with her absence of moral prejudices and almost parvenu indifference to the subtler distinctions, might have bridged the abyss; but she had never opened a book or looked at a picture, and cared for music only because it reminded her of gala nights at the Italiens, in the days of her triumph at the Tuileries. Possibly Beaufort, who was her match in daring, would have succeeded in bringing about a fusion; but his grand house and silk-stockinged footmen were an obstacle to informal sociability. Moreover, he was as illiterate as old Mrs. Mingott, and considered "fellows who wrote" as the mere paid purveyors of rich men's pleasures. (72–73)

In New York, then, the arts have no milieu, no context in which to develop, only a "very thinly settled outskirt" (73). Some old New Yorkers never open a book; there is a rift between society and the arts. None of this is entirely new to Archer:

> He knew that there were societies where painters and poets and novelists and men of science, and even great actors, were as sought after as Dukes; he had often pictured to himself what it would have been to live in the intimacy of drawing-rooms dominated by the talk of Mérimée … But such things were inconceivable in New York, and unsettling to think of. (73)

He puts this state of affairs down to immaturity. France, he thinks, is a more advanced society. With time, America would catch up and there would be a place for art and intellectual life as well as for pleasure. He "knew most of 'the fellows who wrote,' the musicians and the painters" and he has the feeling that the only solution would be "to reach a stage of manners" where they and New York society "would naturally merge" (73).

Edith Wharton held similar views. In "America at War," a lecture delivered in 1918, in which she attempts to make a Parisian audience understand why the United States had entered the Great War, she examines the early history of North America. American civilization grew slowly out of extraordinarily difficult conditions, she said, but the "two groups representing the two principal mobiles of human action—the will to sacrifice everything to intellectual and moral convictions and the desire for wealth and the enjoyment of life"—were soon reconciled:

> These men of iron [the Puritans], and the women who were their equals in stoic resilience, formed the kernel from which our civilization grew. Among them, right from the beginning, were a few individuals with wills equally strong, but with minds less narrow, who overthrew the all-powerful presbyteries and who founded schools and universities, and thus emancipated thought. A hundred years later, Americans were playing games, going to the theatre, thinking about dress, dancing the passepied or the saraband.[22]

Later, Wharton would note in her autobiography that it was "only in sophisticated societies that the intellectual recognize the uses of the frivolous, and that the frivolous know how to make their houses attractive to their betters."[23] In *The Age of Innocence*, France is that sophisticated society and Newland Archer supposes that the United States would one day become another. New York would learn to accommodate frivolousness, and society would no longer frown on "the enjoyment of life" even if it meant ignoring unwritten rules.

M. Rivière, then, is the charming, intelligent, and unfussy product of a sophisticated society, an interesting human being about whom "there was nothing frivolous or cheap" (139). Far more than Ellen Olenska in the novel, he is a symbol of France and his many qualities seem to be the attributes of the country he comes from as much as his own. During a second conversation between Rivière and Archer, this time in New York, Rivière is presented as "serious" (174); he has "tenacity" (177) and he meets Archer's interrogation "sturdily" (174); he is "resourceful" (175); he is also determined and does "not falter" (177); he succeeds "in imposing himself" (176); he is thoughtful: "the young man considered" (175); and, above all, he is sincere: "there was no mistaking the sincerity of his distress" (177). Rivière is also unselfish and speaks not on his own behalf—"on that score I have fully dealt with myself" (174)—but is concerned instead with "abstract justice" (174); he is capable of taking a particular case—that of Madame Olenska—to heart, as his distress, anxiety, and changes of color demonstrate. In short, he is courageous, truthful, generous, and, most important of all, he is unafraid to think for himself— his arguments are his own. In this respect, he is superior to Archer, who still admires and is partly determined by "some deep tribal instinct" (176). Rivière is also more spontaneous than Archer: in the first conversation, he talks frankly and simply about his need to find a new job, and in the second he openly expresses his change of mind concerning Countess Olenska's fate. Archer, on the other hand, never seems to manage to disregard convention, to commit himself, or even to follow his plans through: we are told in the very first pages of the novel that he gets "a subtler satisfaction" "thinking about a pleasure to come" than from its realization (4). He thinks about life with Ellen, in Japan and elsewhere, but, unlike M. Rivière, he never does what he says he will do and hardly ever expresses an idea that is entirely his own. Like him, May lacks spontaneity in both small and great things: in London she worries only about what she is going to wear to dinner and later she quietly, and perhaps only half-consciously, calculates and organizes the expulsion of her cousin. In fact, in *The Age of Innocence*, respect for convention is almost always to be found west of the Atlantic and Ellen, with her experience of European life, shows that she is used to a society where there is less, not more, hierarchy. She tells Archer, for instance, "that her grandmother Mingott and the Wellands objected to her living in a 'Bohemian' quarter." Archer knows that it is "the poverty that her family disliked" (73). And Winsett wonders "how a Countess happens to live in our slum" (87). By contrast, a poor man like Rivière has frequented great men of letters and Ellen Olenska, besides being content to live in a "dishevelled street" where "small dress-makers, bird-stuffers and 'people who wrote' were her nearest neighbours" (47), is on terms of equality—astounding to Archer— with her servant Nastasia: "It was not usual, in New York society, for a lady to address her parlour-maid as 'my dear one,' and send her out on an errand wrapped in her own opera-cloak." Archer tastes "the pleasurable excitement of being in a world where action followed on emotion with such Olympian speed" (116). In spite of her European upbringing, Ellen is both more egalitarian and more spontaneous than old New Yorkers.

But—and here's the rub—M. Rivière, in spite of all his qualities, is nevertheless the emissary—both literally and metaphorically—of the wicked old world: he has been sent by Ellen's estranged husband. As he and Archer talk, the young American's gaze moves back and forth from the Frenchman's face to "the rugged features of the President of the United States," thus placing the exchange squarely within the remit of "the international theme." He and Rivière respond to each other emotionally, aesthetically, and morally as they discuss, or rather step around, a subject that is never named: adultery. "That such a conversation should be going on anywhere within the millions of square miles subject to [the President's] rule seemed as strange as anything that the imagination could invent" (178). We know that the Countess Olenska has "lived and suffered" (73) in a society that is not, to say the least, conducive to domestic bliss. Ellen herself has referred to her former life as devoid of all that is "fine and sensitive and delicate" (169), a life that she calls "shabby," "base," "cheap," "bare," and "poor" (169), full of "the abominations you know of, and all the temptations you half guess" (171). Her reading, too, contributes to this view of her life in France: the books she leaves about her drawing room are by Paul Bourget, Joris-Karl Huysmans, and the Goncourt brothers, all writers of the sort of daring and often desperate novels that Archer also enjoys. But, in this conversation, the reader of *The Age of Innocence* has more to rely on than Archer's flighty imagination or Ellen's perhaps emotional account since M. Rivière himself admits that Ellen is better off in America. Thanks to his talks in Boston with Madame Olenska, Rivière has discovered something he had never thought of before: that she is, after all, an American, that what in France is "part of a general convenient give-and-take" is "unthinkable, simply unthinkable" in the United States (178). His change of heart, coming as it does from a Frenchman—and so a witness for the defense—demonstrates that all is not well in the empire—or by that time, Republic—of France. France may be the home of beautiful furniture, ornament, art, literature, dress, well-run cities, and good food, but it is also the land of unmentionable immorality.

Archer has his own negative memories of European life—they are of Italy rather than France but they color his vision of Madame Olenska's former existence. "Once only, just after Harvard, he had spent a few gay weeks at Florence" (137). As he drives through London with May, he recalls a whole cast of titled ladies, gambling rakes and dandies, magnificent young officers, and elderly dyed wits. The passage, reminiscent of Paul Bourget's *Cosmopolis*—a novel published in 1892 that Archer could certainly not have read, but with which Wharton was familiar—is an unmistakable denunciation of cosmopolitan life:

> [I]t had all seemed to him, though the greatest fun in the world, as unreal as a carnival. These queer cosmopolitan women, deep in complicated love-affairs which they appeared to feel the need of retailing to every one they met ... were too different from the people Archer had grown up among, too much like expensive and rather malodorous hot-house exotics, to detain his imagination long. To introduce his wife into such a society was out of the question; and in the course of his travels no other had shown any marked eagerness for his company. (137)

This memory is placed just before the first flattering description of M. Rivière and just after a description of old New York attitudes to "foreigners," a word that always appears between inverted commas. Mrs. Archer and her daughter Janey "had almost achieved the record of never having exchanged a word with a 'foreigner' other than those employed in hotels and railway-stations" (134). Unsurprisingly, only "queer Europeanized Americans" mix with "cosmopolitans." "Queer Americans"—read not old New Yorkers—are content to frequent an entirely artificial world in France, a world of "hot-house exotics," "as unreal as a carnival," that has little to do with the enjoyment of ordinary French life. All they know is a contrived society, where misbehavior has become a way of life. The France of M. Rivière, the France of the old ways, the country that, in *French Ways and Their Meaning*, Wharton called "the most homogeneous and uninterrupted culture the world has known," remains entirely unknown to them.[24] Like May, most old New Yorkers confuse the real life of France, the life Archer discovers in the person of M. Rivière, with its cosmopolitan variety. His encounter with Rivière, then, instigates a change in Archer: he moves from pride in vague "cosmopolitan views" to the comprehension of—and admiration for—French singularity.

By virtue of its title, the novel examines the old opposition between innocence and experience. Ellen has returned "to wipe out the past" (77) but she finds that New York is no Arcadia, and old New Yorkers are no more innocent, no more devoid of "old European witchery" (6), than France itself. They are, she complains, merely attached to the appearance of innocence, and American houses, with their absence of privacy, paradoxically remind her of that most benighted of French institutions, the convent (94). It is significant that *The Age of Innocence* takes place between two representations of Faust. The Faust legend, as Leslie Fiedler puts it, is about "breaking through all limits and restraints, [about] reaching a place of total freedom where one could with impunity deny the Fall, live as if innocence rather than guilt were the birthright of all men."[25] Faust is promised freedom from old age, from ignorance, from lack of control over nature and fate. Yet, even in America, no matter how much Ellen wounds herself in "her mad plunges against fate" (68), she must, in the end, submit. Between the first representation of Faust and the second two years later, she comes to understand that even west of the Atlantic she cannot live as if "innocence rather than guilt were the birthright of all men." She learns at last (and teaches Archer) that, although Christopher Columbus went to a great deal of trouble, he really did so for nothing—or rather merely to produce more of the same: "It seems stupid to have discovered America only to make it into a copy of another country," she says (168). At the end of the novel, Archer, now an aging widower, thinks of Ellen Olenska, "of the theatres she must have been to, the pictures she must have looked at, the sober and splendid old houses she must have frequented, the people she must have talked with, the incessant stir of ideas, curiosities, images and associations thrown out by an intensely social race in a setting of immemorial manners" (252). What she has gone back to, in Archer's imagination at least, is not to the "matchless terraced gardens at Nice," not the jewels, historic pearls, Sobieski emeralds, sables, pictures, and priceless furniture that so impress her aunt, the Marchioness Manson (114). Instead, she has gone back to the country represented by M. Rivière. Ellen's American family regard, or pretend to "regard her husband's wish to have her back as proof of an irresistible longing for domestic life" (178). Behaving according to "tribal instincts," they send her back to her scoundrel of a husband simply because she is a disturbing element. M. Rivière, on the other hand, rises above his own background. When he considers Madame Olenska's case, he is more rational, more far seeing, and more capable of empathy, than any of the old New Yorkers. He wishes to contribute to Ellen's happiness in spite of his own background and perhaps in spite of his own "tribal instincts." He is capable— in the enlightenment tradition of intellectual speculation—of comprehending American ways and comparing them positively to French ways. He is willing to admit that certain things in French life are "unthinkable" in America and he is able to look at these things with equanimity, rather than to pretend that he lives in an age—or a place—of innocence. He is more modern, more egalitarian, more respectful of women, more human than any of the members of the American tribe. Rivière is, of course, merely a character, but he is the character chosen by Wharton to represent France. At the end of the novel, Dallas Archer, who appears unscathed by old New York's forbidding codes and conventions, and who shares Rivière's modernity, adventurousness, and interest in ideas, shows that, as Wharton made clear in *French Ways*, it was merely a matter of time before New York would catch up with France.

"Isn't that French?" (142). Between its lines, as if in invisible ink, *The Age of Innocence* provides the answer to May Welland's question. May seems to have a rather fuzzy idea of what the epithet implies. In the novel, "French" means new—new ideas, new interior architecture, new clothes, and new inventions, but it also means freedom, independence, courage, and generosity. Wickedness is relegated to the murky world of cosmopolitans. "American," in old New York at least, means conventional, oligarchical, tribal, and immature.

Newland Archer's Doubled Consciousness: Wharton, Psychology, and Narrational Form

Shari Goldberg
Franklin & Marshall College

Psychological readings of Wharton's work can seem inescapable, not to mention unremarkable and tiresome. After pointing out that "a notion of her personal character had always affected responses to her work," Millicent Bell virtually sighs, in 1995: "So, psychology … returns to the study of Wharton's work … [H]er works are now being studied as part of the complex cultural and political dynamics of the early twentieth century."[1] What Bell means by "psychology," in the excerpts above, is mindset: Wharton's writing has been analyzed through the lens of her desires and behaviors, in the first quote, and her absorption of broader social trends, in the second. Candace Waid's introduction to the Norton Critical Edition of *The Age of Innocence* provides apt examples of both, framing the novel as "a return to [Wharton's] own primal scene" by which she also "evoked the era of her own childhood."[2] In such scholarship, Wharton's mind is imagined as having directly transmuted her lived personal experience into her fiction; the task of the reader is, in turn, to discover the pulsing context that made the story happen. Bell signifies her exhaustion with this analysis not because the scope of Wharton's life is too limited—combined, Cynthia Griffin Wolff's explicitly psychological biography, *A Feast of Words*, and Gloria C. Erlich's, *The Sexual Education of Edith Wharton*, run to 500 pages—but because interest in her fictions can never outrun the biography of their author.[3]

Bell's understanding of psychological criticism, while not uncommon in literary studies, is itself reductive: it overlooks psychology as a study of the mind, a discipline devoted to modeling and theorizing permutations of consciousness. Emerging in the latter half of the nineteenth century, psychology undoubtedly formed part of the complex cultural context of Wharton's writing life; the years represented in *The Age of Innocence*, 1870–1900, make up the pre-Freudian period in which the paradigm of hypnosis, with its investigation into different states of consciousness, reigned. Moreover, *The Age of Innocence* is unflinchingly a story about consciousness—about the development of Newland Archer's awareness of his relationship to his environment. Despite these resonances, critics have not viewed the novel as theorizing consciousness along with contemporaneous psychology: as a text that suggests, in concert with its moment, what consciousness means, how it operates, and what such operation implies about the mind and body that give rise to it. This is not to say that the novel's concern with mind has gone unnoticed. Betsy Klimasmith has analyzed the novel's experimentation with memory, and Jill Kress and Pamela Knights have attended to its vision of the public self at the expense of the private individual.[4] Other Wharton works have occasionally been connected with contemporaneous psychological premises, as in Jennifer Haytock's argument that, in *The Reef*, Wharton portrays the mind making sense of fragments, or Jennifer Fleissner's proposal that, in *The House of Mirth*, Lily Bart is physiologically compelled to drift without rest.[5] On the whole, however, Wharton has not been considered a serious psychological thinker who realizes her ideas through the medium of narrative text.

In this essay, I want to offer exactly the kind of psychological criticism that American literary studies have been lacking, by claiming Wharton as a psychological thinker, and, more specifically, a significant psychological prose stylist.[6] Regarding *The Age of Innocence* as a novelistic study of the mind, I argue that Wharton's narrational form—her particular third-person rendering of Newland's thoughts, feelings, and sensations—models a forked approach to consciousness. In this model, Newland's mind is split between a "waking," self-aware consciousness and a secondary one, voiced by the third-person narration, that largely interprets the sensations and perceptions of his bodily experiences. Wharton's narrative model resonates strongly with what Adam Crabtree calls the "alternate-consciousness paradigm,"[7] which evolved from studies of somnambulism and reached its height through research on hypnosis in the latter half of the nineteenth century. Somnambulists exhibited "two very distinct lives, or at least two ways of being," and moreover two separate memory chains, for the waking state could not recall the sleeping one and vice versa.[8] This break in memory, in particular, led to the hypothesis that the somnambulist experienced two different states of consciousness—a doubled consciousness—and hypnosis extended the theory when similar results appeared in inducements of artificial sleep.

My point is not that Wharton intentionally adapted (or even necessarily knew) the work of her peer hypnotists; I rather want to demonstrate how her narrative style inherently constitutes a psychological vision, one that was pertinent and timely, if now largely forgotten. It is worth recollecting in order to expand critical understanding of *The Age of Innocence* as a novel of consciousness and its narration as an innovative psychological development. By understanding how *The Age of Innocence* breaks ground in its representation of mental processes, scholars of American literature can begin to let go of the prejudice that holds that it is only with first-person, stream-of-consciousness writing that fiction begins formally to theorize the mind. As Dorrit Cohn and Ann Banfield noticed more than fifty years ago, and has only recently been registered again, the narrational mode known as free indirect discourse possesses, in Banfield's words, "great significance for the study of language and consciousness."[9] Wharton's prose illuminates how the significance of free indirect discourse inheres in its doubling of consciousness. Even if the alternate-consciousness paradigm has long since expired as currency in the field of psychology, readers bank its value each time they acquaint themselves with the workings of Newland Archer's mind.

From narrator to narration

When critics have discussed Wharton's narration in *The Age of Innocence*, it has generally been to refer to, but not deliberately to explain, her use of free indirect discourse.[10] First recognized in French scholarship as *style indirect libre*, or free indirect style, in 1912, the linguistic term designates narration that indirectly (using no quotation) represents a character's thoughts or speech, but without—free of—the markers, such as "he thought that ...," which might indicate such indirection. "Free indirect style" evolved to "free indirect discourse" to acknowledge that the mode was not personally idiosyncratic but culturally, even internationally, prevalent beginning in the nineteenth century.

In American criticism, the use of free indirect discourse in alternation with a discrete narrator persona has often been analyzed, paradigmatically with regard to Jane Austen, as giving rise to ironic judgment of the character's consciousness represented.[11] Following this tendency, John W. Crowley claims: "The language of *The Age of Innocence* both reflects the veneer of Old New York and tracks the interiority of the protagonist's consciousness by means of free indirect discourse. The knowing sardonic voice of the narrator's commentary undercuts the prevailing rules of conduct and also Newland Archer's rebellious pretensions."[12] Crowley imagines a narrator who moves from Newland's social circle into his mind, directing the story while maintaining a consistently witty perspective.

Margaret Jay Jessee takes a different approach to the text's irony but also argues for the existence of a discrete narrator persona. "The novel's free indirect discourse," she proposes, "creates both a temporal and dramatic irony in which the narrator either knows what Newland is thinking or has Newland seem to have thoughts of the narrator's own."[13] Jessee envisions a narrator with a set of thoughts that it has or "owns" separately from Newland, beyond or in addition to a voice, perspective, or attitude. D. Quentin Miller takes this individuating impulse even further, referring to the narrator, "like Archer," as a "he."[14] Martin Scorsese's film makes the reverse gesture, using Joanne Woodward to give the narrator a feminine voice. But as my friend once asked a mystified scooper of Superman ice cream, why gender it?

It is worth asking what evidence one has for classifying the narrator at all, and especially for identifying it, as Crowley and Jessee presume, as an individuated person-like being, in possession not only of knowledge or views but agency, body, and mind. When the novel opens, for instance, with the sentence: "On a January evening of the early seventies, Christine Nilsson was singing in *Faust* at the Academy of Music in New York,"[15] from whom or what does it come? The reader is introduced to no source, let alone character or persona, that voices the statement; if the reader is a student of literature and pins the statement to something called a narrator, the act of speaking is likely imagined, but the embodied mechanisms through which speech would occur are not present. The reader's engagement only becomes stranger when, a few pages later, it turns out that this entity can reveal, as Cohn writes, "what writers and readers know least in life: how another mind thinks, another body feels."[16] Having no body itself, and, having recounted as its own no set of experiences independent of those described in the tale, this odd entity now slides into Newland Archer's mind and reports on its contents. This first encounter is in direct discourse, or what Cohn calls "quoted monologue":[17] "'The darling!' thought Newland Archer, his glance flitting back to the young girl with the lilies-of-the-valley [May]. 'She doesn't even guess what it's all about'" (5). By the next paragraph, the entity offers no quotation marks or tags to frame a sentence as Newland's thought; although the third-person perspective lets the reader know that it has not disappeared, Newland's thought overtakes the text and begins to propel the story's events. "He did not in the least wish the future Mrs. Newland Archer to be a simpleton" (6): thus the reader meets the magic of free indirect discourse.

I offer this defamiliarization of Wharton's narration in order to put pressure on the idea of the narrator constituted as a figure distinct from Newland. The entity I have described has a less a mind opposed to Newland's own than an expansive function, inclusive of his mental operation. Admittedly, in the first chapter of *The Age of Innocence*, Wharton maintains a separation between the narrator's attitude and Newland's, providing the irony to which Crowley and Jessee refer. Parentheses mark this separation between Newland's unreflective musing on May and the narrator's arch skepticism:

> [H]e meant her (thanks to his enlightening companionship) to develop a social tact and readiness of wit ... If he had probed to the bottom of his vanity (as he sometimes nearly did) he would have found there the wish that his wife should be as worldly-wise and as eager to please as the married lady whose charms had held his fancy through two mildly agitated years; without, of course, any hint of the frailty which had so nearly marred that unhappy being's life, and had disarranged his own plans for a whole winter. (6)

In this passage, the narrator does have a different set of ideas from Newland, given its ability to judge the inadequacy of his self-assessment and to barb—in the very sentence that also represents—his inconvenienced dismissal of his last affair.

But as Lee Clark Mitchell observes, as one reads on, the sentences that blatantly mock Newland begin to disappear,[18] and so do those that undercut his thoughts at the same time that they deliver them, as in the passage quoted above. The narration loses its independent perspective, and its entire quality shifts in turn. What emerges are sentences that guide the reader to follow how Newland's physical sensations become processed as mental perceptions. For example, in chapter 9, when Newland arrives at Ellen's home only to find her absent, the focus is on how he sits, muses, smells, and thinks:

> But since he had come he meant to wait; and he sank into a chair and stretched his feet to the logs.
>
> It was odd to have summoned him in that way, and then forgotten him; but Archer felt more curious than mortified. The atmosphere of the room was so different from any he had ever breathed that self-consciousness vanished in the sense of adventure ... He tried to analyze the trick, to find a clue to it in the way the chairs and tables were grouped, in the fact that only two Jacqueminot roses (of which nobody ever bought less than a dozen) had been placed in the slender vase at his elbow, and in the vague pervading perfume that was not what one put on handkerchiefs, but rather like the scent of some far-off bazaar, a smell made up of Turkish coffee and ambergris and dried roses. (45)

If there is irony in these sentences (and again the parenthetical remark would qualify, about the norms of rose-purchasing), it is limited and lightly cast, and it is not necessarily directed at Newland. The thought may well be his own, with his social circle as the target; he has earlier prickled, with amateur anthropological insight, at the engagement rituals, which included ordering "twelve dozen of everything" for May's trousseau (43). The impossibility of knowing whether the thought of the ten heretically unpurchased roses originates with Newland is one of the hallmarks of free indirect discourse: because the ventriloquized rendering of a character's thoughts tends to alternate with the potentially judgmental speech of an individuated narrator, the writer can be slippery about moving from one to the other, leading the reader to wonder who is judging and who is being judged.[19] In the case of the Jacqueminots, I would argue, the answer does not matter very much—it may indicate an increasing skepticism on Archer's part that is also visible elsewhere. Yet this inconsequence itself is remarkable: what critics are used to recognizing as the ordinary function of free indirect discourse virtually evaporates in this passage.

What replaces irony, or even the potential for irony, is an invitation to sink, to stretch, to feel, to breathe, to puzzle, to sniff with Newland. Whereas the narrator of the early chapters had triangulated between the reader and Newland, now the narration has, as it were, stretched itself out into a kind of bridge, leading the reader into the operations of Newland's mind. This mind has not suddenly developed into a keen and exciting guide: "He tried to analyze the trick [of the room]" lets the reader know that there are limits to what Newland can perceive. Yet, dare I say—risking psychological criticism in another, all but professionally prohibited, dimension—that reading this passage has always seemed to me as pleasant as being in the drawing room seems to Newland. The reader does not sneer at Newland or his circle; she all but inhales with him. Even if Newland's mind has limits, the narration gracefully meets them, turning pedestrian reactions and responses into eloquent formulations: "Archer felt more curious than mortified"; "self-consciousness vanished in the sense of adventure"; "the vague pervading perfume that was not what one put on handkerchiefs." The warmth of the fire, the fading of embarrassment, the breathing of a new atmosphere, the mild puzzling over its composition— it is as if Newland gives these perceptions over, in an utter act of luxury, to narration that renders them in exquisite prose, as if his mind sinks into the narration as his body sinks into Ellen's chair. When the narration identifies the room's scent ("Turkish coffee and ambergris and dried roses"), it has followed Newland's dreamy train of thought to the end, evolving from suppositions to precision. Wharton's narration has shifted, from primarily exposing Newland's inadequacies to unfurling and unfolding his thoughts for him.

This new relation between narration and character not only provides a different tenor from the usual irony of free indirect discourse, it erases the form's frequent hallmark, which is its appearance in alternation with a distinct and knowing narrator. Instead of such alternation, Wharton begins to maintain a narrative voice that consistently records Newland's sensations—what he sees, hears, speaks; how he acts—and interprets his perceptions. As the parenthetical asides at his expense disappear (by my calculation, around chapter 9), so too does the authority of a distinct, person-like entity that could be called, with reference to drama, a narrator. That is, the reader's ability to identify the third-person voice of the novel as a being marked by gender or a particular set of experiences—by a body or mind—evaporates. The passage quoted above becomes representative, in that the physical experiences chronicled belong to Newland's body, and his mental responses become articulated through the narrative voice. Newland sniffs something strange ("a vague pervading perfume"); the narration takes over his wonder at the scent's components. The narration arrives at its answer—"a smell made up of Turkish coffee and ambergris and dried roses"—by riffling through Newland's experiences. To imagine instead a narrator with independent knowledge of Ellen's drawing-room aroma would be truly bizarre: Newland would be puzzling over the perfume that was not what one put on handkerchiefs, that seems exotic (these references appear securely Newland's), when the all-knowing narrator would arrive on the scene to declare, like a Food Network sommelier: "I know! It is Turkish coffee, ambergris, and dried roses!" The narration depends on what Newland has smelled, because the narration has no scent memories of its own—because the narration has no memories of its own, no separate base of experiences; in short, no mind of its own.

Wharton's narration is no narrator. Wharton's narration is no individual. Wharton's narration is what opens the door to Newland's mind, what plumbs his depths but also dredges his shallows, what displays them for the reader, working beyond the character's capacity for self-awareness. Wharton refers to the necessity of such display in *The Writing of Fiction*, published in 1925: "The impression produced by a landscape, a street or a house," she writes, "should always, to the novelist, be an event in the history of a soul."[20] Never referring to a narrator, Wharton demands that even so insignificant an act as waiting for Ellen must reveal and develop Newland's character. As I have argued, such revelations and developments only become legible as such thanks to the narration's lack of personage and its alternative ability to interpret the operations of Newland's soul—what I have called his perceptions or his mind, and will elaborate below as consciousness. I now turn to contextualize Wharton's narration according to the psychological research contemporaneous with the novel.

The original double consciousness

My claim that Wharton's narration fails to qualify as an individual may well seem counterintuitive: how can something that speaks so finely have no mind of its own? This objection likely arises because the model of mind implied—

the possibility of a unique speaker without an individually possessed mental landscape—is so foreign. In the years depicted in *The Age of Innocence*, however, such a model would not necessarily have been disorienting.[21] Indeed, psychologists then involved in hypnosis research were pursuing a line of thinking that nearly reverses the question above. Observing a subject who, induced in an artificial sleep, could talk, act, and think—all without the waking self's notice—they wondered how one physical body could produce two separately conscious beings. In other words, their question was not how something speaking could have no mind, but how an apparently single mind could produce more than one speaker, neither of which was known to the other. Hypnotist-psychologists were fascinated by the consciousness that could carry on a conversation—and be directed to do all manner of silly stunts—precisely without a mind of its own.

When literary scholars use the term double consciousness, they tend to invoke W. E. B. Du Bois's sociological conception of the experience of racial difference as a "sense of always looking at one's self through the eyes of others, of measuring one's soul by the tape of a world that looks on in amused contempt and pity."[22] Yet Du Bois learned the term in William James's psychology classroom, in reference to the splitting of mind originally observed in mesmerism and somnambulism in the 1770s and established as a scientific phenomenon a century later.[23] To invoke a more familiar Jamesian term, double consciousness meant that two streams of consciousness ran from one body, and from one body's set of experiences; the streams maintained their distinction through independent memory chains. Although commonly the somnambulist or hypnotized consciousness could also recall events of the waking self, the reverse did not apply. The implications of this double consciousness were uncanny, even for the researchers devoted to studying it. Alfred Binet opened his 1896 book on the subject by writing: "When we undertake to expound such strange phenomena as those of the doubling of consciousness, at the first blush we naturally provoke astonishment and even doubt. In truth, is not the idea extraordinary, that in hysterical individuals there should exist two distinct personalities, two egos united in the same person?"[24] Similarly, Boris Sidis, another of James's students, began his 1905 *Multiple Personality* with the gambit: "The question 'What is an individual?' seems to be the easiest thing to answer," and then turned to explain how little this was the case: "The individual may be regarded as a complex system of many minds or, more strictly speaking, the psychophysiological individual may be viewed as an organization of many subordinate individuals."[25] Binet and Sidis clarify what is at stake in differentiating Du Bois's notion of double consciousness from its original use. Whereas the sociological term refers to a single self-consciousness that negotiates both an inner and an outside point of view, the psychological term refers to two separate consciousnesses, neither of which is empowered to negotiate over the other. That is to say, the model of double consciousness does not presuppose any overarching consciousness that integrates the separate streams.[26]

In light of this contemporaneous model of mind, the premise of a narration that interprets Newland's thoughts without possessing its own individuality begins to seem less strange. The narration works as Newland's secondary consciousness. It draws from the sensory experiences of his body, producing an account of his mental activity: an interpretive record of his observations, thoughts, and feelings. Yet this secondary consciousness remains, in its third-person perspective, outside of his direct awareness. For Wharton does preserve something like Newland's primary or waking consciousness, a part of his mind that speaks to himself. These instances appear in quotes and are marked by a clumsy, slangy style. On May watching a sexually suggestive gesture at the opera: "The darling! … She doesn't even guess what it's all about" (5). On Ellen's lack of appearance at the announcement of their betrothal: "[May] knows as well as I do … the real reason of her cousin's staying away; but I shall never let her see by the least sign that I am conscious of there being a shadow of a shade on poor Ellen Olenska's reputation" (17). On his annoyance, nevertheless, at her residing in New York: "Hang Ellen Olenska!" (30). On the hope that the first six months of marriage will be the most difficult: "After that I suppose we shall have pretty nearly finished rubbing off each other's angles" (124). These lines represent what Newland hears when he is thinking aloud (he "grumble[s]" [30]), or when he is conscious of his own thought (he "reflect[s]" [17, 124]). Thus Wharton imagines a distinction between how the "waking" Newland composes his thoughts and how the narration—with far more panache—composes his thoughts for him. In addition to the two types of thinking, the other narrated sentences that appear after the novel's early chapters are quoted dialogue (what Newland hears or says) and descriptions of Newland's movements and sensations. That the narration, as a second consciousness, would also know of Newland's primary consciousness and the experiences of his body is coterminous with experiments in hypnosis, as mentioned above.[27]

Wharton's narrative style fits intriguingly with the psychological model of double consciousness that was thrilling researchers during the time that the imaginary Ellen Olenska was thrilling Newland Archer. It would be reductive, to both the text and literary history, to assert an identity, whether intentional or accidental, between science and story. But it is also reductive to fail to register Wharton's production as a novel of consciousness. Novels nearly contemporaneous with *The Age of Innocence*, such as James Joyce's 1922 *Ulysses* or Virginia Woolf's 1925 *Mrs. Dalloway*, qualify as such so universally that Wharton's omission from the category is remarkable, testifying to a deep prejudice, on the part of literary scholars, to conflate the single stream of consciousness with consciousness itself.[28] As Cohn remarked in 1966, it was "only with the first studies of the stream-of-consciousness novel [that] American scholars [began] to analyze the problem of rendering consciousness in a third-person novel,"[29] and the orientation became not only decisive but totalizing. As she explains, novels concerned with consciousness all began to be designated as "stream-of-consciousness," which requires scholars to remember that "William James's original metaphorical meaning has been left far behind, and that the consciousness rendered in modern novels, more often than not, assumes models of the psyche that differ from the one symbolized by James in his river image."[30] I worry that Cohn's second reminder, especially, has become lost—and with it the capacity to read Wharton as having imagined one such alternative model of the psyche. When scholars merely note that *The Age of Innocence* employs free indirect discourse, without exploring the particular workings of its narration, they miss the rich psychological vision of the novel's form.[31]

Who knows what?

I have argued that Wharton's narration serves as Newland's secondary consciousness in order to register *The Age of Innocence* as a psychological novel, in the most sophisticated sense: as a formally innovative engagement with the process of mental perception. Now I want to address the implications of my analysis by responding to two long-standing questions the novel raises. First, does the narration acknowledge or include any perspective other than Newland's own? This question is most pertinent with regard to May, who, the reader ultimately learns, knew of his near-affair with Ellen; does the narration suggest May's knowledge before Dallas informs Newland of it? Second, how much does Newland grow or change from the beginning to the end of the novel? Does his mind evolve, or does it only wear a steadier groove in its original niche? Interpreting these two sets of questions highlights what is at stake in shifting from a notion of narrator to narration, from independent entity to secondary consciousness: the first points at how the reader's experience changes (what is or isn't available for her to know?) and the latter at how Newland's character changes (how can or can't he develop?). I will suggest that Wharton's model of the mind is devoted fully to Newland's process of perception; the narration occludes any other perspective. Yet the novel also leaves obscure any accounting for Newland's gains.

The first question, that of the narration's restriction to Newland's knowledge, arises because of the pressure I am putting on the assumption that *The Age of Innocence* retains an independent narrator. If the novel did so, this entity would not be restricted to interpreting Newland's consciousness, and so might know of, and might suggest to the reader, information beyond Newland's awareness—namely, that others were aware of his emotional affair with Ellen. But if the narration instead functions as Newland's secondary consciousness, then it can have no other position from which to speak or inform or tell. I would argue that the secret remains: that every sentence in the novel may be interpreted as catalyzed by Newland's embodied experience. This is not to say that Newland is aware of, and deliberately formulates, every sentence as a thought. But it is to say that the novel is circumscribed by, encompassed by, the scope of Newland's mind. At Ellen's final dinner party, when "it came over him, in a vast flash made up of many broken gleams, that to all of them he and Madame Olenska were lovers" (200), the suddenness and the broken gleams are the reader's, too.

To claim that there are no sentences that are not, in some sense, Newland's may appear to omit those that physically set the scenes. For example, the narration after Mrs. Archer's dinner party, where Ellen is discussed and Newland's desire sparked, reads as primarily explaining who moves where: "On the drive homeward May remained oddly silent; through the darkness, he still felt her enveloped in her menacing blush ... They went upstairs, and he turned into the library. She usually followed him; but he heard her passing down the passage to her bedroom" (161). It is possible to interpret these as produced by an entity—a narrator—who independently observes and informs the reader of May's silence, the couple mounting the stairs, their separate passages down the hallway. Yet it is just as plausible to read these sentences as part of Newland's consciousness, as his perception of May's silence, their ascent, their separate passages. The latter interpretation has the value of smoothly integrating Newland's feeling of May's blush, as well as the sentence replaced by ellipses above: "What its menace meant he could not guess: but he was sufficiently warned by the fact that Madame Olenska's name had evoked it" (161). What Newland could guess, how he was warned, what he could feel, where May was, where she wasn't: these all constitute Newland's responses to his sensed environment. I have found virtually no phrasing that cannot be subsumed by this formula, that cannot be legitimately regarded as an experience of or response to Newland's sensed environment.[32]

Acknowledging Wharton's rigorous adherence to Newland's consciousness brings into relief the complexity of the narrated interactions between him and May. While May's perspective cannot be admitted—so as to preserve Newland's surprise at Dallas's revelation—her savviness must be plausible, so that Dallas's claim does not strain belief. As the scene after the dinner party progresses, Newland lies about needing to go to Washington on business; May's acquiescent dialogue and request that he visit Ellen is translated into a "mute message," through which he imagines her elaborated, emotional response:

Of course you understand that I know all that people have been saying about Ellen, and heartily sympathize with my family in their effort to get her to return to her husband. I also know that, for some reason you have not chosen to tell me, you have advised her against this course, which all the older men of the family, as well as our grandmother, agree in approving; and that it is owing to your encouragement that Ellen defies us all, and exposes herself to the kind of criticism of which Mr. Sillerton Jackson probably gave you, this evening, the hint that made you so irritable ... Hints have indeed not been wanting; but since you appear unwilling to take them from others, I offer you this one myself, in the only form in which well-bred people of our kind can communicate unpleasant things to each other: by letting you understand that I know you mean to see Ellen when you are in Washington, and are perhaps going there expressly for that purpose; and that, since you are sure to see her, I wish you to do so with my full and explicit approval— and to take the opportunity of letting her know what the course of conduct you have encouraged her in is likely to lead to. (161–162)

This interlude is required, not only because Newland and May never speak of such things frankly, but because May's thoughts are not otherwise available in the course of the narration. "Hints have indeed not been wanting" from her perspective, and from other characters' as well, on matters more than the aptness of Newland's advice, as the reader will learn at her farewell dinner party. Yet the narration cannot fully trace the communication of those hints; it will not know about them until that night, until the vast flash of the broken gleams. The "mute message" above is presumably one such broken gleam; an invented exchange, a social norm decoded, something sensed or felt. Any access to May's mind can only exist at this level, the product of Newland's imagination.[33]

In shifting from narrator to narration, and in reading the narration as Newland's secondary consciousness, traditional notions of omniscience thus become untenable.[34] Yet how or what the narration knows does not thereby become irrelevant; it rather becomes more complex. As I have emphasized, the model of double consciousness that Wharton approximates entails a split, a forking, such that the "waking" Newland that grumbles: "Hang Ellen Olenska!" remains distinct from the one that formulates the thought prompted by May's blush: "What its menace meant he could not guess: but he was sufficiently warned by the fact that Madame Olenska's name had evoked it." Thus, the "waking" Newland is not aware of the passage of the latter, clause by clause, through his mind: such process is not only inconsistent with turn of the century psychology, it is simply too clumsy to entertain as a premise, in story or in life. Still, the idea that "waking" Newland of limited eloquence has absolutely no knowledge of what the narration is up to seems implausible, too. The narration interprets so many of his sensations that it is difficult to imagine how he gets by without some access to its work.

To address the second question raised above, about Newland's evolution over the course of the novel, is to face these contradictory logics. If one follows only the evidence of the "waking" Newland, his explicit grumbles and self-reflections do not become more sophisticated, indicating no progress of character. If one follows only the evidence of the narration, Newland's encounter with Ellen sweeps him outside of his New York circle only to deposit him back into it; the narration is effectively where the novel's plot—of the evolution of Newland's consciousness—is located. Wharton provides no account of how the two streams of consciousness intermingle: she remains true to the alternate-consciousness paradigm, which posits no overarching or integrating self.[35] And yet it is difficult to imagine, especially for the reader who does not divide her novel into alternating strips, that the elements of Newland's mind do not somehow connect, that behind the scenes some mental mechanism does not give his two streams a bit of a stir.

The only evidence that such a stir may ever have occurred appears in the novel's final paragraphs. Seating himself on a bench while Dallas goes up to Ellen's Paris apartment, Newland pictures Dallas's ascent and entry, which is, as usual, relayed by the narration:

> [H]e tried to see the persons already in the room—for probably at that sociable hour there would be more than one—and among them a dark lady, pale and dark, who would look up quickly, half rise, and hold out a long thin hand with three rings on it. ... He thought she would be sitting in a sofa-corner near the fire, with azaleas banked beneath her on a table. (217)

The familiar cadence is interrupted, however, by a line that is as surprising to the "waking" Newland as to the reader attuned to his demarcation from the narration: "'It's more real to me here than if I went up,' he suddenly heard himself say; and the fear lest that last shadow of reality should lose its edge kept him rooted to his seat as the minutes succeeded each other" (217). Newland is not in the habit of intentionally noting, of being aware of, his perceiving mind. Moreover, he has not previously compared the realm of his sensory experience (what is "real to me") with that of his imagination (which the narration generally processes, as in May's mute message). When Newland speaks the line, he vocalizes what he understands thanks, directly, to the narration. This occurs to him passively: Newland "suddenly heard himself say" what he was thinking, and it is as if his waking body has unexpectedly overtaken the narration. He stays rooted to the spot, then, not only to stay the image of Ellen's apartment, but because he wishes to retain "that last shadow of reality" that comes from his imagination. He wishes to retain, in other words, the connection between the waking self that sits and hears itself speak and the one that imagines, in delicate prose, what Ellen's hands look like, and how her flowers come to be arranged in her sitting room.

And so Newland Archer sits in the shadow of his own mind. When Wharton closes the novel, with the "thickening dusk" and the lighting of the lamps, the narration again assumes its proper role, telling the reader how Newland's body moved and why (217). But as he walks away from Ellen's apartment, away, perhaps, from the memory of her New York apartment, the crossing of paths that did not take place between the lovers has occurred—subtly, momentarily—between his two consciousnesses. This brief crossing is no integration, because Wharton's vision, in the final analysis, is not a therapeutic one. It is an image of the mind from the perspective of narration. What it illuminates is the lingering literary legacy of psychology's double consciousness. It shimmers, like an opportunity missed, each time the novel is read, each time a reader sinks into its pages—like Newland into Ellen's chair by the fire—and lets the assured rhythm of the prose take over her mind.

"Trying It On" Again as Affect: Rethinking Feeling in *The Age of Innocence*

Margaret Jay Jessee
University of Alabama at Birmingham

An essay I wrote on Edith Wharton's *The Age of Innocence* was published in *JML: A Journal of Modern Literature* in 2012.[1] As is the case with most literary scholarship, the article was written about two years prior to its publication as it underwent revision, review, and then waiting in the queue to go to press. While it appeared in print in 2012, it was written in 2010. Looking back at that article almost ten years after its composition, I find myself still intrigued with the same concept that drove my initial analysis and claims: the complexity of the way Wharton uses the concept of "trying it on" in the novel. The phrase appears early in the text when Newland Archer first sees Ellen Olenska in the Mingott family opera box. Everyone is aware that Ellen has left her husband, and rumors suggest she has had an affair. She is already considered a social liability before she ever appears in New York. Sillerton Jackson suggests that it is rather shocking the Mingotts would "try it on" by bringing Ellen out in such a public way.[2] Newland quickly adopts Jackson's phrasing as his own, stating that he too did not think the Mingotts would have "tried it on" (11). As I noted in the 2012 article, to "try it on" simultaneously means two things at once: a benign attempt to see if it fits, and a more sinister putting something over on someone or deceiving. In this particular scene, bringing Ellen out at the opera is both an experiment to see how it will go over with the "old New York" social set and a simultaneous plot to deceive the audience, to pretend her past does not prohibit her present and future acceptance into society.

The way I grappled with Wharton's use of "trying it on" ten years ago was through a close reading of the novel itself functioning as a mask formally while it represented, thematically, characters masquerading, or "trying it on." Central to the argument was my reading of the way Newland Archer misunderstands May and Ellen and thus places them into a dichotomous position, one a close reading of the text exposes as a false position. That is, May is far more cunning and conniving than Newland understands, and Ellen is far less worldly and immune to the old New York codes and customs than Newland believes (and hopes). The characters, then, are all "trying it on," and Newland, as our narrative lens, misunderstands the performance. It is in the distance between the narrative voice and Newland, our narrative lens, that readers are able to decipher the masquerade. Readers see through the trying it on, as Sillerton Jackson is able to do.

What intrigues me now as I reread the novel and reconsider this represented world of "trying it on" is the incongruency between the characters' inner feelings and their performed emotions. I am newly interested in the way "trying it on" relates to affect. What makes this such an intriguing example of literary affect is the way Wharton manages to convey the characters' inner feelings despite their performances to disguise their actual emotions—despite their trying it on. As Ben Highmore explains: "affect gives you away: the telltale heart; my clammy hands; the note of anger in your voice; the sparkle of glee in their eyes. You may protest your innocence, but we both know, don't we, that who you really are, or what you really are, is going to be found" in your bodily reaction.[3] Newland Archer, our narrative point of view, confuses the affectation of emotion with the real thing. In fact, Newland obstructs the reader's clear view of affect. Readers must read around Newland in order to understand how other characters feel. Thus, we see characters trying it on, deceiving Newland and others into believing they really feel a certain way when they do not. Yet, through bodily clues, Wharton lets readers know which bodily reaction is the real thing and which is trying it on. For Wharton, the act of understanding another's emotions is an act of misreading, rethinking, and recursively considering feeling.

There are less complex ways than Wharton's to convey a discrepancy between inner feelings and the affected outward expression of those feelings. In other novels, readers know that a character feels a certain way because either readers are privy to the character's inner thoughts or a narrator interprets their feelings for the reader. But Wharton's text manages to convey the characters' real inner feelings by showing readers their outward behavior, even if only through a quick glimpse, before readers see the characters' affected performance of emotion. That is, Wharton conveys emotion as both internal and bodily as well as external and bodily. Conveying such complexity is especially impressive in *The Age of Innocence* because Newland Archer misreads others so frequently. As a result, he often obscures readers' view of other characters and their emotions. Yet Wharton manages to provide these glimpses to the readers despite Newland's inability to correctly read the distinction between the performance of an emotion and the actual emotion. Trying it on, then, is a means of conveying affect as well as affectation. It is only through the attempt to perform a different emotion that readers are able to see the discrepancy between the affect and the affectation.

Wharton's modernist affect

While we may take for granted today that subtly portraying a character as feeling one way and acting in another way is merely a part of representing social beings throughout the whole of literary history, Wharton's depiction of that incongruency is strikingly modern. In her study of realism and affect, *Emotional Reinventions*, Melanie V. Dawson argues that writers in the realist era crafted a more complex and nuanced taxonomy of emotions to capture affect than did their sentimentalist predecessors. Realist-era writers understood, Dawson argues, that, while individual emotions are distinct, they can only be conveyed within the context of other emotions. In large part, this more complex understanding of emotion arose out of the era's more modernized system of representation that was "no longer visible as sentimental representations" as "the diversity of the US Population necessitated a serious consideration of emotional variation."[4]

Modernist understandings of diversity (of place, region, and class status, as examples) meant that the more unifying, singular emotion of sympathy, so prevalent in the sentimental era, could no longer contain the variations of emotional states, nor could it contain the complexities of representation of those emotions. For Dawson, realism "stressed emotional hybridity over ideals of affective purity and emotional flux over a notion of emotional stability."[5]

Key to this hybridity is the realist-era writers' disruption of the notion that emotions are interior feelings that result in direct outward behaviors. If a person is angry, for example, older models of emotional taxonomies suggested that person would, as a result of this inner anger, outwardly show the inner feeling with gritted teeth and clenched fists.

William James refers to the assumption that feelings precede bodily behavior as a misguided "common sense": "we lose our fortune, are sorry and weep; we meet a bear, are frightened and run; we are insulted by a rival, are angry and strike."[6] James calls this sequence of events—first the feeling then the bodily action— quite simply "incorrect." For James, the bodily act is the emotion. Without the physical reaction to the stimulus, "we could not actually feel afraid or angry."[7] The separate notion of bodily and mental experience of emotion, then, was already seen as a faulty separation by the time realist-era writers were tackling literary affect.

The differences between feeling, emotion, and affect are not easily defined, and critics debate the definitions of each concept. The definitions I use here follow Alan Bourassa, who conceives of the relationship between feeling, emotion, and affect as "three concentric circles, feeling enveloped by emotion, emotion by affect."[8] Feeling is quite individual and personal, while emotion is "a more complex term and it forms one of the conditions of possibility for feeling."[9] Emotions, for Bourassa, "are accompanied by feelings, of course, but emotions themselves are more akin to orientations, stances toward the world."[10] Affect incorporates the inner feelings and the outward (or bodily) expression of those feelings, the emotions. Affect does not assume a linear timeline of feelings and emotions—it incorporates it all at once.

For William James, bodily behaviors are the stuff of what we think of as inner emotions. Any attempt to separate the consciousness of a feeling from the bodily symptoms that accompany it results in "nothing left behind, no 'mind-stuff' out of which the emotion can be constituted."[11] Jane F. Thrailkill argues that readers of realist-era fictions were aware that emotions or feelings would involve both the bodily and the mental simultaneously. Emotion is "embodied but not mindless," Thrailkill explains, and emotions are "culturally conditioned" in expression, but that does not mean that there is no biological component.[12] Because emotions are embodied, parsing out which part of an emotional reaction is biological, which is social, and which is mindful or performative is impossible to do in any type of strictly chronological order. Dawson, too, points to complexities inherent in attempts to represent inner emotion through outward expression as a sequence of events.

The bodily may be the stuff of the inner emotion, as James insists, but what is made visible, the outward behavior, can be affected at times. Thus, the affect and the inner motivation are not necessarily congruent because affect and feeling are not necessarily the same thing. There is a distance between emotion and affect, especially in Edith Wharton's old New York. That is, we can think of "trying it on" as the way Wharton's novel captures the distance between actual emotion and affected emotion. In different ways, both Thrailkill's and Dawson's works show that, by the late nineteenth and early twentieth centuries, realist-era fictions began to dismantle the notion that inner feelings manifest simply in a direct sequence of external actions. As Dawson argues, realist-era texts "interrogate the interpretive difficulties that arise when viewers equate actions with underlying emotions."[13] Realist texts blur "the relation between visible and felt experiences of emotion" and, as a result, this literature concluded that observations of bodily signs do not lead to a direct understanding of inner emotion.[14] This is an important point because it is in this era of writing that characters who "try it on" are not always portrayed as clearly villainous to the reader as they were in earlier sentimental and sensational literature. That is, disguising a felt emotion with an incongruent outward behavior does not necessarily mean the character is "bad."

The Age of Innocence uses "trying it on" as a means of separating the outward emotion from the inner motivation, the affect from the feeling and emotion that it encompasses. Importantly, the novel does not suggest separating the performance of emotion from the inner feeling is simple or even possible. As concentric circles, emotion encompasses feelings, and affect encompasses emotion (and feelings). They are not all the same—they are not three different words for the same definition—but they are likewise not easily separated into distinct concepts either. Characters have visible feelings that are in opposition to their performance of emotion (or lack of emotion). They experience feelings, and then they "try it on" in the hopes of conveying an alternative inner feeling. The text blurs the distinction between outward behaviors and underlying feelings as it shows characters who perform outward emotions that are incongruent to their visible experiences of feeling. That is, characters throughout the novel often maintain two emotions: the "real" feelings as congruent with the expressed emotion and the affected outward emotion. The result is a complex web of affect that the reader must interpret in spite of Newland's inability to do so.

Reading around Newland's emotions

In one of her plot outlines for the novel, Wharton describes Newland's reaction to first seeing Ellen at the opera as a one-word sentence: "Horrified" (343). Thus, her opening outline for the plot of the novel is developed through Newland's emotion. In the completed work, the narrator explains that Newland is "content to hold his world view without analysing it, since he knew it was that of all the carefully-brushed, white-waistcoated, buttonhole-flowered gentlemen who succeeded each other in the club box, exchanged friendly greetings with him, and turned their opera-glasses critically on the circle of ladies who were the product of the system" (6–7). Here, Newland is content to hold a "world view" that is common to all the other gentlemen of his set; however, the narrator goes on to explain that "in matters intellectual and artistic," Newland actually feels "himself distinctly the superior of these chosen specimens of old New York gentility; he had probably read more, thought more, and even seen a good deal more of the world than any other man of the number" (7). Newland is able to sustain these competing assessments because "singly, they betrayed their inferiority; but grouped together they represented 'New York,' and the habit of masculine solidarity made him accept their doctrine on all the issues called moral" (7). Whether the narrator believes these men to be inferior is not directly stated, but the use of the word "called" here indicates the group has a morality that exists in name only.

The blending of Newland's thoughts with the narrator's makes the object of ironic critique difficult to parse. Yet, through the repeated phrase, "trying it on," in this same section of the novel, Wharton reveals how Newland arrives at a way of viewing his surroundings. While the other members of the opera box use an opera glass to view Ellen's arrival, Newland feels superior and does not, but he nevertheless tries on what the group sees through that glass. That is, while the narration complicates what is real and what is Newland's misreading, the narrative provides a means of understanding how Newland arrives at his readings: counter to what he believes about himself, Newland is trying on what those around him feel. There is a clear disjunction between the characters' inner feelings and their outwardly expressed emotions.

Newland first has a "tender reverence for [May's] abysmal purity" so that, after marriage, he could educate her and "meant her (thanks to his enlightening companionship) to develop a social tact and readiness of wit enabling her to hold her own with the most popular married women of the 'younger set,' in which it was the recognized custom to attract masculine homage while playfully discouraging it" (6). Newland believes May to be the "young creature whose soul's custodian he was to be" who "knew nothing and expected everything" (28). To Newland, May Welland is a version of the Diana myth: "In her dress of white and silver, with a wreath of silver blossoms in her hair, the tall girl looked like a Diana just alight from the chase" (42). Later, as he sees her acclivity to archery, "In her white dress, with a pale green ribbon about the waist and a wreath of ivy on her hat," Newland notices a "Diana-like aloofness" (128). Newland thinks May "primitive and pure" (115); she is the quintessential virgin, what Elizabeth Ammons calls "America's Dream Girl," referring to notions of the perfect specimen of femininity as articulated at the time in the works of William Dean Howells, Henry James, and Paul John Eakin.[15] He imagines her as a "poor darling" who "doesn't even guess" what the love scenes in Faust "are all about" (4–5). True to his ambivalent nature, what Newland actually wants is for his bride to become "worldly-wise" while maintaining her Diana-like status. "How this miracle of fire and ice was to be created, and to sustain itself in a harsh world, he had never taken the time to think about" (6). Once Newland falls for Ellen early in the novel, however, he finds his "fire" and suddenly the "ice" seems "empty."

Tellingly, we have in Wharton's plot outline of *The Age of Innocence* her conscious decision to craft this very type of disjunction. May offers to give up Newland so that he may be with Ellen. Wharton writes of May in the outline: "she gives him up magnanimously but when she finds that Ellen is the cause she is very bitter, and reproaches Ellen for Ellen too is very much distressed but still," which Wharton later completely crosses out. In its stead, she leaves only what comes after the rejected line: "because she has been taught that 'ladies do not make scenes,' and she continues to pretend that she does not

suspect Ellen of being her rival, till the latter's engagement is announced"
(343). What Wharton decides to strike out is the congruent action following
May's emotion. May feels bitter and accosts Ellen as a reaction to that emotion.
But, by striking out that line and leaving behind only that May will continue to
"pretend," or to continue to try it on, Wharton's finished novel maintains the
disjunction between expressive behavior and inner emotion.

An example of Wharton's complex representation of emotion is Newland's
experience of fear each time he sees that May Welland's emotions are far more
complicated than he first presumes. In a telling scene, May reveals her inner
suspicions that Newland is falling for Ellen Olenska. As Newland is encouraging
May to rush their wedding date, May bows her head, hiding her eyes "under her
conniving hat-brim" (119). "Conniving," like "trying it on," contains a double
meaning: in this case, hiding one's eyes as well as being covert, deceptive. In
the 2012 article, I read this moment as a "narrative dissonance";[16] but now see
that it is May's emotional dissonance revealed here. When Newland asks May
if she realizes that he really does want to marry her, May raises her head, thus
removing the conniving hat brim from between them, and Newland sees "eyes
of such despairing clearness" that he loosens his grip on her waist out of fear
or surprise (120). In this moment, May's emotions are not hidden behind a hat
or even a performative appearance. She shows "despairing clearness," or a full
understanding, and this understanding makes her sad. In response, Newland's
bodily reaction is his emotion—he fears May's clarity.

This scene reveals the dissonance between the characters' performances
of emotion and their inner feelings. As William E. Cain argues, "Newland's
joy in his possession of May Welland" ultimately "enables him to simplify his
sense of what her feelings are."[17] May was already conniving, and Newland
was already performing the role of a bridegroom who anticipates the marriage
with such glee that he does not wish to wait. They have been "trying it on,"
but here, the performance slips and their visible emotions are quite real and
despairing. Their affected emotions give way to their inner feelings, emotions
that are revealed through their bodily actions. Thus, it is not so much that
there is a narrative dissonance here as there is a visible dissonance between
feeling, emotion, and affect.

May recognizes Newland's interest in Ellen early on, and her insecurities
are often misread by Newland as a blankness or "niceness" rather than envy

or jealousy. Yet readers are given glimpses into May's insecurities, despite Newland's misunderstanding. This insecurity becomes particularly apparent in a telling scene when Newland reveals that he "saw some rather gorgeous yellow roses and packed them off to Madame Olenska," then asks May if that was "right" (66). May's response, that "it's odd [Ellen] didn't mention it" because she "spoke of Mr. Beaufort's having sent her wonderful orchids," among other flowers Ellen has received from men, is followed by an equally cunning gesture on May's part: "She seems so surprised to receive flowers. Don't people send them in Europe? She thinks it such a pretty custom" (66). May here deflates any notion Newland might have that he is Ellen's only admirer, suggesting Ellen is pleased to find all of these men in America are sending her flowers, a gesture that works to perfect effect as evidenced by Newland's "irritably" phrased response: "Oh, well, no wonder mine were overshadowed by Beaufort's" (67). Immediately, Newland mentions rushing their wedding date, the first of several times he attempts to trap himself, to force his own inability to be with Ellen. May's retort that others in their set had been engaged much longer, thus why should they rush, strikes Newland as "the traditional maidenly interrogation" and he feels "ashamed" for "finding it singularly childish" (67). Conforming to old New York, something he does and urges Ellen to do, is here deemed "childish" in relation to May. He even wonders "at what age 'nice' women began to speak for themselves" (67), making May the "nice" woman and Ellen—by virtue of her irreverent speaking for herself—not nice.

May asks an important question: "why aren't we very well off as we are?" (67). Newland interprets this question as: isn't it clear that we are already doing well?—an interpretation that might require a pause after the "why": why, aren't we very well off as we are? But May's question also asks: why do you think we are not doing well? Newland's assumption that she is merely concerned with how others in their set handle engagements does not consider May's awareness of his desire for Ellen and his attempt to be what he thinks Ellen desires. Importantly, Newland misreads May's actions. He assumes her behavior reflects an emotional state of blissful ignorance. The reality, of course, is that May is performing her "nice" ignorance. Readers are certainly aware that May is feeling insecure about Newland's interest in Ellen. Similarly, Newland feels insecure in his feelings for both May and Ellen. Both are betraying their actual emotion while attempting to perform ignorance (May) and indifference (Newland).

May is certainly not the only character Newland misunderstands due to the novel's interrogation of outward behavior's ability to reflect inner feeling. In fact, Newland repeats to Ellen: "I don't understand you!" (106, 108). When Ellen tells Newland that he must go ahead with his engagement to May despite his professed change of feelings, he petulantly brings up her friendship with Beaufort in order to cause a specific emotional reaction: "As the words sprang out he was prepared for an answering flare of anger; and he would have welcomed it as fuel for his own" (107). Instead of reacting in anger, however, Ellen "only grew a shade paler, and stood with her arms hanging down before you, and her head slightly bent, as her way was when she pondered a question" (107). Newland is only able to identify that Ellen has a question based on his limited ability to read her outward behavior, yet he is unable to piece together her inner feelings. And that interpretative slippage is because Newland does not understand Ellen's inner motivation. He sees her bodily expression, but what he assumed she would feel—anger—is not what she expresses in this scene. Thus the reader must infer from Ellen's body language what it is she actually feels in this scene and, importantly, whether it is what she feels or whether she is affecting a calm demeanor in order to thwart Newland's attempt to rile her. Wharton may here portray Ellen as feeling resigned after coming to a new and saddening understanding of Newland's inability to comprehend the impossibility of their situation. But the text describes her "tone" and her "look" as "enveloped" in "a soft inaccessibility" (107). Ellen's feelings are shrouded from Newland and, as a result, the reader tries to read around Newland, almost wishing he could step aside at times to stop obstructing the view.

The function of Newland as the narrative point of view is ostensibly to demonstrate that, just as he is obstructing, he is misreading his place and role in his social status. That is, Newland's attempt to separate himself from the old New York set results in his misreading or misunderstanding of May's and Ellen's emotional states. He resists empathy with May because Newland actually fears that he is much like May. Newland's disavowal is an attempt to identify as an outsider like Ellen, not a representative of old New York like May. He misreads Ellen's empathy with him because he misreads their shared status as "outsiders." Dawson argues that realist writers' characters often display a desire to feel the emotional satisfaction that attends a gesture of fellow feeling, even as they are repeatedly disappointed by their lack of sympathetic connection with those outside of their social milieu. Dawson names the desire "interrogative energy," which captures the nature of realist thought, with its recursive intertwining of feeling, thinking, thinking-about-feeling, and feeling-about-thinking.[18] For Dawson, it is only "when lifestyles and ideologies are shared" that "empathy ... occurs";[19] otherwise, feeling across differences in station appears "challenging, unsatisfying, and ultimately impossible."[20] He wants to be like Ellen, or he wants to be like he thinks Ellen is. By not understanding May's emotions, he is able to maintain his insistence that he is really an outsider, that he is really more like Ellen. Looking at New York through Ellen's lens, Newland realizes that "viewed thus, as through the wrong end of a telescope," his world looks "disconcertingly small and distant" (62). Newland's old New York turns into a distant, foreign place when he is looking at it with Ellen.

Indeed, before Newland's desire for Ellen begins to shift his perspective on May's potential absence of any real emotion, Newland and May feel similarly about each other. They each respect the other's feelings. Lee Clark Mitchell argues that May and Newland are able to communicate with each other early in the novel because they share the narrowness of the old New York society. This narrowness "allows for a certain emotional closeness and instant mutual understanding."[21] Because their emotions are contained within the same tightly constructed world, "communication occurs without the need for words at all," but it is Ellen's advent that "leads him to undervalue this subtle capacity, and only rarely thereafter do he or we wonder about May" (207). It is in his desire for Ellen that Newland loses his interest in what May is feeling, in her emotional state. Earlier in the novel, Newland is consistently checking in with May's feelings, trying to read her inner feelings through her expressed emotion. But after his desire for Ellen becomes intense, he is no longer interested in trying to understand May's emotions.

And Newland's inability to understand May's feelings, while rooted in a general lack of interest in her at the height of his desire for Ellen, becomes reassuring for Newland because he equates not understanding May with not being like May. Newland tries on Ellen's position as outsider. He doesn't want to belong to the "hieroglyphic world where the real thing was never said or done" (29). After knowing and loving Ellen, Newland remembers thinking before that the world of more bohemian artists and eccentrics was probably just as small as his own world. But when he is "reminded of this by trying to picture the society in which the Countess Olenska had lived and suffered" he also imagines she has "tasted mysterious joys" (65). Suddenly, remembering the Mingotts' concern over her bohemian lifestyle "amuses" Newland. He even acknowledges to himself that Ellen has "reversed his values" (66). If he feels the way Ellen feels, then he can consider himself outside of May's world, a fantasy that has more to do with how he misreads the women than with himself.

William E. Cain makes a point that really should be obvious to any reader but can actually lie beneath the narrative surface because the narrative point of view follows Newland: "What Newland does not do is to wonder what May's feelings were when he and she had sex, which he does not have with Ellen."[22] That is, readers know that May and Newland are having sex because May becomes pregnant. And though Newland is shocked to learn this, everyone, including May, assumes he and Ellen have also had sex. Thus, it never occurs to Newland to wonder what May must have been feeling having sex with a man who is betraying her (so she thinks). He never considers how May feels about their marital sex, though he realizes she has feelings about his presumed sexual relationship with Ellen.

Manners as hereditary affect

It is rather fitting, perhaps, that I arrive at my argument here by rethinking my earlier article on the novel—*The Age of Innocence* itself is a reflection on the past. Because the novel is set in the 1870s but was published in 1920, the narrative lens is focused backward, shaping the reader's view of events, actions, and emotions through memory and reconsideration. "Wharton," Nir Evron argues, "did not identify with Archer the man but rather with the predicament in which he finds himself in the final chapter: outliving the world that had shaped him."[23] Realist-era writers like Wharton were certainly invested in the way emotions shape people and, in particular, how past emotion affects immediate responses and reflections. As Newland's son, Dallas, describes the previous generation to his aged father after twenty-six years have passed since the action of the novel, "you never did ask each other anything, did you? And you never told each other anything. You just sat and watched each other, and guessed at what was going on underneath" (214). The novel explores that very act of guessing what the dissonance was between the outer behavior to be "watched" and the inner feelings "going on underneath" from a backwards-looking point of view.

With the era's intense interest in the origins of man, following the work not only by Charles Darwin but other prominent scientists of the time like Jean-Baptiste Lamarck and Herbert Spencer, the literature in the late nineteenth and early twentieth century also reflected the interest in the origins of emotion.[24] Dawson argues that fiction interested in emotion's origins "probed the dynamic of cause and effect by considering processes from the past that were tied to emotion effects in the present."[25] Realist writers like Wharton dealt with the causal relationship between past emotion and present behavior—both the long term and the immediate. This, Dawson argues, "multiplied the importance of emotion's narrative work as authors considered the basis of emotional habit."[26] By analyzing an emotional past, these writers sought to understand contemporary behaviors. Emotions were seen as leaving a trace on the present actions. Just after Dallas tells Newland that their generation had to sit and guess each other's inner feelings, he does admit that the older generation knew "more about each other's private thoughts" than the younger generation would "ever have time to find out" about their own (214). The disruptions between the expressive behaviors and inner motives are a part of the past, a part of Dallas's family history, that has left an imprint on him.

There is an important difference between *fin de siècle* literary writers' and scientists' interest in past emotion, Dawson argues. While the era's evolutionists like Darwin and Spencer believed studying the origins of emotions could give scientific insight into human behavior, literary writers explored the "possible *disjunctions* between expressive behaviors and inner motives as part of an individuated emotional past."[27] In addition to Darwin, Spencer, and various psychologists and anthropologists, Wharton also read biologists, something Dawson uses to explain Wharton's "intellectual interest in tracing habits, abilities, and tendencies back to familial contexts," which Dawson then applies to "the question of emotional expression" largely because hereditary questions had been linked to emotions since at least Darwin in 1872.[28] Wharton is interested, then, in both culturally habituated behaviors as they are passed down as well as the biological (what we might now call genetic) familial influence on emotions and behaviors. While Dawson's study uses *Ethan Frome* to explore this notion, tracing these familial habits and tendencies, I argue, is another way of conceiving of the role of emotions or affect in the novel of manners.

As a novel of manners, *The Age of Innocence* grapples throughout with the customs and codes passed from one generation to the next. And while it can be easy to assume these customs and codes are merely "taught" from parent to child, Wharton's texts certainly suggest a greater familial or biological shape to the way characters feel or express emotion. As Newland laments when considering May: "he had long given up trying to disengage her real self from the shape into which tradition and training had moulded her" (196). Her past, and the past that led to her past, create a type of emotional ancestry that characters are "moulded" by, one that they can never be separated from. Learning a behavior can easily be separated from the individual. But expressed emotions, ones that are deeply connected to an inner feeling, carry far more of a genetic or biological element. One person may be said to "take after" their father if they cry at sentiment or their mother if they always blush when made the center of attention. Part of what Wharton's novel of manners interrogates is how much an individual is permanently "moulded" by their past, by their heredity as well as their social conditioning.

Interestingly, this notion of heredity is part of what repels Newland from May and toward Ellen. It is May's heredity of manners that Newland actually fears about May. Newland spends much of the novel anxious about the fact that May is nothing more than a replica of her mother, Mrs. Welland, and that she will remain "in look and tone, the simple girl of yesterday" (115). Newland considers May's "look" as "primitive and pure" (115). She is a part of the past, a relic of some previous generations. Newland "asks himself if May's face was doomed to thicken into the same middle-aged image of invincible innocence" of Mrs. Welland because "he did not want May to have that kind of innocence, the innocence that seals the mind against imagination and the heart against experience!" (119). Newland is terrified that May is "simply ripening into a copy of her mother, and mysteriously, by the very process, trying to turn him into a Mr. Welland" (177). It is this concept of "niceness," which Newland views as a contagious emptiness, that Newland fears May has inherited from her mother (129).

Ellen's status as "outsider" makes her alluring to Newland because she may be able to deviate from what he sees as the hereditary certainty of a general lack of feeling, an absence of emotion, a "niceness." It is Ellen's unique position as an outsider that allows Newland to see her behavior as severed from the old New York genealogy, not reliant on a heredity of manners. As a child, Ellen wears "crimson merino and amber beads, like a gipsy foundling" and otherwise "gaudy clothes" (38). To be a "gypsy" is to be without a grounding in familial place, and to be a "foundling" is to be without a defined heredity. From her earliest presence in old New York society, Ellen never achieves acceptance, a status highlighted by her lack of propriety. Ellen—shockingly—"was allowed to wear black satin at her coming-out ball" (26), a choice Mrs. Welland calls "almost prophetic" (118). She is "allowed" to transgress the ritual of purity by Medora Mason who, by virtue of her own status as outsider, does not pass down the heredity of manners.[29]

Ellen is surprised to learn that New York, with its "big honest labels on everything," is actually a part of the "old pattern" she thinks she's escaped. For Newland, Ellen's "mysterious faculty of suggesting tragic and moving possibilities outside the daily run of experience" was "a part of her, either a projection of her mysterious and outlandish background or of something inherently dramatic, passionate and unusual in herself" (73). Her experience, her lack of virgin innocence, created in her an "odd absence of surprise" that excites Newland. It is in Newland's sense of Ellen "having been plucked out of a very maelstrom" that he sees her as inhabiting a space outside of his old New York. As a result, "the things she took for granted gave the measure of those she had rebelled against" (73). As a "part of her," Ellen's refusal (or inability) to be the "nice" woman is not affectation, according to Newland's system. Instead, she is inherently antithetical to the old New York women. Thus, for Newland, he and Ellen do not have the hereditary or genetic feelings that the Mingotts and others in their old New York circle share. Newland is trying to rewrite his own affective past into an outside so that he can be like Ellen and not like May.

The last scene of the novel to precede the twenty-six-year gap in time coincides with a moment of clarity for Newland about how May actually feels. After May has effectively driven Ellen back to Europe, Newland sees triumph in May's eyes. His own emotions cannot be affected as he begins to tell May he wants to leave her. Newland fails "to speak with the indifference of a man who longs for a change, and is yet too weary to welcome it" (205). May's voice becomes "unsteady" as she decides to tell him that she is pregnant. May's "color" burns "deeper" when Newland suggests she told Ellen she was pregnant before she actually knew she was, but she continues to hold his gaze. In this scene, May and Newland fail to "try it on" with each other successfully. They both realize how the other really feels because their bodily reactions convey their inner feelings without the successful use of an affected performance of emotion. And it is in this moment that Newland commits himself to remain with May, for the bulk of their lives, which readers never see but understand has happened within the gap of time the novel does not cover. Contemporary reviews of the novel certainly suggest a reading of May and Ellen precisely as Newland reads (or misreads) them. Carl Van Doren argues that Newland and Ellen make a tragic sacrifice because May is "incapable of understanding that there is anywhere anything larger or freer" and that she is "unimaginative" to her own and to others' detriment, and Vernon L. Parrington, Jr. calls May "physically magnificent but mentally equipped with no more than the clan negations."[30] While readers tend to be savvier than Newland is at reading May accurately, in particular, it is interesting to note Wharton's subtlety of affect, her ability to reveal through concealing.

Fractured emotion

The final scenes of the novel refocus on Newland's perception of Ellen's feelings rather than on Ellen's actual emotions. Newland's imagination of Ellen is his "more real" encounter with her at the end of the novel. In the final famous scene of the novel, instead of going up to her rooms with Dallas and seeing Ellen for the first time in decades, Newland stays outside, looking up at her window. He imagines that "a dark lady, pale and dark ... would look up quickly, half rise, and hold out a long thin hand with three rings on it" (217). Newland's image of how Ellen would behave comes from his past experiences with her, yes, but also from his experiences with what is considered proper ritual for a woman greeting a guest. It is both Ellen's behavior and socially acceptable behavior. What does not come through in this final scene, and perhaps what gives the final scene part of its tragic tone, is that Newland does not express what Ellen's inner emotion upon seeing Dallas might be. Unusual for his character, he does not venture a guess as to what Ellen might feel when she sees someone who looks and behaves much like a young Newland, someone Ellen has never met because May's pregnancy with him caused the final ritualized banishment of Ellen from the old New York set. As Mitchell reads the ending, it is "the not going up" that "allows him to appreciate how much his conception of Ellen, his investing of her with his romantic aspirations, has compelled him to live up to his own best self."[31] Readers are left only with Newland's image of her behavior, and there is no access to Ellen's or to Newland's inner feelings. The novel ends with an emotional ellipsis.

To return to the article I wrote almost ten years ago, part of my search for meaning in Wharton's use of "trying it on" had to do with my genuine appreciation of the novel as conveying multiple levels of irony, of conveying meaning through opposition to linguistic content. This tendency is what lends the work to close reading, to analyses that attempt to show how the thematic and the formal work in a semiotic relationship. What intrigues me even more today is the way Wharton's novel represents characters who are "trying on" various affected emotions but still revealing inner feelings. Thus, both readings are interested in what is on and beneath the surface at once and in Wharton's unique ability to disrupt the clear separation between the two spaces.

It seems fitting that this novel—written just after World War I but set in the 1870s—should present fractures and fissions in the surface that separates the expressed from the underlying, the interior from the exterior, the individual subject from a singular humanity. It is neither clear nor easy to craft a unifying sentiment or emotion in texts written in a post-Great War world, as Wharton's novel suggests. Unlike the sentimental novel's attempt to keep a unified, intact national emotion through sympathy, Wharton's novel expresses the modern dissonance between feelings, emotions, and behaviors, thus breaking any unified notion of affect.

Innocence and Scandal in Edith Wharton's Old New York

Hildegard Hoeller
CUNY

"I'm not at all nervous about the success of my book—my publisher tells me I have no need to be—but I am afraid of its being a succès de scandale."[1]

As for the Columbia Prize, the kind Appletons have smothered me in newspaper commentary; & when I discovered that I was being rewarded— by one of our leading Universities—for uplifting American morals, I confess I did despair.

Subsequently, when I found the prize shd [*sic*] really have been yours, but was withdrawn because your book (I quote from memory) had "offended a number of prominent persons in the Middle West," disgust was added to despair. (Letter to Sinclair Lewis, August 6, 1921)[2]

Un-scandalous again!

When, as a 14-year-old girl, Edith Wharton finished her first novella, *Fast and Loose*, she attached mock reviews that dismissed the text as school-girl-like sentimentality. Belying its racy title, the novella had turned out to be anything but scandalous. "Apparently," one such fictional reviewer lamented, "the author's well-meant intention was that everybody & everything should be fast & loose"; however, the "hero evaporates into a vacillating sentimentalist," and the "heroine, who we are informed is the fastest woman in London, does nothing that would have raised a blush on the rigid countenance of an elderly Quakeress."[3] Years later, Wharton reimagined the publication of that novelette in her short story "Expiation" (1904) in very similar terms. Her author, Mrs. Fetherel, who has just published her novel *Fast and Loose*, is humiliated by having her "scandalous" book not be the "succès de scandale" she had feared (and hoped) it would be, instead being praised by a reviewer as "sweetly inoffensive" with a "pure fresh view of life" and an "altogether unfashionable regard for the reader's moral susceptibilities."[4] As if in a self-fulfilling prophesy, Wharton's experience of receiving the Pulitzer Prize for "uplifting American morals" mirrored what she had imagined twice with *Fast and Loose*.

At what could be seen as the moment of her greatest triumph, the celebration of her work came with the very same "criticism" she had launched at herself as a child penning her first fiction and then later as a published writer in "Expiation." Wharton's fiction, now in a real rather than imagined moment, was praised for its morality within the context of the "welter of cant & sentimentality" she abhorred.[5] Like *Fast and Loose*, *The Age of Innocence* betrayed its promise of a scandalous plot and was praised and rewarded for its much detested "moral uplift." Perhaps, for this reason, Wharton responded to being given the coveted prize for "uplifting American morals" with "despair" and "disgust."

Immediately following *The Age of Innocence*, Wharton returned to the subject of old New York and wrote four novellas that would be published together in book form under the title *Old New York* (1924)—the very title she had originally planned for *The Age of Innocence*. These novellas, revisiting the world of *The Age of Innocence*, are significantly more scandalous than the novel. Indeed, they foreground scandal and reveal the side of *The Age of Innocence* that Wharton had envisioned in her early conceptions of the novel but from which she had pulled back in the novel's final execution. These novellas, particularly "The Old Maid" and "New Year's Day," revisit the world of the novel deliberately to focus on scandals, revealing Wharton's own reflections on her earlier novel's innocence and giving us a lens through which to reread *The Age of Innocence*.

Throughout her career, Wharton thought about the relation between scandal and art; the idea of a *succès de scandale*, mocked in her early writing, would remain important to Wharton's ambition as a writer. In her 1934 autobiography, *A Backward Glance*—a book that leaves out her affair with Fullerton and can, on first sight, be read as evasive and safe—she emphasizes the importance of scandal for her career as a writer. Beginning with a quote from Goethe's *Venezianische Epigramme* (1796), Wharton links her old New York to Goethe's own high-bourgeois German environment and reflects on the limited possibilities for creativity within such "good" society: "Gute Gesellschaft hab ich gesehen; man nennt sie gute Wenn sie zum kleinsten Gedicht nicht die Gelegenheit giebt."[6] She elaborates that scandal is at the heart of her work as an artist when she recounts her mother's mention of their cousin George Alfred whose scandalous life had made him "vanish," "that is," she explains, "out of society, out of respectability, out of the safe daylight world of 'nice people' and reputable doings."[7] In George Alfred's doings with "some woman," Wharton saw her

> earliest glimpse of the poetry that Goethe missed in the respectable world of the Hirschgraben, and that my ancestors assuredly failed to find, or to create, between Battery and Union Square. The vision of poor featureless unknown Alfred and his siren, lurking in some cranny of my imagination, hinted at regions perilous, dark, and yet lit with mysterious fires, just outside the world of copy-book axioms, and the old obediences that were in my blood; and the hint was useful—for a novelist.[8]

Wharton's language highlights how difficult and "useful" it was to her as an artist to seek out these scandalous regions in order to move beyond the world of "copy-book axioms" and obediences; only through scandal could she tap into a realm of passion and mystery that was both essential to her art and antithetical to her upbringing and "blood."

In an astounding move, Wharton further emphasizes the importance of scandalous writing for her life as an artist, when she links her earliest memory of actually reading a book to a scandalous text:

> One day I was found sitting under a table, absorbed in a volume which I did not appear to be using for improvisation. My immobility attracted attention, and when asked what I was doing, I replied: "Reading." This was received with incredulity; but on being called upon to read a few lines aloud I appear to have responded to the challenge, and it was then discovered that the work over which I was poring was a play by Ludovic Halévy, called "Fanny Lear," which was having a succès de scandale in Paris owing to the fact that the heroine was what ladies of my mother's day called "one of those women."

> Thereafter the books I used for "making up" were carefully inspected before being intrusted to me ... now that I could read I divided my time between my own improvisations and the printed inventions of others.[9]

Looking at the non-dated holograph manuscript of *A Backward Glance* reveals that Wharton made several, significant alterations to the passage: she inserted the name of the play, "Fanny Lear," in the manuscript and she later added the phrase *succès de scandale* for the published version.[10] The insertion of "Fanny Lear" did not only specify the play and the idea of a courtesan as a heroine of a text; it also referenced the notorious American demi-monde figure Hattie Blackford who had adopted the name Fanny Lear and become legendary for her affair with the Grand Duke Nicholas Constantinovich, nephew of Tsar Alexander II of Russia.[11] Wharton located the beginnings of her reading and writing in the context of the less than respectable woman figure and the public's fascination with such figures and literary *succès de scandale*. From her juvenile writings to her final autobiographical account of her life's work, scandal remained at the heart of her art; and yet, as if repeating the imagined fate of her juvenile *Fast and Loose*, so many years later, her most prestigious novel, while conceived around a scandal, ended up being rewarded for its "innocence."

The possibility of scandal in *The Age of Innocence*

Such innocence had not been part of the original plan, or title. On the contrary, Wharton's initial conception of the novel, which she submitted to Appleton for the contract, was much more scandalous than the published novel. Appleton's American advertisement for *The Age of Innocence* in *Publisher's Weekly* highlighted the theme of scandal. "Was She Justified in Seeking a Divorce?" Appleton's advertisement teased:

> Why was this American girl forced to leave her brutal Polish husband? Why did Ellen, Countess Olenska, return to New York, seeking to forget? Whispers came all too soon that she had been compromised in the artistic continental society from which she had fled. But in the narrow New York society of the 1870's [*sic*] she was welcomed back, and the whispery of far

off Europe ignored, until she and Newland Archer are swept together by mutual attraction, and the old, old question is renewed, shall she create a *scandal* just because she is unhappy? (emphasis mine)[12]

The publisher clearly enticed American readers to think of *The Age of Innocence* in light of its potentially scandalous nature. The wording of the advertisement—"brutal Polish husband," "swept together," "scandal"— suggests the plots of racy novels. For Wharton, the final question the advertisement raised was at the forefront of her own thinking about the novel: how scandalous should it be?

The three outlines of the novel that Wharton drafted and left in her papers each provide a different answer to that question, but each answer contains a more scandalous plot than the final published novel, whose title she ultimately changed from "Old New York" to *The Age of Innocence*.[13] Noting that Wharton "preserved the outlines for posterity in her papers, carefully labeling and dating them," Jennifer Rae Greeson argues: "it appears that Wharton herself intended that her outlines be studied by future scholars and readers interested in her creative process as she composed *The Age of Innocence*"; it also, Greeson adds, "suggests [Wharton's] own interest in the documentation of how her narrative developed."[14] Wharton left clear traces that she particularly tampered with the "scandalous" part of the novel, envisioning different scenarios about how far Archer and Ellen would be "swept" together and how "scandalous" their "mutual attraction" would become. In light of her secret self-critique in both *Fast and Loose* and "Expiation," and her later reflection on the centrality of scandal for her art in her autobiography, these synopses give us a glimpse into Wharton's struggle with the extent to which she wanted her writing about old New York—the "Gute Gesellschaft" of her childhood—to become more sexually explicit and morally troubling, how much it should delve into those "dark, perilous regions" that are "lit with mysterious fires."

In her "first plan," Ellen's own experience and sexual explicitness doom the two lovers. Wharton notes that Ellen had not only been in a bad marriage "but it was also said that she had been 'fast' & 'talked about.'" Archer falls in love with Ellen, breaks his engagement with May, and gets engaged to Ellen; "Archer, his struggle over, is sublimely, supremely happy. He urges Ellen to marry him at once. She shocks him deeply by proposing that they should first 'go off for a few weeks' so that he can be sure he is not making a mistake."[15] Ellen relents and marries Archer, but she soon realizes how dull a life with Archer would be; she returns to Europe and Archer consents to a separation. Archer ultimately immerses himself in business, and "he returns to live with his mother & sisters. May Welland marries someone else, & nothing ever happens to him again."[16] In this version, Ellen's "fastness" is incompatible with Archer's dullness. As in most of Wharton's fiction, marriage itself becomes a dull, unsatisfying, even deadly trap, and the lovers part ways.[17]

In the second outline, Wharton imagines a secret adulterous affair between Ellen and Archer, and she specifically mentions a comparison of the sexual intimacy between Archer and May to that between Archer and Ellen. Archer falls in love with Ellen (now called Clementine) but marries May. When he comes back from his honeymoon, he sees Clementine frequently, May has a baby, and "at last he & Clementine fly together (contrast between bridal night with May & *this* one)." They stay together for a while, managing to go South:

> Arrange somehow that all this is done *very secretly*. No one knows they are together. Both get tired—she of the idea of living in America, he of the idea of a scandal & a dislocation in his life ... They return to N.Y. separately, & the last scene is a dinner which the happy May (who has had a boy) insists on giving to her cousin Mme Olenska before the latter sails.[18]

Greeson rightly points out that these differences from the published version were fundamental, particularly because they redirected the focus of the novel; "including a consummated affair between the two characters would have required that Wharton focus more explicitly on sex," and it would also have highlighted the incompatibility of the two lovers, who were separating on their own accord, not because of the pressures old New York put on them.[19] Such a novel would have left the reader with more sexual descriptions and significantly less "moral uplift."

In the final outline Wharton once again imagines a sexual affair between Clementine and Langdon Archer, this time facing the impossibility of divorce as the final hindrance for the two lovers. Clementine returns to New York, and she "& Langdon Archer meet & fall madly in love with each other." Archer does not dare break his engagement with May and marries her. After he returns to a boring life in New York, Clementine "falls into Archer's arms, & they go off secretly & meet in Florida, where they spend a few mad weeks. (But Mme. Olenska cannot divorce as she & her husband are Roman Catholics)." Archer cannot live "as an outcast with another man's wife," and Clementine grows tired of the affair. Clementine returns to Europe and "May (who is going to have a baby, & who suspects nothing) insists on giving her cousin a farewell dinner, at which all of old New York is present."[20] In this version, too, Wharton would have dealt with sexual intimacy; furthermore, she imagined tackling the issue of divorce—which the Appleton advertisement highlighted—as well as the lack of attraction a man like Archer—and America itself—would hold for the Ellen figure.

In the end, Wharton backed away from these more scandalous trajectories, leaving her readers' sense of old New York and marriage somewhat intact and shying away from any more explicitly sexual themes. Wharton had buried the scandalous versions of the novel in Newland Archer's limited point of view and range of actions. Alan Price theorizes that:

> [S]urely one reason for the shift of focus from the Countess to Archer was that although Mrs. Wharton was sympathetic to Ellen, she could not be confident that her readers would share her sympathy for a woman who broke up the engagement of a nice girl, suggested a trial marriage, and then abandoned her husband because she thought New York's seasonal social life was dull. Also, Ellen's situation came dangerously close to that of Edith Wharton herself: she had divorced her husband seven years earlier, had long since chosen to live "a real life" in Paris rather than return to her own family in New York or Teddy Wharton's in Boston, and had been quite explicit about her distaste for a settled New York existence. Ellen as a heroine ran the risk of being seen as a woman who could not get along with a bad European husband and now cannot get along with a good American one. The novel with Ellen as a liberated heroine would have been an exciting, perhaps even more interesting one, but Mrs. Wharton recognized the practical artistic problem of making her heroine acceptable to her readers.[21]

Wharton's motives for her changes in the novel are a matter for speculation. She apparently left no definite explanation for the final changes. Her correspondence with Rutger Jewett, as well as Appleton's American advertisement of the novel, suggest that Appleton believed that readers would be interested in a more scandalous version of the text and had accepted the novel—also for serialization—based on the synopses given. Yet Wharton and Jewett do not discuss the alterations in their correspondence, and we are left without definitive answers. Joseph Candido, in his careful study of Wharton's final emendations to the galleys, finds that Wharton consistently reins the novel in; revisions, he concludes, "[suggest] that she is trying to draw Ellen in a more restrained fashion."[22] Overall, he reveals a "general tendency ... to blur deliberately the bold outlines of personality, to depict in less detail the external actions and features of a character to draw him more subtly."[23] Wharton, he argues, aims to make her characters visible yet ambiguous, shying—even on the sentence level—away from the more explicit treatment of Ellen and Archer's relationship.

In the end, while we do not know exactly why Wharton abandoned the more scandalous synopses of her novel, it is impossible to imagine that Wharton would have been awarded the Pulitzer Prize for "uplifting American morals" had she followed any of these outlines. Perhaps her "disgust" and "despair" at receiving the Pulitzer Prize for being "morally uplifting" were connected to her earlier biting critiques of herself in *Fast and Loose* and "Expiation." The innocence of *The Age of Innocence* rendered it anything but a *succès de scandale*.

Prequel, sequel: Old New York and its scandals

Right after the publication of *The Age of Innocence*, Wharton returned to the subject of *Old New York*, first in her novella "The Old Maid"—where she once again focuses on the love triangle involving two cousins—and then in "New Year's Day" where she offers us a different look at the 1870s in old New York society than she had offered in *The Age of Innocence*. Both novellas, combined with two additional novellas, would ultimately comprise a volume bearing the title she had initially envisioned for *The Age of Innocence*: *Old New York*. Breaking up the historical omniscience of the narrator in *The Age of Innocence*, Wharton now offered "four point of views on four decades": "False Dawn" for the forties, "The Old Maid" for the fifties, "The Spark" for the sixties, and "New Year's Day" for the seventies. The old New York emerging from these novellas is clearly the same world Wharton had described in *The Age of Innocence*, but it is also far less innocent, bearing more resemblance to the world of the outlines than the published version of the novel. Sequels in terms of composition and prequels in terms of narrated time, these novellas depict worlds full of scandals, offering revisions to the novel's more innocent depiction of old New York.

While the change in form might have obscured the close link between the texts, it can also be read as a direct response to her earlier novel and the criticism of it in terms of its historicity. Annoyed at the readers' complaints about the historical accuracy of the novel, she explained in a letter to Rutger Jewett:

> What I was trying to do, and what I believe every novelist who write [*sic*] an "historic" novel should do, was to evoke the intellectual, moral, and artistic atmosphere not of one year but of ten years: that is to say my allusions range from, say, 1875 to 1885. Any narrower field of evocation must necessarily reduce the novel to a piece of archeological pedantry instead of a living image of the times.[24]

Wharton's old New York novellas exemplify that method to perfection; each novella, devoted to a different decade, "[evokes] the intellectual, moral, and artistic atmosphere not of one year but of ten"; together, they offer four vignettes rather than a sustained, linear narrative that might suggest the kind of "archeological pedantry" Wharton wanted to avoid. The method of evocation rather than chronicling is made even more explicit since each novella is also told from a different point of view; Wharton thus eliminates the possibility of one authoritative narration that should and could be examined for historical accuracy.

Critics have generally agreed that no sequel to *The Age of Innocence* exists. Lee reports that Wharton intended a sequel, now told from the perspective of Fanny Archer, about Fanny's marriage to Dallas, "called 'Homo Sapiens' or 'The Age of Wisdom,' in which she would show 'the omniscient youth of the present date who has settled in advance all social, religious, and moral problems, and yet comes to grief over the same old difficulties.'"[25] Lee also notes that Wharton was asked to write a sequel to *The Age of Innocence* but declined: "In November [1921] she had the idea for a group of 'Old New York' stories, including 'The Old Maid.' And she was planning a sequel to *The Age of Innocence*, which she did not write."[26] Neither Lee nor other critics have contemplated that this group of novellas could be a sequel in plain sight.[27] Clearly, in these novellas Wharton expanded on the themes that she had started to contemplate in her composition of *The Age of Innocence*. She also chronologically designed the novellas to be prequels to her novel, giving us glimpses into the preceding decades. In *Old New York*, using multiple points of view and covering many decades, Wharton retells the stories of old New York society in a bolder way: exposing its scandals, allowing desires to be consummated, voices to be heard, and enemies to be confronted. Particularly in "The Old Maid" and "New Year's Day," Wharton revisits the questions of adultery, passion, love, and sexual desire she had contemplated in her novel, and more directly in her three outlines for *The Age of Innocence*.[28]

The novella, as a genre, was particularly suited for such a scandalous revision of her earlier novel. Here, too, Goethe's influence is central because, as one of the few theorists of the novella, he defined it as the literary form most directly concerned with scandal. Wharton herself was rereading the works of Goethe before and during the 1920s, and she particularly referenced Johann Peter Eckermann's *Conversations with Goethe*, in which Goethe formulates his famous definition of the novella: "Was ist die Novelle anders als eine sich ereignete unerhoerte Begebenheit? [What else is a novella but an incident that happened and is unheard-of]."[29] "Unerhoert," or literally "unheard-of," means "scandalous" in German; the literal translation, "unheard-of," further emphasizes that the novella focuses on silenced, scandalous incidents of the past. The novella, in other words, goes where the novel does not; it delves into the scandalous places that the larger tapestry of the novel might hide. Wharton employs the novella form in precisely such a way in *Old New York*. She uses the novella form to foreground the very plots she had silenced in her earlier novel.

The opening and closing passages of *The Age of Innocence* hint at these silences as well as Goethe's influence. The novel starts with an operatic performance of *Faust*, and Archer's fantasy about reading *Faust* to May once they are married: "'we'll read Faust together … by the Italian lakes …' he thought, somewhat hazily confusing the scene of his projected honeymoon with the masterpieces of literature which it would be his manly privilege to reveal to his bride." It ends with Dallas Archer's view of his parents' life as one of silence: "You never did ask each other anything, did you? And you never told each other anything. You just sat and watched each other, and guessed what was going on underneath. A deaf-and-dumb asylum, in fact."[30] *Old New York* reverses the silence of *The Age of Innocence* and delves into the "unerhoerte" or unheard-of "perilous regions" of Wharton's old New York. In these novellas, Wharton's characters are finally facing and living scandals in the way she had initially begun to envision in her plot synopses of *The Age of Innocence.*

Embodied scandal: "The Old Maid" and the end of innocence

Whereas *The Age of Innocence* had received the Pulitzer Prize for "uplifting American morals," Rutger Jewett informed Wharton that he had trouble placing "The Old Maid." Lewis notes that "the editor of the *Ladies Home Journal* said of 'The Old Maid': 'it is a bit too vigorous for us.' The spokesman for the *Metropolitan Magazine* declared it to be powerful but too unpleasant." It was rejected "on the grounds of distasteful sexuality."[31] A much more daring piece than the novel, the novella, composed immediately after *The Age of Innocence*, connects clearly to its prequel/sequel. It, too, tells the story of two cousins, Delia and Charlotte Lovell, enmeshed in a triangular plot. Confined by Archer's point of view, we never see Ellen and May truly confront each other; in "The Old Maid," on the other hand, we witness Charlotte and Delia's confrontations. Wharton lets us see that not all things were dealt with in silences in the way she describes it in *The Age of Innocence*. Instead, focusing on the two women and their relationship to each other, Wharton is able to write a more disconcerting and challenging story that leaves little unrevealed.

It seems inconceivable, given the façade of *The Age of Innocence*, that such a confrontation could have taken place. More accurately, though, it is merely Archer's central point of view that hides those confrontations.[32] May, after all, does let Archer know that she has "talked" to Ellen: "I stayed and had a long talk with her. It was ages since we'd had a real talk …";[33] "we've talked things over yesterday—";[34] "you know I told you we'd had a long talk one afternoon—."[35] These talks, hidden in the ellipses and dashes, will become the focus of her "Old Maid" novella. Dispensing with her male characters, Wharton gives the two cousins center stage and has her readers hear their conversations and confrontations.

By focusing on the illegitimate child, Tina, Wharton further makes any return to innocence impossible. Tina takes the place of the male figure in the triangular plot, while Tina's father, Clem Spender, remains off-stage. Both Delia and Charlotte loved Spender, an artistic youth who Delia rejected in order to marry the safer and richer Jim Ralston. Charlotte, in turn, spends a night with Spender and has his child, whom she adores and hides in an orphan asylum. On the verge of being married to Joe Ralston, a cousin of Jim Ralston, Charlotte confesses her motherhood to Delia and that she will not leave her child in the orphanage. Delia arranges that the marriage will not take place, Delia's husband Jim Ralston dies, and, in Part Two, Wharton focuses her novella on the three women: Delia (who has become the adoptive mother), Charlotte (posing as her daughter's maiden aunt), and the daughter Clementina, who ultimately is being integrated into old New York society through Delia's adoption. By giving the daughter a name close to that which Wharton had originally chosen for Ellen (Clementine), Wharton links the two texts. Through Delia and Charlotte Lovell, Wharton revisits the May/Ellen relationship, this time casting Delia Ralston in the role of May and Charlotte, the old maid, in the role of Ellen.

Immediately, Wharton addresses the silences of old New York society. Whereas Archer reveres the silent communication that marks the delicacy of his class, Wharton offers a markedly different view here:

> To "do things handsomely" had always been a fundamental principle in this cautious world, built up on the fortunes of bankers, India-merchants, shipbuilders and ship-chandlers. Those well-fed slow-moving people … lived in a genteel monotony of which the surface was never stirred by the dumb dramas now and then enacted underground. Sensitive souls in those days were like muted key-boards, on which Fate played without a sound.[36]

Wharton demystifies the world of her earlier novel, focusing on the base (the economic underpinnings) rather than the superstructure (the opera) of old New York. While narrative irony allows us to see Archer's misconceptions to some degree, here Wharton leaves no doubt that the enforced silence of this society is far from the "atmosphere of faint implications and pale delicacies" Archer sees.[37] The phrase "muted key-boards" belies the presence of music— the operatic voice we hear at the beginning of the novel—as well as the delicate communication Archer attributes to the silences of the audience. We see instead dysfunction, a machine not allowed to operate on its own terms. We see monotony, sluggish bodies, fat wallets, and crippled, muted, sensitive souls. Amidst this dysfunction, Wharton insists, scandals happen.

May Welland's child—and her premature "confession" of her pregnancy to Ellen—becomes crucial in avoiding the scandal of an adulterous love affair between Archer and Ellen. In "The Old Maid," the illegitimate child, Tina, the physical embodiment of an extramarital affair—something Wharton did not even imagine in the synopses for *The Age of Innocence*—becomes the given of the story that prevents the return to a sense of "innocence" and instead must be reckoned with. While Delia takes care of Charlotte and her child, she also prevents Charlotte's marriage and adopts Tina, usurping Charlotte's place as her mother. Tina, standing in for her father, becomes the object of desire in the text, and both women are fiercely and passionately attached to her. Delia, in possession of money and her married/widowed status, keeps the upper hand. Wharton makes clear that Delia's love for Tina is deeply connected to her love for Clem Spender. After her own children leave, "Delia Ralston sometimes felt that the real events of her life did not begin until both her children had contracted—so safely and suitably—their irreproachable New York alliances."[38] This sense of "real life" as connected to a relationship outside of marriage, a love relationship like no other, surfaces again and again in Wharton's own writings about her affair with Morton Fullerton and also in Archer's response to Ellen. "You gave me my first glimpse of a real life," he tells Ellen.[39] For both women, Tina stands in for her father, Clem Spender; she embodies a sexual encounter with him, and her future becomes vicariously that of the two mothers/lovers. When Charlotte asks Delia to move into the room next to Tina after Delia's daughter got married and vacated that room, Delia feels bereft.

> In truth Delia had looked forward more than she knew to the quiet talks with Tina to which the little boudoir lent itself. While her own daughter inhabited the room, Mrs. Ralston had been in the habit of spending an hour there every evening, chatting with the two girls while they undressed, and listening to their comments on the incidents of the day. She always knew beforehand exactly what her own girl would say; but Tina's views and opinions were a perpetual delicious shock to her. Not that they were strange or unfamiliar; there were moments when they seemed to well straight up

from the dumb depths of Delia's own past. Only they expressed feelings she had never uttered, ideas she had hardly avowed to herself; Tina sometimes said things which Delia Ralston, in far-off self-communications, had imagined herself saying to Clement Spender. And now there would be an end to these evening talks … A pang went through Delia at the thought that henceforth she would be cut off from the means of keeping her hold on Tina.[40]

Wharton's language links Delia's motherly feelings for Tina to her erotic desires for Clement Spender. The "delicious shock" Tina's utterances give her, and the way in which Tina reconnects Delia to the "dumb depths of her past," suggest an erotic dimension to her relationship with her adoptive daughter, as the latter becomes the stand-in for the lover and for the Delia who loved and desired him. Then, later, on the evening before Tina's wedding, the two cousins look ahead to a long life together without the love of their lives. "On the following evening the house would be empty: till death came, she and Charlotte would sit together beside the evening lamp."[41] It would become a "marriage" without a "lover"—a marriage like Archer's to May Welland.

While the complexities of May's feelings for Ellen are hidden, Wharton lets us see them in Delia's character. May keeps reiterating how "dear" Ellen is to her, and yet Archer wonders whether May does not hate her cousin.[42] In Delia, Wharton depicts a mix of these emotions all the way to the end. They all come to the forefront when, on the final evening before Tina's departure, the two women must decide who will take the role of the mother and have that last "talk" with Tina. While in *The Age of Innocence* we are never privy to those "real talks" May had with Ellen, in "The Old Maid" Wharton fills in these gaps, showing that—even in the fifties—confrontations did take place. When Charlotte suggests telling Tina that she is her mother, Delia is horrified. Charlotte responds:

"If I did, should you hate me as much as all that?"

"Hate it? What a word between us!"

"Between us? But it's the word that's been between us since the beginning—the very beginning! Since the day when you discovered that Clement Spender hadn't quite broken his heart because he wasn't good enough for you; since you found your revenge and your triumph in keeping me at your mercy, and in taking his child from me!" Charlotte's words flamed up as if from the depth of the internal fires; then the blaze dropped, her head sank forward, and she stood before Delia dumb and stricken.[43]

Wharton shows us all the fire and fury that lie behind the muted world of old New York; in her old maid figure, Wharton brings out the language of passion, love, hate, and rage that can no longer be silenced. And while Delia at first fights back ("You wicked woman—you are wicked")[44] she later begins to see the truthfulness of Charlotte's attack: "As the truth stole upon Delia, her heart melted with the old compassion for Charlotte. She saw that it was a terrible, a sacrilegious thing to interfere with another's destiny."[45] In this confrontation, Wharton lets us in on the hidden desires of Delia's life, and also the helpless way in which both women are tied to each other. Charlotte understands that she cannot reveal her motherhood to Tina now and therefore lets Delia take the mother's role for the last task with Tina, and Delia feels for Charlotte's pain and realizes that, sitting with Tina, "[she] must not, for her own pleasure, prolong that tragic vigil."[46] Wharton's eroticization of illegitimate motherhood offers us a scandalous response to the ordering role that May's pregnancy provides in *The Age of Innocence*. Both "mothers" in "The Old Maid" find outlets for their thwarted desires in Tina, and we witness the full force of their struggle to remain connected to some form of "real life"—a life of passion. That, Wharton says, is the "internal fire" that smolders under the surface of old New York society.

"The Old Maid" ends in public silence, as Tina will be passed into New York society, her illegitimate origins covered up by her adoption; however, Wharton lifts the veil of that silence. We must now encounter the seventies through the lens of these fifties—as if they had begotten the Clementine that would become Ellen Olenska. Indeed, Sillerton Jackson, after coming back from a trip to Paris, insinuates that there might be some resemblance between Tina and Ellen: whereas "he complimented [Delia Ralston] on the rosy beauty of her own Delia … after dinner he confided to the older ladies that there was something 'very French' in the girl's way of doing her hair, and that in the capital of all the Elegances she would have been pronounced extremely stylish."[47]

Back in the seventies: Scandal in plain sight and the problems of innocence in "New Year's Day"

Wharton's novella devoted to the seventies, entitled "New Year's Day," invites us most directly to revisit *The Age of Innocence* and to face the idea of the scandal. Paralleling many scenes in the two texts, Wharton makes possible a comparative reading that reveals her specific revisions of her earlier vision. The novella's heroine, Mrs. Hazeldean, can be read against Ellen Olenska in startling ways: she is self-determined, outspoken, and—like the Clementine of the outlines—sexually experienced. Replacing the perspective of Archer with that of the next generation—just as she had intended for the sequel to the novel—Wharton reveals the silences of her earlier novel and creates a female character that is neither Ellen nor May. Sexually knowledgeable, confident, loving, and strong, Mrs. Hazeldean gives us a new view of the old New York of the seventies and troubles the opposition between scandal and innocence.

Wharton opens the novella with a revision of the opera scene in *The Age of Innocence* by replacing the opera Faust with the spectacle of the burning Fifth Avenue Hotel. In *The Age of Innocence*, we are told that Archer has delayed his entrance into the opera and arrives just as "Madame Nilsson's 'M'ama!' thrilled out above the silent house." Archer's gaze turns toward May Welland's response to the love scene:

> A warm pink mounted to the girl's cheek, mantled her brow to the roots of her fair braids, and suffused the young slope of her breast to the line where it met a modest tulle tucker fastened with a single gardenia. She dropped her eyes to the immense bouquet of lilies-of-the-valley on her knee, and Newland Archer saw her white-gloved finger tips touch the flowers softly. He drew a breath of satisfied vanity and his eyes returned to the stage.[48]

The irony of the scene is marvelous, as the aria about love "thrilled the silent house" filled with muted old New Yorkers. Archer's gaze on May is a turn toward silence and safety, away from the world of passionate love declarations and betrayals that the opera depicts and that—perhaps– drew him to come to the opera at that precise moment of heightened emotion. He watches in delight as the "scandalous" opera reddens May's skin just enough to reveal her innocence and whiteness. Later in that scene, against the backdrop of crude gossip about the scandal surrounding Ellen's marriage and her escape ("she left him," "he's an awful brute," "she bolted with his secretary"),[49] Archer imagines the beauty of his silent communication with May: "The persons of their world lived in an atmosphere of faint implications and pale delicacies, and the fact that he and she understood each other without a word seemed to the young man to bring them nearer than any explanation would have done."[50] In this opening scene, Wharton juxtaposes the operatic language of scandal and the crude, gossipy language of domestic violence and adultery with the "language" of silence that Archer prefers and sees as the hallmark of his old New York society. He comes to the opera to see scandalous ruin on stage while enjoying the innocence and purity of May in contrast, tracing only the vague imprints of the opera on May's white skin.

In "New Year's Day," Wharton has us revisit this scene, as we now see spectators again gazing at a "scandalous" woman—this time through the exposure of the Fifth Avenue Hotel fire. It tells the story of Lizzie Hazeldean, whose adulterous affair with Henry Prest becomes public when they both are seen fleeing the burning hotel. Later, as the young narrator puts together the story, we learn that Mrs. Hazeldean prostituted herself to Prest under the guise of an affair in order to finance the health care of her sick and dying husband. The novella begins with a blunt sentence: "She was *bad* ... always" and "*They used to meet at the Fifth Avenue Hotel.*"[51] Wharton's italicization mirrors the operatic M'ama of the earlier novel, while Mrs. Hazeldean in this analogy replaces Madame Nilsson as Marguerite. Archer himself is replaced with the young narrator who looks at Mrs. Hazeldean and the gazing crowd. This replacement gets at the core of the revision that "New Year's Day" offers to *The Age of Innocence*. Mrs. Hazeldean replaces Marguerite—as well as Ellen Olenska and May Welland—and, through her figure, Wharton explodes the values that Archer puts on each woman. Whereas the opera and the commentary on Mrs. Hazeldean offer discourses on the fallen woman and female virtue, Mrs. Hazeldean, seen through the eyes and words of the admiring young narrator, defies these traditional categorizations. The novella moves from a clear moral judgment ("she was bad") to a conclusion that blurs the line between innocence and scandal.

By using the accident of the Fifth Avenue Hotel fire, Wharton has her *Old New York* characters witness a transgression they had long suspected and kept below the surface. Moving from internal to external fires, she literally burns the roof off of old New York, exposing the hidden scandals behind the walls of the notorious hotel—as well as hidden in plain sight in the backgrounds of her earlier great New York novels, *The House of Mirth* and *The Age of Innocence*. In "A Theory of Scandal," Ari Arut defines scandal as "the disruptive publicity of transgression."[52] As he shows in the case of Oscar Wilde, private deviant behavior can long be tolerated as a private action but becomes a scandal when publicized. "Ruthless repression of publicly enacted deviance," he writes, "can go hand in hand with an extensive lenience of the same transgression in silence."[53] "A publicized transgression can hence transmute into the litmus test of the vigor of the violated norm—a discomfiting and even dangerous ordeal for the authorities."[54] Even as a child, the narrator recognizes exactly that: "The group in our window continued to keep an embarrassed silence. They looked almost frightened; but what struck me even more deeply was that not one of them looked surprised. Even to my boyish sense it was clear that what they had just seen was only the confirmation of something they had long been prepared for."[55]

In *The Age of Innocence*, scandals or transgressions are kept in the background, silenced by a common agreement not to publicize or condemn in the very moral language that opens "New Year's Day": "She was bad." In her novella, Wharton explores the idea of transgression through the mode of scandal—confronting her readers with a more scandalous view of the old New York of her youth and revising the gender dynamics and societal norms upheld by Archer's point of view in *The Age of Innocence*. For example, in "New Year's Day," Wharton also revisits the language of flowers she employed in *The Age of Innocence*. This time, it is Mrs. Hazeldean, not Archer, who goes to the florist:

> She paused before the florist's window, and looked appreciatively at the jars of roses and forced lilac, the compact bunches of lilies-of-the-valley and violets, the first pots of close-budded azaleas. Finally she opened the shop-door, examining the Jacqueminots and Marshal Niels, selected with care two perfect specimens of the silvery-pink rose, waited for the florist to wrap them in cotton-wool, and slipped their long stems into her muff for more complete protection.[56]

The scene is reminiscent of Archer's visit to the florist when he orders, as usual, the lilies for May and then, in an after-thought, a "cluster of yellow roses" for

Ellen Olenska.[57] When Lizzie Hazeldean returns home, she finds a florist's box with roses on her dressing table. And after burning the envelope with a card, she "pushed the flowers aside,"[58] mirroring Ellen's refusal of Beaufort's bouquet in *The Age of Innocence.* [59] Later, when Mrs. Hazeldean enters her husband's library, she "drew the roses from her muff, tenderly unswathed them, and put them in a slim glass on her husband's writing-table."[60] The arrangement reminds us of the "two Jacqueminot roses (of which no one ever bought less than a dozen)" which "had been placed in [a] slender vase" in Madame Olenska's apartment when Archer first visits her.[61] Employing the language of flowers, Wharton revises the floral exchanges to give Mrs. Hazeldean more agency. By giving, receiving, and rejecting flowers, the latter asserts a role that mixes up the roles of Archer, Ellen, and May. Just as Ellen does, Mrs. Hazeldean rejects the flowers of an unwelcome lover or suitor, but she also gives flowers to the one she loves, foreshadowing that her adultery is also a form of loyalty, her prostitution a form of innocence.

Nowhere could the differences and revisions be more apparent than in the pivotal moment of confrontation between Ellen and Archer, and Mrs. Hazeldean and Henry Prest. When Ellen and Archer discuss how they might come together, in their most open exchange of the novel, Ellen asks Archer:

> "Is it your idea then, that I should live with you as your mistress—since I can't be your wife? ..."
> The crudeness of the question startled him: the word was one that women of his class fought shy of, even when their talk flitted closest about the topic. He noticed that Madame Olenska pronounced it as if it had a recognized place in her vocabulary, and he wondered if it had been used familiarly in her presence in the horrible life she had fled from.[62]

While Wharton's outlines had imagined variations on the question of marriage or an affair, in the end Wharton settles for this confrontation to show that Archer is not capable of "real talk," and that his idea of femininity is deeply connected to silence. Archer reduces the question to an issue of "vocabulary" and considers Ellen's language to be a result of her "horrible" life abroad. He later realizes that, to everyone else, she indeed had been his mistress: "And then it came over him, in a vast flash made up of broken gleams, that to all of them they were lovers, lovers in the extreme sense peculiar to 'foreign' vocabularies."[63] To Archer, such a notion of a "foreign language" is the nature of his innocence and his idea of female virtue.

In "New Year's Day," Wharton repeats this scene, but with an even more "vigorous" transgression of female reserve. Mrs. Hazeldean confronts her lover, Prest, when he comes to see her after her husband's death and wants to ask her to marry him:

> "Well, then, you thought I loved you, I suppose—"
>
> He smiled again, revived his moustache with a slight twist, and gave a hardly perceptible shrug. "You … ah … managed to produce the illusion …"
>
> "Oh, well, yes: a woman *can*—so easily! That's what men often forget. You thought I was a lovelorn mistress; and I was only an expensive prostitute."
>
> "Elizabeth!" he gasped, pale now to the ruddy eyelids. She saw that the word had wounded more than his pride, and that, before realizing the insult to his love, he was shuddering at the offence of taste. No one reproved coarseness of language in women more than Henry Prest; one of Mrs. Hazeldean's greatest charms (as he had just told her) had been her way of remaining, "through it all," so ineffably "the lady."[64]

Mrs. Hazeldean's language goes even further than Ellen's; Wharton shows us the range of female language, emotions, and sexuality. Prest, a despicable character, nonetheless shares Archer's distaste for "language in women" that gets to the realities of female experience. Wharton, topping the earlier scene from *The Age of Innocence*, shows that women can and must speak about their lives in ways that men will find distasteful. Mrs. Hazeldean's response to Prest is also a response to the spectators in the beginning who pronounced her "bad." Her "prostitution," it turns out, is a form of sacrifice since she "prostitutes" herself in order to keep her beloved husband alive and comfortable. It is, in that sense, a form of innocence, but not the kind of "morally uplifting" innocence that would fill Wharton with "disgust" and "despair." Mrs. Hazeldean's control over her life, body, emotions, and finances marks her as a grown-up woman who cannot afford to adhere to prescribed versions of virtue and innocence, and who feels pride in her ability to face reality. She is not a fallen woman, not a mistress, not an innocent victim of seduction or a crude husband; she is a challenge to the discourse of innocence. In Mrs. Hazeldean, Wharton creates a phenomenal figure that defies the ideas of corruption and purity that still underlie *The Age of Innocence* and Faust. Mrs. Hazeldean is no May Welland, no Marguerite or Gretchen, and no Ellen Olenska.

In the end, Wharton returns to the image of the opera box. When the narrator joins Mrs. Hazeldean there, he learns that Mrs. Hazeldean lives on the margins of respectable society, but, "not openly classed with Fanny Ring, our one conspicuous 'professional' ... out of respect for her social origin."[65] No lady joins her in the box, but she is also not entirely isolated. Unlike Ellen, she has not been excommunicated. Instead, labelled by the narrator's friend as a "jolly" woman, she inhabits a place in society that is somewhere in-between inclusion and exclusion. "One always felt at Lizzie Hazeldean's," the narrator notes, "that the next moment one's grandmother and aunts might be announced; and yet so pleasantly certain that they wouldn't be."[66] The narrator, defying notions of innocence, adores Mrs. Hazeldean both as a former lover and a friend.

> For she was really too lovely—too formidably lovely. I was used by now to mere unadjectived loveliness, the kind that youth and spirits hang like rosy veil over commonplace features, an average outline and a pointless merriment. But this was something calculated, accomplished, finished—and just a little worn. It frightened me with my first glimpse of the infinity of beauty and the multiplicity of its pit-falls. What! There were women who need not fear crow's feet, were more beautiful for being pale, could let a silvery hair or two show among the dark, and their eyes brood inwardly while they smiled and chatted? But then no young man was safe for a moment! But then the world I had hitherto known had been only a warm, pink nursery, while this new one was a place of darkness, perils and enchantments ...[67]

This long passage is a love declaration to a woman with sexual knowledge and experience, who defies notions of scandal or innocence. In Mrs. Hazeldean, Wharton draws a model of a scandalous woman that is "too formidably lovely" to be judged by the moralistic language with which the narrative began. In creating Mrs. Hazeldean, and having us see her through the sympathetic and adoring eyes of her young narrator, Wharton rewrites the very idea of innocence.

To scandalize skillfully

"New York Society in my youth was a small affair," writes Wharton to Rutger B. Jewett on February 21, 1923, "and I shall have exhausted it fully by the time my 'Old New York Stories' are done."[68] Even as she would still write memoirs, Wharton's comment to Jewett gives a palpable sense of conclusion and completeness, a sense that she had "exhausted" the subject to its fullest. Certainly, in *Old New York* she had revisited the innocence of *The Age of Innocence*, expanded her scope of voices, and pushed her view beyond the limits of Archer's perspective into the "perilous regions" she later described in *A Backward Glance* as the places where poetry and fiction reside. She had filled in the silences of the earlier text and presented the passions and scandals that made her old New York a more complex and morally disturbing place than her novel had suggested.

In his influential article "Gossip and Scandal," Max Gluckman theorizes the purpose of gossip and scandals via Colson's work on Makah Indians.

> To be a Makah, you must be able to join in the gossip, and to be fully a Makah you must be able to scandalize skillfully. This entails that you know the individual family histories of your fellows; for the knowledgeable can hit at you through your ancestry, and you must be able to retort in kind. You also have got to have some knowledge of the old ways of the Makah tribe.[69]

"To scandalize skillfully" is a wonderful description of the novella form as Goethe saw it and as Wharton employed it in *Old New York* in order to make us resee her "Age of Innocence." By scandalizing such, she also re-asserted her own roots and membership in the old New York society even as she composed her writings in France, her chosen country of residence.

Both in "The Old Maid" and "New Year's Day," Wharton implicates herself biographically. In "The Old Maid," she has Tina and her future husband Lanning Halsey enact her parents' own courtship as she would later describe it in *A Backward Glance*. She casts herself as Tina's child, a product of an old New York less innocent than Archer's.[70] In "New Year's Day," Wharton also inscribes her own past. Lee notes that the Fifth Avenue Hotel was owned by the Stevens family, the family of Harry Stevens with whom Wharton had been rumored to have a romantic entanglement. The Joneses disapproved of the Stevens and their hotel, "whose gaudy goings-on were in the Jones's family's eye, across the street, all through Edith's childhood."[71] Wharton then had seen the gaze she describes in the first scene, and part of her had wanted to be engaged in the forbidden world of the Fifth Avenue Hotel. Gluckman notes in his discussion on scandals that the right to speak of them "is a privilege which is only extended to a person when he or she is accepted as a member of a group or set. It is a hallmark of membership."[72] Perhaps for this reason, Wharton implicates herself in the novellas in unheard-of ways. In *Old New York* she scandalizes her life, her tribe, the "Gute Gesellschaft" of her youth. Here we see old New York without its "innocence." Beyond the "copy-book axioms" and "old obediences," scandal, too, is in the blood of old New York; and scandal is the bloodline of art itself. *Old New York*, finally, is her *succès de scandale*.[73]

The Age of Dissonance

Beth Nguyen

University of Wisconsin, Madison

I had no business reading *The Age of Innocence*. I knew that from the moment I first opened the book, in high school. I had never been to New York and wouldn't for years; I knew nothing about opera or hothouse flowers or what it meant to call on someone; I had no idea why men drank port after dinner and what was port, anyway? Someone like me, a Vietnamese girl, a refugee, the child of refugees living in a conservative, mostly white town in Michigan, had no place in any of the books I kept reading—like Austen's *Pride and Prejudice* and James's *The Wings of the Dove*. Someone like me would never have even crossed these characters' minds. Yet I reached for these faraway worlds because they were faraway, and perhaps because I also lived in the shadows of what my stepmother often said to me: who do you think you are? According to her, I was too big for my britches.

What drew me to *The Age of Innocence* wasn't the wealth porn or the mysterious lives of rich white people, though I was fascinated by the long dinners that involved things like canvasbacks. It wasn't the love triangle of Ellen, Newland, and May, though I lingered over the tensions and learned from them what silence can accomplish in a work of fiction. It was the idea of language, the particular ways in which these folks did and didn't communicate, a system that Wharton describes as "a kind of hieroglyphic world."[1] It was the fact that the manners and etiquette served less as practical functions and more as practical gatekeepers, identifying those who belonged and those who did not.

I was obsessed with the idea of belonging. My family didn't like to talk about being refugees but I understood that it meant you didn't belong anywhere, exactly. Your original home was no longer yours. You had to go where you could and start over, which meant a lifetime, generations even—of trying to fit into a country, city, and culture that didn't want you in the first place. I didn't feel any sense of belonging in the conservative town where we had been resettled. Increasingly, I didn't feel I belonged in my own family, where I was called too quiet, too shy, a nerd who spent too much time reading.

***

When I was about 8 years old, a friend invited me to her house after school to play and have supper. I was nervous because my friend was blonde, blue-eyed, and proper—meaning her clothes were clean and unwrinkled, her mom regularly baked cookies, and the family lived in a suburb of two-story, colonial-type houses. I knew I was not proper; my family was not proper because we were refugees, and I was desperately trying to pretend that we weren't.

I'm sure that my friend didn't know my family's story; I had never spoken of it. I was trying to be as Midwestern American as they were. But the moment I stepped into my friend's house, with its freshly vacuumed beige carpets and don't-touch living room, I saw that I was lost. I didn't know the rules of behavior. I took off my shoes, which is what everyone in my family did the moment they came home because shoes were dirty and why would we bring the outdoors inside? My friend gave me a funny look. I had never worn shoes inside a house before, but I put mine back on even though it felt wrong.

At home, I lived with my siblings, father and stepmother, grandmother, and uncles. My grandmother cooked Vietnamese stews, curries, and stir-fries with fresh rice in the rice cooker. At dinner we served ourselves, then found a place at the dining table that was always partly covered in newspapers. Sometimes we ate together and sometimes we didn't. But we always ate fast, with chopsticks, bowls held close to our faces. Napkins were piled in the middle of the table, or forgotten altogether. And if we wanted something to drink? Well, there were probably clean cups in the kitchen.

My friend's house introduced me to what I imagined was the ideal American way of life: the table set with matching dishes and utensils, tablecloths and placemats, a napkin folded at each place. The father sat at the head of the table. The mother cooked and served. No one could eat until everyone was seated, and ready, and a prayer was spoken. I learned that the hard way when

I immediately started in on the beef stroganoff set before me and the mother said, with sharpness in her voice: "In this house, we pray before we eat."

I remember that dinner as both delicious and excruciating. I was glimpsing and experiencing something I had only seen on television, which I had tried to study. I understood that I didn't fit in here, that I had affirmed myself as an object of difference and foreignness. They could see it in me before I did a single thing. The fact of my face, my Vietnameseness in this white world, signaled to them that I could be no more than a strange visitor. I vowed, then, to learn these ways, to learn these unspoken rules. One day, I would belong so deeply that no one would know where I came from.

***

In *The Age of Innocence*, Ellen Olenska does and doesn't belong to old New York. She has lived a glamorous, European life just long enough to be considered foreign. Upon her return to New York, her clothing is scrutinized. The old New Yorkers notice that she chooses to live in a "strange quarter" of the city, among "dressmakers, bird-stuffers, and 'people who wrote'" (65). But most damning of all is the fact that she has fled a terrible husband and wants to get a divorce. Ellen, we see, makes herself an object of difference and foreignness and pity. Does she realize it? Does she do it on purpose?

Newland Archer falls in love with Ellen because of this, because she represents the opposite of the conventional life he has grown to expect with his future bride, May Welland, who happens to be Ellen's cousin. When Ellen says to Newland "I don't speak your language," it is a barb and a taunt—a reminder to him that he is conventional (131). No matter how many books he orders from abroad, he cannot know the life she has known.

The novel's love triangle forms and hinges on language. It exists because of language, and manners, and the customs of this particular, small society. May is the keeper of these ways; Ellen is the outlier; Newland is the one who cannot decide where he wants to be. When Wharton describes him as a dilettante, she's getting at his inability to commit, his desire to have it all without the consequences of having it all. He is a conformist who thinks he wants to be a non-conformist.

Of course, I identified more with Ellen (who doesn't?) because she's the unpredictable rebel figure. She is a little too big for her britches. More than that, I felt like I understood the complications of her desires. I had to admire her restraint. Newland doesn't make the real decisions because it's Ellen and May who have all the control. In the end, it is the women who all agree, without ever saying so, to uphold the old New York system.

In one form or another, we all live in coded worlds. Some of us know intimately and intuitively how to code-switch long before we know the meaning of that term. This is how I spent my growing-up years, switching from the Vietnameseness of family to the whiteness of school. It's a balance I still have to maintain.

When I first read *The Age of Innocence*, I was 16 or 17. Afterwards, I kept rereading it every couple of years. Each time, I saw a little more how fucked up I was at 16 or 17, going into *The Age of Innocence* without context, with barely a clue about what the Gilded Age even was. It was one thing to feel a loss of belonging in real life, but to replicate that feeling in the reading of a book? I was a fucked-up reader with a scared, assimilationist mindset, buying into the idea that refugees and immigrants could only belong in America if they did what they were told and followed all the unclear rules set by other people. I thought the key was to decipher the undecipherable code without ever acknowledging that there was a code. I thought that, if I could know how things worked, exactly, I could know how to be. There is, after all, comfort in rules: you know the napkin goes in your lap; you know where to go right after dinner; you know how to get good grades; you know whom to talk to, and when. How ambitious to think I could learn all of this well enough to seem natural-born. I was, as ever, too big for my britches.

The message of *The Age of Innocence* is clear: the social code is strict and unforgiving. It doesn't bend to outsiders. When Ellen Olenska finally figures this out, all she can do is go back to Europe and stay there.

In the novel, as in life, it is the passage of time that wears away tradition. In the end, many years later, Newland's son Dallas is engaged to one of "Beaufort's bastards" and teasingly describes his father as "prehistoric" (341, 359). We see that the social order has shifted, but Newland has not. He and Dallas are in Paris, where they are supposed to visit Ellen, but Newland walks away from the chance to see her. As a reader, I really want him to see her; every time I want him to see her. But Newland affirms what we have known all along: he is old-fashioned. He is the conformist he always was. He is a full product and participant of the social code that made him, so much so that he cannot change. May has been dead for years but still she speaks to him without saying a word. Newland walks away from the future and chooses, instead, the past.

***

If you were to see me in real life today you wouldn't recognize me as a girl who hid, taking notes in her mind, a refugee and child of refugees trying to figure out the systems in place. I teach; I write; I parent; I go to meetings and conferences and get-togethers. I code-switch so well you won't know I'm doing it; often, I don't recognize it either. I am constantly trying to choose the future while still trying to understand and reckon with the past.

The first reading of a book is an adventure; the rereadings are an immersion and a gaining of agency. To read a novel about whiteness, to be saturated in such whiteness, is risky and precarious for any reader of color. You risk feeling fucked up about it. The rereading actually helps because you already know what's going to happen: you're prepared, and therefore can learn in unexpected ways; you can gain a greater sense of control and understanding over these dominant landscapes and identities. This kind of experience is rarely had in actual life.

Rereading makes me feel stronger; it makes me assess what I thought I knew and reminds me that I'm the one who gets to interpret. The text stays the same but the reading of it changes. We change, because the reading changes us and later we change the reading. When I return to *The Age of Innocence* it is to see, with renewed perspective, the old characters I think I know so well, to cozy up in their dining rooms and parlors, to envision seaside Newport and the "wilderness near the Central Park" where Mrs. Mingott resides, and to imagine a city, a time, and a place that are almost as foreign to me as the place I was born (10). The journey into this old New York has a bit of nostalgia—a fond, somewhat bittersweet retreading of somewhere that is no longer—but it is also a way to go back to my own old self. When I reread, I remember myself as I was in high school, and then in college, and then as an adult, a teacher, a professor, a mother, a woman lying in bed on a rainy day, recalling all the places where she has loved reading books, recalling all the ways in which she read to escape, to learn, to yearn. Maybe we all have an age of innocence, which is to say an age of dissonance, though we don't know it until we get beyond it and recognize, with astonishment, how much time has gone by.

Notes

Introduction

1   William Lyon Phelps, "As Mrs. Wharton Sees Us," *New York Times* October 14, 1920, 26, 31.

2   Examples include Robert McCrum, "The 100 Best Novels in English," *Guardian*, August 17, 2015: https://www.theguardian.com/books/2014/jul/28/100-best-novels-age-of-innocence-edith-wharton-robert-mccrum; "100 Best Novels," Modern Library, http://www.modernlibrary.com/top-100/100-best-novels; David Handlin, "One Hundred Best American Novels, 1770 to 1985 (a Draft)," *American Scholar*, July 16, 2014: https://theamericanscholar.org/one-hundred-best-american-novels-1770-to-1985-a-draft/#.XDj2mc9KglL; Ta-Nehisi Coates, "The Age of Awesome," *Atlantic*, April 20, 2011: https://www.theatlantic.com/entertainment/archive/2011/04/the-age-of-awesome/237588; Roxane Gay, "Roxane Gay's 10 Favorite Books," *Vulture*, March 15, 2018: https://www.vulture.com/2018/03/roxane-gays-10-favorite-books.html.

3   In *The Letters of Edith Wharton*, ed. R. W. B. Lewis and Nancy Lewis (New York: Scribner's, 1988), 445.

4   Meredith Goldsmith, "Of Publicity, Prizes, and Prestige: The Middle-Zone of the Marketplace in *Hudson River Bracketed*," *American Literary Realism* 48.3 (2016): 232–250.

5   Edith Wharton, "The Great American Novel," *Yale Review* (July 1927): 647–649.

6   Alessandra Stanley, "Scorsese, From the Mean Streets to Charm School," *New York Times*, June 28, 1992: https://www.nytimes.com/1992/06/28/movies/film-scorsese-from-the-mean-streets-to-charm-school.html.

7   Appleton advertisement in *Publishers' Weekly*, quoted in Edith Wharton, *The Age of Innocence: Norton Critical Edition*, ed. Candace Waid (New York: W.W. Norton & Co., 2003), 378. Subsequent references to this volume are listed as: Waid, *Age of Innocence*.

8   Edith Wharton, *The Letters of Edith Wharton*, ed. Richard Warrington Baldwin and Nancy Lewis (New York: Collier Books, 1988), 481.

9   Janet Flanner, "Dearest Edith," *New Yorker*, March 2, 1929: https://www.newyorker.com/magazine/1929/03/02/dearest-edith.

10 Edith Wharton and Ogden Codman, *The Decoration of Houses* (New York: Scribner's, 1897), 165.

11 Edith Wharton, *The Age of Innocence* (New York: D. Appleton & Co., 1920), 364. All subsequent citations from the novel in this introduction are parenthetical and use this edition.

12 Eric Burns, *1920: The Year That Made the Decade Roar* (New York: Pegasus, 2015), 198.

13 Quoted in Jane Mayer, "The Making of the Fox News White House," *New Yorker*, March 11, 2019: https://www.newyorker.com/magazine/2019/03/11/the-making-of-the-fox-news-white-house.

14 Alexandra Svokos, "Viral Photo of Woman's Abortion Protest Sign Will Make You Laugh Then Cry," *Elite Daily*, October 4, 2016: https://www.elitedaily.com/news/politics/woman-abortion-protest-poland/1632496.

15 While at work on *The Age of Innocence*, Wharton wrote to her friend Sara Norton: "I am steeping myself in the nineteenth century, which is such a blessed refuge from the turmoil and mediocrity of today." In R. W. B. Lewis, *Edith Wharton: A Biography* (New York: Harper and Row, 1975), 424.

16 Wharton herself deliberately muddied the exact time period of the novel in order to avoid its being read as a mere costume drama or set piece, writing to Rutger Jewett: "What I was trying to do, and what I believe every novelist who write [*sic*] an 'historic' novel should do, was to evoke the intellectual, moral, and artistic atmosphere not of one year but of ten years: that is to say my allusions range from, say, 1875 to 1885. Any narrower field of evocation must necessarily reduce the novel to a piece of archeological pedantry instead of a living image of the times." In Edith Wharton, *The Age of Innocence*, ed. Michael Nowlin (Peterborough, ON: Broadview Press, 2002), 351. Early reviewers such as the anonymous reviewer from the *Literary Digest* mistakenly took this deliberate conflation as authorial error: "the book is full of anachronisms which are so sure to be noticed by old New-Yorkers that we shall only mention one or two," in Waid, *Age of Innocence*, 392. Betsy Klimasmith identifies the deliberateness of this vague temporality and its consequences, suggesting that Wharton's sense of historical time in the novel is shaped by modern theories of simultaneity and relativity drawn from philosopher Henri Bergson and physicist Albert Einstein, which amount to an example of what Rita Felski calls "the hybrid temporality of the modern." Quoted in Betsy Klimasmith, "Salvaging History: Modern

Philosophies of Memory and Time in *The Age of Innocence*," *American Literature* 80.3 (2008): 556–581 (557).

17 Z. Ramadan, "The Gamification of Trust: The Case of China's 'Social Credit,'" *Marketing Intelligence & Planning* 36.1 (2018): 93–107.

18 Alex Ward, "Pence Says US 'Will Not Back Down' from China's Aggression in Fiery Speech," *Vox*, October 4, 2018: https://www.vox.com/2018/10/4/17936514/pence-china-speech-text-hudson.

19 Bing Song, "The West May Be Wrong About China's Social Credit System," *Washington Post*, November 29, 2018: https://www.washingtonpost.com/news/theworldpost/wp/2018/11/29/social-credit/?noredirect=on&utm_term=.57d5633e25f7.

20 Elizabeth Ammons argues that the sexual temptation posed by Ellen jeopardizes Newland's idea of civilization in "Cool Diana and the Blood-Red Muse: Edith Wharton on Innocence and Art," *American Novelists Revisited: Essays in Feminist Criticism* (Boston, MA: G. K. Hall, 1982), 209–224.

21 Carl Van Doren, "An Elder America," *Nation*, November 3, 1920: 111.

22 Nancy Bentley cites the dinner scene in which Ellen Olenska is cast out of the "tribe" in connection with work on tribalism by the contemporary anthropologist Bronislaw Malinowski, writing "[May's] family has issued what anthropologists in their fondness for classifying species of magic termed a 'conditional curse,' a protective spell that calls down in advance the punishment that will befall anyone who transgresses it." "Realism, Relativism, and the Discipline of Manners," in Waid, *Age of Innocence*, 447–460 (458).

23 Shinan Govani, "How 'Crazy Rich Asians' Splash Their Cash," *Daily Beast*, July 7, 2015: https://www.thedailybeast.com/how-crazy-rich-asians-splash-their-cash.

24 *Gossip Girl*, "The Age of Dissonance," Robby Hull (writer), Jim McKay (director), CW (March 16, 2009).

25 Wharton's use of novel-of-manners conventions is so precise and unsparing that Nancy Bentley associates *The Age of Innocence* with the social scientific tradition in the emerging fields of ethnography and anthropology. See Bentley, "Realism, Relativism." See also Gary Lindberg, *Edith Wharton and the Novel of Manners* (Charlottesville, VA: University Press of Virginia, 1975).

26 Coates, "The Age of Awesome."

27 Harry Hartwick, *The Foreground of American Fiction* (New York: American Book Co., 1934). Erika W. Smith, "Everything Countess Ellen Olenska Wears in 'The Age of Innocence,'" *Medium*, June 7, 2016: https://medium.com/@erikawynn/everything-countess-ellen-olenska-wears-in-the-age-of-innocence-f84e6cc2d5c7.

28 For a study of *The Age of Innocence* as a *roman à clef*, see Gwendolyn Morgan, "The Unsung Heroine—A Study of May Welland in *The Age of Innocence*," *Heroines of Popular Culture*, ed. Pat Browne (Bowling Green, OH: Popular, 1987), 32–40; and Julia Ehrhardt, "To Read These Pages Is to Live Again," in Waid, *Age of Innocence*, 401–412. In her autobiography, *A Backward Glance*, Wharton writes: "The low order, in fiction, of the genuine roman a clef (which is never written by a born novelist) naturally makes any serious writer of fiction indignant at being suspected of such methods. Nothing can be more trying to the creative writer than to have a clumsy finger point at one of the beings born in that mysterious other-world of invention, with the playful accusation: 'Of course we all recognize your aunt Eliza!,' or to be told (and this has more than once happened to me): 'We all thought your heroine must be meant for Mrs. X., because their hair is exactly the same colour.'" Edith Wharton, *A Backward Glance* (New York: Scribner's, 1964), 211.

29 See, for example, "Snapshot of EW smoking taken in Lenox, Mass. in 1905 by Kate Haven (later Mrs. William Osborn), daughter of Mrs. J. Woodward Haven," Edith Wharton Collection, box 64, folder 1790 (New Haven, CT: Beinecke Library, Yale University).

30 Morgan writes: "May Welland … is a character of much potential. Intelligent, intuitive, loving and a survivor, she could have been the heroine of *The Age of Innocence*." Morgan, "Unsung Heroine," 38.

31 At the end of the novel, Newland is 57—the same age as Wharton at the time of the novel's composition, as Carol Singley points out in her essay here before describing their many differences. Like Ellen, Wharton left New York to become "Europeanized" as a girl and then again, for good, after the dissolution of her marriage. Critically, Elizabeth Ammons associates Wharton with Ellen in "The War," *Edith Wharton's Argument with America* (Athens, GA: University of Georgia Press, 1980), 125–156. Gloria Erlich, Jean Witherow, and Nir Evron associate Wharton with Newland. Gloria Erlich, *The Sexual Education of Edith Wharton* (Berkeley, CA: University of California Press, 1992); Nir Evron, "Realism, Irony and Morality in Edith Wharton's *The Age of Innocence*," *Journal of Modern Literature* 35.2 (2012): 37–51; Jean Witherow, "A Dialectic of Deception: Edith Wharton's 'The Age of Innocence,'" *Mosaic: An Interdisciplinary Critical Journal* 36.3 (September 2003): 165–180. Candace Waid and R. W. B. Lewis see in May Wharton's own knowledge of "what it meant to be sacrificed to an ideal that required women to suffer from what her protagonist Newland Archer reveres and condemns as 'abysmal purity'" both in Candace Waid's "Introduction," in Waid, *Age of Innocence*, xiv.

32 EW to Teddy, Wednesday July 6, 1910. Edith Wharton Papers, box 30, folder 941 (New Haven, CT: Beinecke Library, Yale University).

33 Rebecca Solnit, "Men Explain Things to Me," in *Men Explain Things to Me and Other Essays* (Chicago, IL: Haymarket Books, 2014), 1–18.

34 Brian A. Primack, A. Shensa, J. E. Sidani, E. O. Whaite, L. Y. Lin, D. Rosen, J. B. Colditz, A. Radovic, and E. Miller, "Social Media Use and Perceived Social Isolation Among Young Adults in the US," *American Journal of Preventive Medicine* 53.1 (2017): 1–8.

35 Mark Zuckerberg is the founder of the social media network Facebook.

36 Elsewhere I write about representational desire with a bit more specificity, describing how Wharton critiques the replacement of authentic sexual desire with its representations in popular culture in *The Custom of the Country* (1913). See Arielle Zibrak, "The Woman Who Hated Sex: Undine Spragg and the Trouble with 'Bother,'" *Edith Wharton Review* 32.1–2 (2016): 1–19.

37 Emily Orlando, *Edith Wharton and the Visual Arts* (Tuscaloosa, AL: Alabama University Press, 2006), 174.

38 Ammons argues, on the contrary, that the martriarchy of the *Old New York* depicted in the novel is undermined by Mrs. Mingott's ultimate deference to her son and lawyer. (Ammons, "The War".)

39 Vernon L. Parrington, Jr., "Our Literary Aristocrat," *Pacific Review*, June 1, 1921, reprinted in Waid, *Age of Innocence*; and Carl Van Doren, "An Elder America," *Nation*, November 3, 1920, also reprinted in Waid, *Age of Innocence*.

40 Edith Wharton, *The House of Mirth* (New York: Scribner's, 1905), 108; Edith Wharton, *A Backward Glance* (New York: Simon & Schuster, 1998), 119.

Chapter 1

1 R. W. B. Lewis, *The American Adam* (Chicago, IL: University of Chicago, 1955).

2 Edith Wharton, *The Age of Innocence* (New York: Scribner's, 1968), 347. Subsequent page references to this volume appear parenthetically in the text.

3 Sacvan Bercovitch, "The Problem of Ideology in American Literary History," *Critical Inquiry* 12.4 (Summer 1986): 631–653.

4 Robert E. Spiller, Willard Thorpe, Thomas H. Johnson, and Henry Canby, eds., "Address to the Reader," in *Literary History of the United States*, 4th ed., 2 vols. (New York: Macmillan, 1948), 1: xxi.

5 Ibid., xxii.

6   F. O. Matthiessen, *The American Renaissance: Art and Expression in the Age of Emerson and Whitman* (New York: Oxford University Press, 1941), vii.

7   Lewis, *American Adam*; Richard Chase, *The American Novel and Its Tradition* (Baltimore, MD: Johns Hopkins University Press, 1957 [1933]).

8   Richard Poirier, *A World Elsewhere: The Place of Style in American Literature* (Madison, WI: University of Wisconsin Press, 1985), 8.

9   Carolyn Porter, *Seeing and Being: The Plight of the Participant Observer in Emerson, James, Adams, and Faulkner* (Middletown, CN: Wesleyan University Press, 1981), xx.

10 "Chairman Ben Bernanke Delivers Remarks Before the Greater Omaha Chamber of Commerce," CQ Transcripts Wire, *Washington Post*, February 6, 2007: http://www.washingtonpost.com/wp-dyn/content/article/2007/02/06/AR2007020600882.html.

11 John Cawelti, *Apostles of the Self-Made Man* (Chicago, IL: University of Chicago Press, 1965), 44. Quoted in Aaron Barlow, *The Cult of Individualism: A History of an Enduring Myth* (Santa Barbara, CA: Praeger, 2013), 37.

12 Ralph Waldo Emerson, "Manners," in *Emerson: Essays and Poems*, ed. Joel Porte, Harold Bloom, and Paul Kane, Library of America College Editions (New York: Literary Classics, 1996), 514–515.

13 Richard Weiss, *The American Myth of Success* (New York: Basic Books, 1969), 175. Quoted in Barlow, *Cult of Individualism*, 131.

14 Emerson, "Manners," 515.

15 Ibid., 515.

16 Ralph Waldo Emerson, "Civilization," *The Complete Works of Ralph Waldo Emerson*, ed. Edward Waldo Emerson, 12 vols. (Boston, MA: Houghton Mifflin, 1904).

17 Ralph Waldo Emerson, "Nature," in *Emerson: Essays and Poems*, ed. Joel Porte, Harold Bloom, and Paul Kane, Library of America College Editions (New York: Literary Classics, 1996), 10.

18 Edgar Allan Poe, "The Tell-Tale Heart," in *The Selected Writings of Edgar Allan Poe*, ed. G. R. Thompson (New York: Norton, 2004), 317.

19 Edith Wharton, *A Backward Glance* (New York: Scribner's, 1934), 68.

20 Poe, "The Imp of the Perverse," in *The Selected Writings of Edgar Allan Poe*, ed. G. R. Thompson (New York: Norton, 2004), 404.

21 Daniel H. Borus, *Twentieth-Century Multiplicity: American Thought and Culture, 1900–1920* (Lanham, MD: Rowman & Littlefield, 2009), 127.

22 Ibid., 129–130.

23 Barlow, *Cult of Individualism*, 26–27.

24 Borus, *Twentieth-Century Multiplicity*, 137.

25 Emerson, "Nature," 9.

26 Hector Saint John de Crèvecoeur, *Letters from an American Farmer* (New York: E. P. Dutton, 1957 [1782]), 39.

27 Barlow, *Cult of Individualism*, 34.

28 Randolph Bourne, "Trans-National America," *Atlantic Monthly* 116 (July 1916): 88. Quoted in Barlow, *Cult of Individualism*, 34.

29 Barlow, *Cult of Individualism*, 34.

30 Ralph Waldo Emerson, "The American Scholar," in *Emerson: Essays and Poems*, ed. Joel Porte, Harold Bloom, and Paul Kane, Library of America College Editions (New York: Literary Classics, 1996), 65.

31 William James, *Principles of Psychology* (Cambridge, MA: Harvard University Press, 1983 [1890]), 281–284. Quoted in Borus, *Twentieth-Century Multiplicity*, 132.

32 Borus, *Twentieth-Century Multiplicity*, 135.

33 Edith Wharton to Corrine Roosevelt Robinson, April 29, 1923, in *The Letters of Edith Wharton*, ed. R. W. B. Lewis and Nancy Lewis (New York: Scribner's, 1988), 466.

Chapter 2

1 Edith Wharton to Rutger B. Jewett, July 20, 1933, Appleton MSS, Box 22, Folder 7 (Bloomington, IN: Lilly Library, Indiana University). Courtesy of the Lilly Library, Indiana University.

2 Scott Marshall, "Edith Wharton on Film and Television: A History and Filmography," *Edith Wharton Review* 13.2 (1996): 16.

3 Parley Ann Boswell, *Edith Wharton on Film* (Carbondale, IL: Southern Illinois Press, 2007), 84.

4 Edith Wharton to Rutger B. Jewett, August 23, 1921, Appleton MSS, Box 21, Folder 3 (Bloomington, IN: Lilly Library, Indiana University). Courtesy of the Lilly Library, Indiana University.

5 William Lyon Phelps, "As Mrs. Wharton Sees Us," in *Edith Wharton: The Contemporary Reviews*, ed. James W. Tuttleton, Kirstin O. Lauer, and Margaret P. Murray (Cambridge: Cambridge University Press, 1992), 284.

6 Katherine Perry, "Were the Seventies Sinless?," in *Edith Wharton: The Contemporary Reviews*, ed. James W. Tuttleton, Kirstin O. Lauer, and Margaret P. Murray (Cambridge: Cambridge University Press, 1992), 283.

7   Brigitte Peucker, "Rival Arts? Filming *The Age of Innocence*," *Edith Wharton Review* 13.1 (1996): 19.

8   Ibid., 19.

9   Linda Costanzo Cahir, "Wharton and the Age of Film," in *A Historical Guide to Edith Wharton*, ed. Carol Singley (Oxford: Oxford University Press, 2003), 212.

10 Boswell, *Edith Wharton on Film*, 94.

11 Cahir, "Wharton and the Age," 219.

12 A. S., "Wax Flowers and Horse Cars," Review of *The Age of Innocence* (1934), *New York Times*, October 19, 1934, 27.

13 Margaret B. McDowell, "Edith Wharton's 'The Old Maid': Novella/Play/Film," *College Literature* 14.3 (Fall 1987): 250–252.

14 Marshall, "Edith Wharton on Film," 18.

15 Boswell, *Edith Wharton on Film*, 96.

16 Linda Costanzo Cahir, *Literature into Film: Theory and Practical Approaches* (Jefferson, NC: McFarland, 2006), 27.

17 Robert Stam, "Beyond Fidelity: The Dialogics of Adaptation," in *Critical Visions in Film Theory: Classic and Contemporary Readings*, ed. Timothy Corrigan, Patricia White, and Meta Mazaj (Boston, MA: Bedford/St. Martin's, 2011), 545.

18 Ibid.

19 Ibid., 547.

20 Cahir, "Wharton and the Age," 226.

21 Boswell, *Edith Wharton on Film*, 86.

22 Ibid.

23 Bethany Wood, "Gentlemen Prefer Adaptations: Addressing Industry and Gender in Adaptation Studies," *Theatre Journal* 66.4 (December 2014): 560–561.

24 Boswell, *Edith Wharton on Film*, 88.

25 *The Age of Innocence* [Film], dir. Philip Moeller (USA: Warner Bros., 1934). All quoted dialogue from the film is taken from the Warner Bros. DVD (2011) and will hereafter be cited by director's last name (Moeller).

26 The Hays Production Code insisted that "the sanctity of the institution of marriage and the home shall be upheld." Rule Number One under the heading "Sex" states that "Adultery, sometimes necessary plot material, must not be explicitly treated, justified, or presented attractively." See "The Motion Picture Production Code (as published 31 March, 1930)," in Richard Maltby, *Hollywood Cinema*, 2nd ed. (Hoboken, NJ: Blackwell, 2003), 595.

27 Edith Wharton, *The Age of Innocence* (Oxford: Oxford University Press, 2006), 241. All further page references to the novel will be cited parenthetically and refer to this edition.

28 A. S., "Wax Flowers," 27.

29 Rudolf Arnheim, *Film as Art* (Berkeley, CA: University of California Press, 1957), 9.

30 Sergei Eisenstein, "Film Language," in *Film Form: Essays in Film Theory*, ed. and trans. Jay Leyda (San Diego, CA: Harcourt, 1949), 108.

31 Ibid., 115.

32 Béla Balázs, *Béla Balázs: Early Film Theory: Visible Man and The Spirit of Film*, ed. Erica Carter, trans. Rodney Livingstone (New York: Berghahn Books, 2010), 17.

33 Ibid., 19.

34 Ibid., 23.

35 Hugo Münsterberg, *The Photoplay: A Psychological Study* (Scotts Valley, CA: CreateSpace Independent Publishing, 2013), 84.

36 Sergei Eisenstein, "Dickens, Griffith, and the Film Today," in *Film Form: Essays in Film Theory*, ed. and trans. Jay Leyda (San Diego, CA: Harcourt, 1949), 195.

37 Balázs, *Béla Balázs*, 23.

38 Eisenstein, "Dickens," 213.

39 Sarah Y. Mason and Victor Heerman, *The Age of Innocence Estimating Script*, RKO, Inc. (Bloomington, IN: Lilly Library, Indiana University, March 24, 1934), 1. Courtesy of the Lilly Library, Indiana University.

40 Ibid., 1.

41 Ibid.

42 In "Adapting Traditions: Laucane Surrounding the 1934 Film Adaptation of Edith Wharton's *The Age of Innocence*," *Edith Wharton Review* 34.2 (2018): 105, Bethany Wood describes the genesis of this montage, which originally appeared in the 1933 screenplay titled *Without Sin*, by Melville Baker and Jack Kirkland. Wood argues that the producers ultimately went with the montage in order to make Wharton's nostalgia-driven work more accessible to the 1934 viewer.

43 Soviet montage differs from the type of montage editing more common in US cinema, which is used to compress time and keep the plot moving forward at a quick pace.

44 Arnheim, *Film as Art*, 98.

45 Boswell argues that these images evoke "the raging, roaring twenties" (*Edith Wharton on Film*, 95), while Wood persuasively argues that they are more specifically tied to 1934 ("Adapting Traditions," 105).

46 Moeller, *The Age of Innocence*.

47 Wood, "Adapting Traditions," 105.

48 Balázs, *Béla Balázs*, 38.

49 Claudia Gorbman, "Classical Hollywood Practice," in *Critical Visions in Film Theory: Classic and Contemporary Readings*, ed. Timothy Corrigan, Patricia White, and Meta Mazaj (Boston, MA: Bedford/St. Martin's, 2011), 168–169.

50 Ibid., 169.

51 Balázs, *Béla Balázs*, 183.

52 Sabine Haenni, "Geographies of Desire: Postsocial Urban Space and Historical Revision in the Films of Martin Scorsese," *Journal of Film and Video* 62.1–2 (Spring/Summer 2010): 78.

53 Peucker, "Rival Arts," 21.

54 Christopher Arnott, "Hartford Stage's Lush, Elegant 'Age of Innocence' Adapted to Be Freshly Relevant," *Hartford Courant*, April 16, 2018.

55 Quoted in Christopher Arnott, "'Age of Innocence' Love Story Drives Hartford Stage Adaptation," *Hartford Courant*, April 6, 2018.

Chapter 3

1 Henry James, *Theory of Fiction: Henry James*, ed. James E. Miller, Jr. (Lincoln, NE: University of Nebraska Press, 1972), 37.

2 Edith Wharton, *The Age of Innocence*, ed. Cynthia Griffin Wolff (New York: Penguin, 1996), 52 and 4. All further references to the novel will be cited parenthetically and refer to this edition.

3 Donald Pizer, "American Naturalism in Its 'Perfected' State: *The Age of Innocence* and an American Tragedy," in *The Theory and Practice of American Literary Naturalism: Selected Essays and Reviews* (Carbondale, IL: Southern Illinois University Press, 1993), 161.

4 Janet Beer and Avril Horner, "'The Great Panorama': Edith Wharton as Historical Novelist," *Modern Language Review* 110.1 (January 2015): 81.

5 Matthew Jockers and Gabi Kirilloff, "Understanding Gender and Character Agency in the 19th Century Novel," *Cultural Analytics* "Genre" cluster (December 2016): doi: 10.31235/osf.io/sw85; and Gabi Kirilloff, Peter Capuano, Julius Fredrick, and Matthew Jockers, "From a Distance 'You Might Mistake Her for a Man': A Closer Reading of Gender and Character Action in *Jane Eyre, The Law and the Lady*, and *A Brilliant Woman*," *DSH: Digital Scholarship in the Humanities* 33.4 (December 2018): 821–844.

6 Margaret Jay Jessee, "Trying It On: Narration and Masking in Edith Wharton's *The Age of Innocence*," *Journal of Modern Literature* 36.1 (2012): 37–52; Evelyn

Fracasso, "The Transparent Eyes of May Welland in Wharton's *The Age of Innocence*," *Modern Language Studies* 21.4 (1991): 43–48; and William E. Cain, "Edith Wharton and the Second Story," *New England Review* 29.2 (2008): 95–106.

7   Jessee, "Trying It On," 49.

8   Jean Witherow, "A Dialectic of Deception: Edith Wharton's 'The Age of Innocence,'" *Mosaic: An Interdisciplinary Critical Journal* 36.3 (2003): 170.

9   Mark Nicholls, "Male Melancholia and Martin Scorsese's *The Age of Innocence*," *Film Quarterly* 58.1 (2004): 26.

10 For examples of this style of work, see Franco Moretti, *Graphs, Maps, Trees: Abstract Models for Literary History* (London and New York: Verso, 2005); Ted Underwood, *Why Literary Periods Mattered: Historical Contrast and the Prestige of English Studies* (Stanford, CA: Stanford University Press, 2013); and Matthew Jockers, *Macroanalysis: Digital Methods and Literary History* (Champaign, IL: University of Illinois Press, 2013).

11 The term "distant reading" is widely attributed to Franco Moretti; however, examining syntactical patterns and trends across texts has a rich history within literary studies. Though it has become almost synonymous with text analysis, "distant reading" does not necessitate the use of computational methods. For a thorough history, see Ted Underwood, "A Genealogy of Distant Reading," *Digital Humanities Quarterly* 11.2 (2017): http://www.digitalhumanities.org/dhq/vol/11/2/000317/000317.html.

12 This corpus contains works by many of Wharton's contemporaries, including Willa Cather, Henry James, and Theodore Dreiser.

13 *The Valley of Decision* (1902), *The House of Mirth* (1905), *The Fruit of the Tree* (1907), *The Reef* (1912), *The Custom of the Country* (1913), *Summer* (1917), *The Marne* (1918), *The Age of Innocence* (1920), *The Glimpses of the Moon* (1922), *A Son at the Front* (1923), *The Mother's Recompense* (1925), *Twilight Sleep* (1927), *The Children* (1928), *Hudson River Bracketed* (1929), and *The Gods Arrive* (1932) were included. In her chronology of Edith Wharton's works, Shari Benstock lists the above as Wharton's non-posthumously published novels. Given that the nineteenth-century corpus is composed of novels, I chose, for consistency's sake, to only select texts Benstock had labeled as novels (rather than novellas or short story collections). I attempted to avoid works, such as *Ethan Frome* (1911), that have been categorized as both novels and novellas; however, the methods I outline in this essay could be applied to other texts by Wharton. See Shari Benstock, *No Gifts from Chance: A Biography of Edith Wharton* (Austin, TX: University of Texas Press, 2004).

14 Some of the code used in this project was recycled from the nineteenth-century project; consequently, it was written by both Jockers and Kirilloff. In addition, Jockers provided assistance in rerunning the portions of this project that needed to be executed on the Holland Computing Center's Computer Cluster and the University of Nebraska-Lincoln. In both the nineteenth- and twentieth-century corpora, the novels range in genre and included popular and literary fiction. Most of the texts selected were well known. The number of female and male authors in this corpus is evenly split.

15 A model was trained on 75 percent of the subject verb pairs. For the remaining 25 percent of the pairs, the model "guessed" the gender of each pronoun based on the verb being performed by that pronoun. For a more detailed explanation of the methods see Jockers and Kirilloff, "Understanding Gender."

16 It is often impossible to cleanly demarcate specific historical periods in terms of their ideological commitments—e.g., liberal feminism can be traced back to the eighteenth century—however, several critics and historians have noted that the turn of the nineteenth century was characterized by changing and unstable gender roles. For example, Showalter discusses the ways in which the figure of the "New Woman" and the onset of feminist causes redefined "masculinity" and "femininity" during this period. See Elaine Showalter, *Sexual Anarchy: Gender and Culture at the Fin de Siecle* (New York: Penguin, 1991).

17 Ted Underwood, David Bamman, and Sabrina Lee, "The Transformation of Gender in English-Language Fiction," *Cultural Analytics* "Genre" cluster (February 2018): doi: 10.31235/osf.io/fr9bk.

18 Judith Butler, *Gender Trouble: Feminism and the Subversion of Identity* (New York: Routledge, 1990), 145.

19 Paula Rothenberg, *Race, Class, and Gender in the United States: An Integrated Study* (New York: St. Martin's Press, 1998), 593.

20 Underwood et al., "The Transformation of Gender," n.p.

21 Among the nineteenth-century novels, 738 exhibited predominantly misclassified female pronouns (female pronouns performing actions more indicative of male pronouns), while 531 of the novels exhibited predominantly misclassified male pronouns (male pronouns performing actions more indicative of female pronouns). Among the twentieth-century novels, 38 of the 100 novels exhibited predominantly misclassified female pronouns, including Willa Cather's *Sapphira and the Slave Girl* and Henry James's *The Ambassador*. Only 10 novels exhibited predominantly misclassified male pronouns, including Zona Gale's *Miss Lulu Bett* and Dorothy Canfield Fisher's *The Bent Twig*.

22 Nancy Jay, "Gender and Dichotomy," *Feminist Studies* 7 (1981): 45.

23 It is worth noting that, in the nineteenth-century study, female authors were more likely to write male characters that performed unconventional actions, while male authors were more likely to write female characters that behaved unconventionally. While it is unclear if this pattern would persist across an equally large corpus of twentieth-century texts, Wharton's work does defy this trend.

24 See Arielle Zibrak, "The Woman Who Hated Sex: Undine Spragg and the Trouble with 'Bother,'" *Edith Wharton Review* 32.1–2 (2016): 1–19. Zibrak notes that Wharton's novels have long been associated with misogyny, a view that has continued into the twenty-first century, especially in the public conception of Wharton. Scholars such as Cynthia Griffin Wolff, Elizabeth Ammons, Judith Fetterley, and Wai-Chee Dimock have challenged this view, focusing on Wharton's insights into the social structures of the early twentieth century. The highly varying views on Wharton's engagement with gender are reflected in individual readings of her plots and characters. For example, in *The Female Imagination*, Spacks reads Lily's death as an "escapist fantasy of motherhood" (241), while in "The Death of the Lady (Novelist)" Showalter reads this scene as emblematic of "Lily's awakened sense of loving solidarity and community" (145). See Patricia Meyer Spacks, *The Female Imagination* (New York: Alfred Knopf, 1975) and Elaine Showalter, "The Death of the Lady (Novelist): Wharton's House of Mirth," *Representations* (Special Issue) no. 9 (Winter 1985): 133–149.

25 This result also should not be understood as indicating that the misclassified novels are somehow more similar to one another than the novels that were correctly classified. There are important differences between these novels. This result simply points to one area of similarity that may be interpreted in multiple ways.

26 The other three novels are Sinclair Lewis's *Main Street* and Agatha Christie's *The Mysterious Affair at Styles* and *The Secret Adversary*.

27 Edith Wharton, *The Marne* (New York: D. Appleton and Co., 1918), 21.

28 Ibid., 10.

29 Troy does actually "cry" in the novel, but these cases are in the sense of "crying out" not "crying tears."

30 William Blazek, "French Lessons: Edith Wharton's War Propaganda," *Revue Francaise D'Etudes Amerricaines* 115.1 (2008): 11.

31 Wharton, *The Marne*, 45.

32 Ibid., 60.

33 Ibid., 94.

34 Ibid., 106.

35 Dianne Chambers, *Feminist Readings of Edith Wharton: From Silence to Speech* (New York: Palgrave Macmillan, 2009), 10–11.

36 Mrs. van der Luyden, Mrs. Mingott, and Mrs. Beaufort all "throne." Interestingly, Wharton also links this action with Mr. Letterblair—"the accredited legal adviser of three generations of New York gentility, throned behind his mahogany desk"— this association further links this verb with prestige and power (75).

37 Nancy Bentley, "'Hunting for the Real': Wharton and the Science of Manners," in *The Cambridge Companion to Edith Wharton*, ed. Millicent Bell (Cambridge: Cambridge University Press, 1995), 50.

38 Wharton makes the unreliable nature of the verb "seemed" clear to the reader when Ellen comments on her naivety about New York society: "New York simply meant peace and freedom to me: it was coming home. And I was so happy at being among my own people that every one I met seemed kind and good, and glad to see me" (140).

39 See Gwendolyn Morgan, "The Unsung Heroine—A Study of May Welland in *The Age of Innocence*," in *Heroines of Popular Culture*, ed. Pat Browne and Ray B. Browne (Bowling Green, OH: Bowling Green State University Popular Press, 1987), 32–40.

40 Jessee, "Trying It On," 38.

41 Fracasso, "Transparent Eyes," 43.

42 Cain, "Edith Wharton and the Second Story," 95.

43 When measuring the number of auxiliary verbs per sentence, the average for Wharton's novels was higher than the rest of the twentieth-century corpus. On average, for every ten sentences, Wharton uses approximately seven auxiliary verbs compared to the corpus average of approximately five.

44 An examination of the other stylistic and syntactical differences between Wharton and her contemporaries (including her high-level usage of auxiliary verbs) would make for an interesting future study.

45 Morgan, "Unsung Heroine," 35.

46 Parley Ann Boswell, *Pregnancy in Literature and Film* (Jefferson, NC: McFarland & Co., 2014), 49.

47 Katherine Joslin-Jeske, *Women Writers: Edith Wharton* (London: Macmillan, 1991), 103.

48 Interestingly, Newland and May are the only two characters in the novel described as "boyish." May is described as boyish twice: 116 and 156, and Newland once: 193.

49 If, as Capuano argues, the novelistic depiction of needlework functions as the fictional embodiment of the separate spheres ideology, then it is especially telling that May's large hands, so adept for outdoor physical activity, are unsuited for needlework. See Peter Capuano, *Changing Hands: Industry, Evolution, and the Reconfiguration of the Victorian Body* (Ann Arbor, MI: University of Michigan Press, 2015).

50 See John Dudley, *A Man's Game: Masculinity and the Anti-Aesthetics of American Literary Naturalism* (Tuscaloosa, AL: University of Alabama Press, 2016), 128.

51 John Dudley links Ellen with the New Woman and notes that "Ellen is more of a 'man'—aesthetically speaking—than Newland can ever hope to be" in part because of her desire for personal freedom. Ibid., 119.

52 Edmund Wilson, "Justice to Edith Wharton," in *Edith Wharton: A Collection of Critical Essays*, ed. Irving Howe (Englewood Cliffs, NJ: Prentice-Hall, 1962), 26–27.

53 Beer and Horner, "Great Panorama," 75.

54 Dudley, *Man's Game*, 116.

55 Ibid., 17.

56 On a more obvious level, the predominance of Newland feeling, knowing, and seeing also highlights the extent to which Wharton is thematically concerned with his role as an observer, and privilege his perceptual agency over Ellen's and May's.

57 Tara McDonald, *The New Man, Masculinity and Marriage in the Victorian Novel* (New York: Routledge, 2016), 1.

58 Witherow, "Dialectic of Deception," 171.

59 McDonald, *New Man*, 16–17.

60 In the final chapter of the novel, Wharton underscores the fact that both Newland and May are necessary, transitional links between "old" and "new" social values by highlighting their close relationship with Dallas and Mary. Newland notes that people say that Dallas "took after him" and Mary "was so like her mother" (297 and 284). In describing Mary, Wharton writes that "her feats of athleticism could not have been performed with the twenty-inch waist that May Archer's azure sash so easily spanned" (287). Though Mary's body is larger than May's, and thus capable of greater physical activity, this passage recalls Mrs. Mingott's observation that "modern" sports were spreading May's joints, making her hands larger.

61 Rick Altman, *A Theory of Narrative* (New York: Columbia University Press, 2008), 15.

Chapter 4

1   Sigmund Freud, *Malaise dans la Civilisation* (Paris: Presses universitaires de France, 1971), 68 (my translation).

2   Vladimir Nabokov, *Lectures on Literature* (New York: Harvest, 1980), 98.

3   Edith Wharton, *The Age of Innocence* (London and New York: Oxford, 2008), 22. All page references to the novel will be cited parenthetically and refer to this edition.

4   Arbitrary signs: the idea that signs are purely conventional, that there is no connection between a specific form and a specific meaning, was developed by the Swiss semiotician Ferdinand de Saussure (1857–1913) in his description of language and soon taken up in the budding fields of anthropology and sociology. Newland Archer could not have been familiar with Saussure's work, which was published posthumously in 1916, but by 1920 his creator may well have been.

5   According to the OED, the word "milieu" was first used in French, in the sense of "social environment," in 1842. In English, George Eliot appears to have been the first to use it in 1854. See OED Online (June 2019), https://www-oed-com.ezproxy.u-bordeaux-montaigne.fr/view/Entry/118407?redirectedFrom= milieu. In *The Age of Innocence* the word is used twice (76), in italics, as if it were a French word, perhaps borrowed from Hippolyte Taine's "Introduction" to his *Histoire de la littérature anglaise*, vol. 1 (Paris: Hachette, 1863) in which he famously laid out his approach to literary criticism: "la race, le milieu, et le moment" (inherited temperament, social and geographical environment, and historical background), he said, could explain a work of art (iii–xlviii).

6   Stephen Fender, "Introduction," in Henry James, *Daisy Miller and Other Stories* (London: Penguin Books, 2016), xiii.

7   Ibid., xiv.

8   Edmond Jaloux, "La Vie littéraire: Au temps de L'innocence par Madame Edith Wharton," *La Revue hebdomadaire* 43 (1921): 505–508 (508).

9   A few dates may be in order here: the French Revolution (1789–1799) put an end to the monarchy and the *Ancien Régime*; the First Empire (1804–1815) began when Napoleon Bonaparte was crowned "Emperor of the French" and was named Napoleon I: a yellowing print of his coronation (from a painting by Jacques-Louis David) hangs in Mr. Letterblair's dining room (69); Josephine was Napoleon I's wife until their divorce in 1809; Napoleon I's nephew, Louis-Napoleon Bonaparte, was elected President of the Second Republic in 1848; in 1852, he was proclaimed Emperor Napoleon III, reigning until the fall of the

Second Empire in 1870. The balls in the Tuileries Palace were annual events
throughout the Second Empire to which many foreigners were invited.

10 For French—and more particularly Paul Bourget's—*anglomanie* see Daniel
    Karlin, *Proust's English* (Oxford and New York: Oxford University Press, 2005),
    especially chapter xx.

11 Translated into English as *Outre-Mer: Impressions of America* (New York:
    Scribner's, 1895).

12 Asphalt is not the only example in the novel of European—as opposed to
    American—modernity. Later, "one of the new stylographic pens" (164)—invented
    by a Roumanian but patented in Paris—and cab-stands, "still a foreign novelty"
    (165), make an appearance.

13 Jaloux, "La Vie littéraire," 506.

14 Edith Wharton, *French Ways and Their Meaning* (Lee, MA: Berkshire House,
    1997), 110.

15 *Monsieur de Camors* (1867) was written by one of the Empress Eugenie's favorite
    novelists and playwrights, Octave Feuillet (1821–1890).

16 As well as admirable but less well-known religious paintings, William-Adolphe
    Bouguereau (1825–1905), a mostly forgotten and now often derided academic
    painter, produced, between 1865 and 1887, over 200 works for the English and
    American art markets. These included the "much discussed nude" (Wharton, *Age
    of Innocence*, 16), "Love Victorious." For Bouguereau's reputation as an academic
    painter, see Laurier Lacroix, "Bouguereau, une question de sensibilité," https://
    www.erudit.org/fr/revues/va/1984-v29-n115-va1170294/54250ac.pdf.

17 The OED gives "domination by a romantic or unreal conception of oneself" as
    the definition of bovarism (alternate spellings include bovarysme and Bovarism)
    from the name of the novel by Gustave Flaubert, Madame Bovary, whose heroine
    is deluded by her reading. See OED Online (June 2019), https://www-oed-com.
    ezproxy.u-bordeaux-montaigne.fr/view/Entry/22167?redirectedFrom=bovarism.

18 For another view of the effect of Archer's reading, see Emily J. Orlando,
    "Rereading Wharton's 'Poor Archer': A Mr. 'Might-have-been' in 'The Age of
    Innocence,'" *American Literary Realism, 1870–1910* 30.2 (1998): 56–76. For a
    more general examination of reading in Wharton, see Agnès Berbineau-Dezalay,
    "Reading and Readers in Edith Wharton's Short Stories," *Journal of the Short
    Story in English* 58 (Spring 2012): 93–108.

19 Archer repeatedly, and perhaps significantly, imagines love scenes in which
    one of the protagonists has his or her back turned: in "one episode [in *The
    Shaughraun* at Wallack's theater] that held the house from floor to ceiling" (81)

"the actress … was standing near the mantelpiece and looking down into the fire"; later "Madame Olenska did not move when he came up behind her" (116); and again Archer finds Ellen "in the pagoda … leaning against the rail, her back, to the shore" (151).

20 Prosper Mérimée (1803–1870) was also intimately connected with the Second Empire: an old friend of the Empress Eugenie's mother, he became part of the imperial circle at the Tuileries Palace.

21 Arthur Symons, *The Symbolist Movement in Literature* (London: Carcanet, 2014), 145.

22 Edith Wharton, "America at War: Explaining the National Character in 1918," *Times Literary Supplement*, February 16, 2018: https://www.the-tls.co.uk/articles/public/america-at-war-wharton.

23 Edith Wharton, *A Backward Glance* (New York: Library of America, 1990), 855.

24 Wharton, *French Ways*, 32.

25 Leslie Fiedler, *Love and Death in the American Novel* (New York: Penguin Books, 1984), 143.

Chapter 5

1 Millicent Bell, "Introduction: A Critical History," in *The Cambridge Companion to Edith Wharton*, ed. Millicent Bell (Cambridge: Cambridge University Press, 1995), 15.

2 Candace Waid, "Introduction," in *The Age of Innocence* by Edith Wharton (New York: Norton, 2003 [1920]), xv, xiv.

3 As Laura Rattray summarizes: "Biography has long been the showcase genre of Wharton scholarship, which in certain regards proves both a blessing and a curse: it opens up the critical vista on a life, while indirectly perpetuating determinedly biographical readings of her work." Laura Rattray, *Edith Wharton in Context* (Cambridge: Cambridge University Press, 2012), 8.

4 Betsy Klimasmith, "Salvaging History: Modern Philosophies of Memory and Time in *The Age of Innocence*," *American Literature* 80.3 (2008): 555–581; Jill M. Kress, *The Figure of Consciousness: William James, Henry James, and Edith Wharton* (New York: Routledge, 2002); Pamela Knights, "Forms of Disembodiment: The Social Subject in *The Age of Innocence*," in *The Cambridge Companion to Edith Wharton*, ed. Millicent Bell (New York: Cambridge University Press, 1995), 20–46.

5   Jennifer Haytock, *Edith Wharton and the Conversations of Literary Modernism*
     (New York: Palgrave Macmillan, 2008), 44; Jennifer Fleissner, *Women,*
     Compulsion, Modernity: The Moment of American Naturalism (Chicago, IL:
     University of Chicago Press, 2004), 197–199.

6   Even if Wharton was not well-read in contemporary psychology (as she was
     in anthropology), the term figures often in her reflections on writing. See, for
     example, Edith Wharton, *The Writing of Fiction* (New York: Scribner's, 1925),
     66. Wharton writes of Proust: "No one else has carried as far the analysis of
     half-conscious states of mind, obscure associations of thought and gelatinous
     fluctuations of mood" (Wharton, *Writing of Fiction*, 155); we have no reason to
     assume that she herself was not also engaged in such an enterprise. Wharton read
     Proust between 1913 and 1927. See Hermione Lee, *Edith Wharton* (New York:
     Vintage, 2007), 283–285.

7   Adam Crabtree, *From Mesmer to Freud: Magnetic Sleep and the Roots of*
     Psychological Healing (New Haven, CT: Yale University Press, 1993), 283.

8   Ibid., 284.

9   Ann Banfield, "Where Epistemology, Style, and Grammar Meet Literary History:
     The Development of Represented Speech and Thought," *New Literary History*
     9.3 (1978): 453. Jonathan Kramnick's *Paper Minds: Literature and the Ecology*
     of Consciousness (Chicago, IL: University of Chicago Press, 2018) emphasizes
     the significance of free indirect discourse for the study of consciousness within
     the contemporary university. He presents it as a literary form for representing
     consciousness that cannot be reduced to, or otherwise made commensurate with,
     neurological or biological models for doing the same. My focus here is on the
     particular vision of consciousness as doubled that such narration implies.

10   For a more considered analysis of the narration in *The House of Mirth*, see
     Michael J. O'Neal, "Point of View and Narrative Technique in the Fiction of Edith
     Wharton," *Style* 17.2 (1983): 270–289.

11   For criticism that acknowledges and adds nuance to the affiliation of irony
     and free indirect discourse in Austen, see Casey Finch and Peter Bowen,
     "'The Tittle-Tattle of Highbury': Gossip and the Free Indirect Style in *Emma*,"
     Representations 31 (1990): 1–18; Frances Ferguson, "Jane Austen, *Emma*, and the
     Impact of Form," *Modern Language Quarterly* 61.1 (2000): 157–180; and
     D. A. Miller, *Jane Austen, or The Secret of Style* (Princeton, NJ: Princeton
     University Press, 2003).

12   John W. Crowley, "Revaluation: *The Age of Innocence* and the Electronic
     Revolution," *The Sewanee Review* 121.3 (2013): 428.

13 Margaret Jay Jessee, "Trying It On: Narration and Masking in Edith Wharton's *The Age of Innocence*," *Journal of Modern Literature* 36.1 (2012): 40.

14 D. Quentin Miller, "'A Barrier of Words': The Tension between Narrative and Vision in the Writings of Edith Wharton," *American Literary Realism, 1870–1910* 27.1 (1994): 20. Lee also claims, more generally, that Wharton "often uses an observant, dispassionate man as her narrator" (Lee, *Edith Wharton*, 186).

15 Edith Wharton, *The Age of Innocence* (New York: Norton, 2003 [1920]), 3. Further references to this text are cited parenthetically.

16 Dorrit Cohn, *Transparent Minds: Narrative Modes for Presenting Consciousness in Fiction* (Princeton, NJ: Princeton University Press, 1978), 5–6.

17 Ibid., 58.

18 Lee Clark Mitchell, "Enamored with an Embodied Style in Edith Wharton's *The Age of Innocence*," *Literary Imagination* 20.2 (2018): 205.

19 In her essay on Melville's *Benito Cereno*, Peggy Kamuf raises these questions with regard to the racialized images, which may be attributed either to the narrator or to Amasa Delano: "Who is speaking? Who is offering up these unreliable tropes and eliciting trust in their sure value?" Peggy Kamuf, *The Division of Literature, or, The University in Deconstruction* (Chicago, IL: University of Chicago Press, 1997), 193. See also, on the slipperiness of the narrative text, D. A. Miller's exquisite reading of Emma, in which he notices that one sentence—"Emma could not forgive her"—appears at the end of one chapter in free indirect discourse (as part of Emma's thinking) and at the start of the next in standard narrative prose (declaring a state of events). Miller, *Jane Austen*, 64–65.

20 Wharton, *Writing of Fiction*, 85.

21 I refer to "mind" without a definite article to underscore that it does not have existence as a known concrete object—to distinguish mind, that is, from less abstract nouns such as the Academy of Music.

22 W. E. B. Du Bois, "From the Souls of Black Folk," in *The Norton Anthology of American Literature*, 7th ed. vol. C, ed. Nina Baym (New York: Norton, 2007), 896.

23 Henri Ellenberger, *The Discovery of the Unconscious* (New York: Basic, 1970), 53 and Alan Gauld, *A History of Hypnotism* (Cambridge: Cambridge University Press, 1995), 297.

24 Alfred Binet, *On Double Consciousness: Experimental Psychological Studies* (Chicago, IL: Open Court Publishing Co., 1905), 10–11.

25 Boris Sidis and Simon P. Goodhart, *Multiple Personality: An Experimental Investigation into the Nature of Human Individuality* (New York: D. Appleton, 1905), 3, 52.

26 Because, as I explain in note 35, the alternate-consciousness paradigm would
be nearly eclipsed by the far more familiar psychoanalysis, readers may be
curious as to how researchers omitted an overarching "self"-consciousness.
Crabtree summarizes Pierre Janet's philosophy, which Freud directly countered:
"Janet believed that a person can have a number of centers of consciousness
operating subconsciously. He had no problem accepting the notion of multiple
streams of conscious mental activity operating simultaneously. He described
these separately functioning streams as one might describe independent minds
of different people" (Crabtree, *From Mesmer to Freud*, 358; see also 359).
Although Janet would not have done so, one might apply this view to ordinary
life by acknowledging both the waking and the dream consciousness without
considering either primary.

27 The ability of the secondary consciousness to know of the first is nicely illustrated
by Morton Prince in his 1906 *The Dissociation of a Personality*. The secondary
consciousness, who is eventually named Sally, not only knows of the first one's
past, but naughtily does things, like smoking cigarettes, that will irritate it.
Morton Prince, *The Dissociation of a Personality* (New York: Longmans, 1906),
40, 96. Although it has been argued that cases of multiple personality, chronicled
in Prince's book and Sidis's, mark a break with the alternate-consciousness
paradigm (see Ian Hacking, *Rewriting the Soul: Multiple Personality and the
Sciences of Memory* [Princeton, NJ: Princeton University Press, 1998]), the
behavior of the secondary consciousness in relation to the first in this instance
is broadly representative. On American literature's failure to conform to the
supposed break, see my "A New Chapter in the Story of Trauma: Narratives of
Bodily Healing from 1860s America," *American Literature* 91.4 (2019).

28 Wharton would have been satisfied to be held apart from Joyce and Woolf, as
she famously detested stream-of-consciousness writing; she associated it with
realism's unwillingness to select only the key narrative details. Yet she never
rejected the effort to represent consciousness wholesale. See also Klimasmith's
essay, which points out that, although the "genre, style, setting, and author [of
The Age of Innocence] have disqualified it from consideration as a modernist text,"
Wharton engages Bergson's ideas of memory and Einstein's of time. Klimasmith
thus finds in the novel "a version of modern consciousness in which behavior
and emotion, public and private time, tradition and inspiration all coexist."
Klimasmith, "Salvaging History," 557.

29 Dorrit Cohn, "Narrated Monologue: Definition of a Fictional Style," *Comparative
Literature* 18.2 (1966): 102.

30 Ibid., 108.

31 Although I have used the term free indirect discourse throughout this essay
    to conform to critical discourse, the psychological implications of Wharton's
    narration are more congruent with the German account of such narration:
    erlebte Rede. Erlebte Rede, or "experienced discourse," refers to the writer's (and
    ultimately the reader's) ability to imaginatively enter the consciousness of the
    character. While neither *erlebte Rede* nor *style indirect libre* is native to English,
    and while Cohn and Banfield circulated both in the 1960s and 1970s, the latter
    linguistic term became dominant in American criticism. Yet it may be worth
    reviving the qualitative difference between the two, in order to understand just
    how consciousness is implied in third-person narrative writing.

32 It would be a stretch to include, however, the early sentences that ironize
    Newland's lack of self-awareness. I also have one caveat, which occurs in a
    discussion between Newland and May with terms different from the one
    examined below. Having the opportunity to meet Ellen in New York, Newland
    lies about no longer needing to go to Washington: "Their glances met for a
    second, and perhaps let them into each other's meanings more deeply than
    either cared to go" (170). The pluralizing of the subject—so that both learn
    something about the other's mind—is anomalous. Yet the "perhaps" makes what
    is experienced impossible to certify. Further, the fact that the novel is in the
    past tense makes it possible to read this line as, still, Newland's later reflection
    on the conversation—on what she must have been thinking. Such moments,
    where Newland's future knowledge becomes evident in the past-tense narration
    of his thinking, are very common in Henry James's late novels but not part of
    Wharton's style. See Ruth Bernard Yeazell, "Remembrance of Things Present
    in *The Ambassadors*," *The Henry James Review* 38.3 (2017): 231–237. Indeed,
    she repeatedly has Newland notice May's "transparent eyes" (94, 194), even
    though he will later learn them to have been hiding—or himself to have been
    misreading—quite a bit.

33 May's story is not thereby limited to what the "waking" Newland consciously
    guesses about her. For a well-developed account of how May's and Ellen's stories
    are legible within the confines of the novel's narration, see Kathy Miller Hadley,
    "Ironic Structure and Untold Stories in *The Age of Innocence*," *Studies in the Novel*
    23.2 (Summer 1991): 262–272.

34 In *The Uncanny*, Nicholas Royle makes the welcome point that the premise of
    omniscient narration is tied to notions of religion, not fiction. But his suggestion
    that omniscience be exchanged for concepts of telepathy or clairvoyance does

not go far enough, in my view, in undoing the anthropomorphizing of narrative voice. Nicholas Royle, *The Uncanny: An Introduction* (Manchester: Manchester University Press, 2002).

35   For literary scholars more familiar with psychoanalysis than its precursors, the idea that two consciousnesses run through the entire novel, and that one never subsumes the other, will likely seem odd—as will the very pluralization of consciousness. As Crabtree explains, Freud's major departure from the alternate-consciousness paradigm was to argue that consciousness is unique and unitary: "each person can have but one" (Crabtree, *From Mesmer to Freud*, 358). Thus, rather than admit, as the researchers I have cited here did, two (and later more) consciousnesses, Freud insisted on one consciousness and relegated all other mental activity to unconsciousness (Crabtree, *From Mesmer to Freud*, 358–359). The gesture was decisive in substituting for multiple consciousnesses, each with its own tendency, a binary (and in turn hierarchical) relation of consciousness and unconsciousness. In identifying Wharton's narration with the earlier paradigm, I am responding to the dualism of the "waking" Newland and the third-person account of his perceptions, their difference in kind and tendency and style. Each reads to me as a version of Newland, a way of "doing" him, rather than a derivative section of his mental landscape. I am also making a case, which is in part but not exclusively a historicist one, for recognizing pre-Freudian models of consciousness and critically employing them, without apologetic anticipation of their eventual lack of influence.

Chapter 6

1   Margaret Jay Jessee, "Trying It On: Narration and Masking in Edith Wharton's *The Age of Innocence*," *Journal of Modern Literature* 36.1 (2012): 37.

2   Edith Wharton, *The Age of Innocence: Norton Critical Edition*, ed. Candace Waid (New York: W.W. Norton & Co., 2003), 9. Subsequent page references to this edition appear parenthetically in the text.

3   Ben Highmore, "Bitter After Taste: Affect, Food, and Social Aesthetics," in *The Affect Theory Reader*, ed. Melissa Gregg and Gregory J. Seigworth (Durham, NC: Duke University Press, 2010), 118.

4   Melanie V. Dawson, *Emotional Reinventions: Realist-Era Representations Beyond Sympathy* (Ann Arbor, MI: University of Michigan Press, 2015), 12.

5   Ibid., 27.

6   William James, "What Is an Emotion?," *Collected Essays and Reviews* by William James (New York: Longmans, Green, & Co., 1920), 190.

7   Ibid., 190, emphasis in original.

8   Alan Bourassa, *Deleuze and American Literature: Affect and Virtuality in Faulkner, Wharton, Ellison, and McCarthy* (New York: Palgrave Macmillan, 2007), 42.

9   Ibid., 42–43.

10 Ibid., 43.

11 James, "What Is an Emotion?,"193.

12 Jane F. Thrailkill, *Affecting Fictions: Mind, Body, and Emotion in American Literary Realism* (Cambridge, MA: Harvard University Press, 2007), 16.

13 Dawson, *Emotional Reinventions*, 32.

14 Ibid.

15 Elizabeth Ammons, "Cool Diana and the Blood-Red Muse," in *American Novelists Revisited: Essays in Feminist Criticism*, ed. Fritz Fleischmann (Boston, MA: Hall, 1982), 209. Reprinted in Wharton, *Age of Innocence*, 433–447 (438).

16 Jessee, "Trying It On," 43.

17 William E. Cain, "Edith Wharton and the Second Story," *New England Review*: *Middlebury Series* 29.2 (2008): 96.

18 Dawson, *Emotional Reinventions*, 10.

19 Ibid., 248.

20 Ibid., 247–248

21 Lee Clark Mitchell, "Enamored with an Embodied Style in Edith Wharton's *The Age of Innocence*," *Literary Imagination* 20.2 (2018): 201–214 (207).

22 Cain, "Edith Wharton," 103.

23 Nir Evron, "Realism, Irony and Morality in Edith Wharton's *The Age of Innocence*," *Journal of Modern Literature* 35.2 (2012): 37–51 (39).

24 Dawson, *Emotional Reinventions*, 114.

25 Ibid., 114.

26 Ibid., 115, emphasis in original.

27 Ibid., 116, emphasis mine.

28 Ibid., 130.

29 Medora is described as an outsider because she was foolish enough to marry despite the "insanity recurring in every second generation of the Albany Chiverses, with whom their New York cousins had always refused to intermarry—with the disastrous exception of poor Medora Manson, who, as everybody knew … but then her mother was a Rushworth" (7).

30   Vernon L. Parrington, Jr., "Our Literary Aristocrat," *Pacific Review*, June 1, 1921, reprinted in Wharton, *Age of Innocence*, 393; and Carl Van Doren, "An Elder America," *Nation*, November 3, 1920, reprinted in Wharton, *Age of Innocence*, 386.

31   Mitchell, "Enamored with an Embodied Style," 213–214, emphasis in original.

Chapter 7

1   Edith Wharton, "Expiation," in *The Muse's Tragedy and Other Stories*, ed. Candace Waid (New York: Signet Classic, 1990), 198.

2   Edith Wharton, *The Letters of Edith Wharton*, ed. R. W. B. Lewis (New York: Collier Books, 1988), 445.

3   Edith Wharton, *Fast and Loose*, ed. Viola Hopkins Winner (Charlottesville, VA: University of Virginia Press, 1977), 118.

4   Wharton, "Expiation," 208.

5   Wharton, *Letters*, 445.

6   Edith Wharton, *A Backward Glance* (New York: Scribner's, 1985), 1. The quote remains untranslated in Wharton's text. In English it means: "I have seen 'good' society; it is called 'good' when it does not give opportunity for even the smallest little poem" (translation mine).

7   Ibid., 23.

8   Ibid., 24–25.

9   Ibid., 35–36.

10   The manuscript version reads: "My unusual immobility attracted attention, + when asked what I was doing with the book, I replied quietly that I was reading it. This was received with incredulity; when challenged (crossed out and replaced with 'when called upon') to read ('I apparently' crossed out) a few lines aloud I appear to have met the challenge, + it was then discovered that the work over which I was poring was a play by Ludovic Halévy (inserted 'Fanny Lear'), the heroine of which was a lady of easy virtue." Edith Wharton Papers, box 2, folder 26 (New Haven, CT: Beinecke Library, Yale University), 19.

11   Henry Meilhac's and Ludovic Halévy's comedy *Fanny Lear* opened in Paris in the theater of Gymnase on August 13, 1868, and then was produced again in Paris in two additional theaters opening on April 24, 1875, and February 14, 1889. Henry Meilhac and Ludovic Halévy, *Fanny Lear* (Paris: Calman Lévy, 1889), unpaginated opening page. Andrew de Tenant places the play in a wave of mid-nineteenth-

century French plays about courtesans. He describes the plot of *Fanny Lear* as follows: "the heroine … is an Englishwoman of loose morals who has a strong desire to become a lady of title and enter Parisian society. She obtains the title with her ill-gotten earnings, but is furious when she discovers that the old noble husband she has paid for so dearly is nearly insane. Fanny Lear finds that it is impossible to force open the doors of Parisian drawing-rooms by entering on the arms of a half-mad husband, and conceives the idea of marrying the nobleman's daughter to a dissipated fellow who will consent to live under the same roof as herself. The woman's little plans, however, are ultimately foiled." Andrew de Tenant, "The Courtesan on the French Stage," *The Westminster Review* 154.6 (July–December 1900): 671–684 (676). The Philadelphia-born Harrie Blackford assumed the name Fanny Lear and published her own account of her affair with the Grand Duke under the title "Le Roman d'une Americaine en Russie" in 1875. In it, she defends her own love story with the Grand Duke; the editors of the first English edition, Eva and Daniel McDonald, note that the book "was an instant best seller until the French police acting on a request by the Russian Government succeeded in confiscating as many copies of the book in Paris bookshops that they were able to find." Eva and Daniel McDonald, eds., *Fanny Lear: Love and Scandal in Tsarist Russia* (Bloomington, IN: iUniverse, 2011), xi. In their 1951 historical novel, *The Scandalous Mrs. Blackford*, authors Harnett T. Kane and Victor Leclerc write: "Perhaps no American woman of her day or ours had a career such as Mrs. Blackford; yet few people have heard of her. She is a remarkable, almost forgotten figure in the untold history of the last century." Harnett T. Kane and Victor Leclerc, *The Scandalous Mrs. Blackford* (New York: Julian Messner, 1951), vi. The examples of the real Hattie Blackford and the fictional Fanny Lear are telling since Wharton is able to write scandal in, for example, the case of Charity Royall in *Summer*. This essay is about Wharton's struggle to highlight and foreground a scandalous woman of high-bourgeois society of her old New York. We see such women in the background in her two old New York novels, *The House of Mirth* and *The Age of Innocence*; but, in the former her heroine remains a virgin suicide, while in the latter Wharton refrains from making Ellen the mistress and lover she envisioned in her initial plot synopses of her novel.

12 Appleton advertisement in *Publishers' Weekly*, quoted in Edith Wharton, *The Age of Innocence: Norton Critical Edition*, ed. Candace Waid (New York: W.W. Norton & Co., 2003), 378.

13 Even Wharton's last synopsis still bears the title "Old New York." She ultimately corrects that title on the second outline, adding the new title "in ink at some

later date." Jennifer Rae Greeson, "Wharton's Manuscript Outlines for *The Age of Innocence*: Three Versions," in Wharton, *Age of Innocence*, 415.

14   Ibid., 414.

15   Ibid., 415.

16   Ibid., 415.

17   Wharton once equated marriage with suicide in her diaries. In 1913 she composed the following exchange: "'Did you know that John + Susy committed suicide together on Tuesday?' 'What? No.—How?' 'They got married.'" Edith Wharton, "Diaries (1905–1934)," Edith Wharton Collection, box 51, folder 1521–1523 (New Haven, CT: Beinecke Library, Yale University), quoted in Hildegard Hoeller, *Edith Wharton's Dialogue with Realism and Sentimental Fiction* (Gainesville, FL: University Press of Florida, 2000), 140. Kathy Miller Hadley notes via Virginia Blum that Archer and May's wedding is "cast in funereal language," and concludes: "With this imagery, Wharton juxtaposes the two traditional nineteenth-century novel endings: marriage and death become one." Kathy Miller Hadley, "Ironic Structure and Untold Stories in *The Age of Innocence*," *Studies in the Novel* 23.2 (Summer 1991): 262–272 (267). During the composition of *The Age of Innocence*, Wharton initially confused wedding and funeral ceremonies. She writes to Rutger Jewett on November 13, 1920: "Words fail me when I think of this confusion in wedding and funeral ceremonials … I suppose, however, I was so appalled with the fate of May Welland and Newland Archer when they started for the church altar that I would have accepted sections of the temple ceremonial from Aida." Quoted in Michael Nowlin, "Appendix B: Wharton's Correspondence About *The Age of Innocence*," in Edith Wharton, *The Age of Innocence*, ed. Michael Nowlin (Peterborough, ON: Broadview Press, 2002), 350.

18   Greeson, "Wharton's Manuscript Outlines," 416.

19   Ibid., 418.

20   Ibid., 416–417.

21   Alan Price, "The Composition of Edith Wharton's *The Age of Innocence*," *The Yale University Library Gazette* 55.1 (July 1980): 22–30 (24–25).

22   Joseph Candido, "Edith Wharton's Final Alterations of *The Age of Innocence*," *Studies in American Fiction* 6.1 (Spring 1978): 21–31 (31).

23   Ibid., 24.

24   Quoted in Nowlin, "Appendix B," 351.

25   Hermione Lee, *Edith Wharton* (New York: Alfred Knopf, 2007), 575. Lee does call *Old New York* a "companion volume" (566).

26 Ibid., 600.

27 My research found no critical readings of the connections between *The Age of Innocence* and *Old New York*. Wharton left many other traces of the connection between the texts. We are recognizably in the same world as in *The Age of Innocence*, with the same characters reappearing, such as Mrs. Lovell, the Mingotts, the Beauforts, Fanny Ring, the van der Luydens, Jackson Sillerton, Mrs. Struthers, the Lannings, and the Dagonets.

28 Wharton left fragments of eloquent writing about sexual encounters. Her "Life Apart" is a diary about her affair with her lover Morton Fullerton. The "Beatrice Palmato Fragment," which she left with "Life Apart," is a sexually explicit description of an incest scene between father and daughter. Lee dates the composition of the fragment close to *The Age of Innocence* and *Old New York* (Lee, *Edith Wharton*, 586). She also notes that Wharton, at the time, was "extremely preoccupied … with how to write about the truths of female sexuality, the cruelty that is marriage, and taboo subjects like incest, homosexuality, prostitution, adultery, the horrors of repression, and the baleful effect of silencing" (Lee, *Edith Wharton*, 590). She also comments on the irony of *The Age of Innocence* at the same time being awarded the Pulitzer Prize and its emphasis on wholesomeness (Lee, *Edith Wharton*, 590).

29 Quoted in Siegfried Weing, *The German Novella: Two Centuries of Criticism* (Columbia, SC: Camden House, 1994), 24. For a fuller discussion of Wharton's reading of Goethe and her use of his definition of the novella in *Old New York*, see Hildegard Hoeller, "Invisible Blackness in Edith Wharton's *Old New York*," *African American Review* 44.1–2 (Spring/Summer 2011): 49–66, esp. note 30 on 64–65.

30 Wharton, *Age of Innocence*, 6, 214.

31 R. W. B. Lewis, *Edith Wharton: A Biography* (New York: Harper & Row, 1975), 435, 436. Previously, I further argued that Wharton writes more "vigorously"—to use the *Ladies Home Journal*'s phrase—about the tribalism and consolidation of old New York. Whereas in *The Age of Innocence* we see a society that culturally draws its lines and defends its tribe, in "The Old Maid" Wharton describes the consolidation of old New York in physical, racial terms. The Ralstons are engaged in a kind of eugenic engineering campaign to consolidate their race and whiteness, but the novella ultimately describes their extinction. See Hoeller "Invisible Blackness."

32 Kathy Miller Hadley, in her article "Ironic Structure and Untold Stories," argues that Wharton consistently gives us hints at the two women's own stories, even while hiding them behind Archer's perspective. "Wharton undermines her own form

throughout the novel, writing beyond the story about Newland Archer to convey a sense of the women characters that her attention to her audience and to acceptable forms removed from center stage." Hadley, "Ironic Structure and Untold Stories," 264.

33 Wharton, *Age of Innocence*, 188–189.

34 Ibid., 195.

35 Ibid., 205.

36 Edith Wharton, *Old New York* (New York: Scribner's, 1924), 83. For further references to silencing in "The Old Maid," see Wharton, *Old New York*, 83, 84, 88, 94–95, 101, 102, 136, 145.

37 Wharton, *Age of Innocence*, 12.

38 Wharton, *Old New York*, 132.

39 Wharton, *Age of Innocence*, 148. For example, Wharton writes in her "Love Diary," which she composed about her affair with Morton Fullerton: "of, my adored, my own Love, you who have given me the only moments of real life I have ever known." Quoted in Kenneth M. Price and Phyllis McBride, "'The Life Apart': Texts and Contexts of Edith Wharton's Love Diary," *American Literature* 66.4 (December 1994): 663–688 (683).

40 Wharton, *Old New York*, 135–136.

41 Ibid., 170.

42 Wharton, *Age of Innocence*, 189.

43 Wharton, *Old New York*, 174. Also: "Yes: it was true that the sweetness and peace of Tina's bridal eve had been filled, for Delia, with visions of her own unrealized past … All these last days she had been living the girl's life, she had been Tina, and Tina had been her own girlish self, the far-off Delia." Wharton, *Old New York*, 177.

44 Ibid., 175.

45 Ibid., 187.

46 Ibid., 180.

47 Ibid., 129.

48 Wharton, *Age of Innocence*, 5.

49 Ibid., 11. This language also mirrors the language of the Appleton advertisement for the novel.

50 Ibid., 12.

51 Wharton, *Old New York*, 237.

52 Ari Arut, "A Theory of Scandal: Victorians, Homosexuality, and the Fall of Oscar Wilde," *American Journal of Sociology* 111.1 (July 2005): 213–248 (219).

53 Ibid., 222.

54 Ibid., 222.

55 Wharton, *Old New York*, 244.

56 Ibid., 248.

57 Wharton, *Age of Innocence*, 51.

58 Wharton, *Old New York*, 252.

59 Wharton, *Age of Innocence*, 101.

60 Wharton, *Old New York*, 251.

61 Wharton, *Age of Innocence*, 45.

62 Ibid., 174.

63 Ibid., 200.

64 Wharton, *Old New York*, 292–293. Lee writes about Wharton's difficulty of placing her "prostitution story" in a market that is looking for the "clean, wholesome, and happy" (Lee, *Edith Wharton*, 596).

65 Wharton, *Old New York*, 304.

66 Ibid., 305.

67 Ibid., 302–303.

68 Wharton, *Letters*, 464.

69 Max Gluckman, "Papers in Honor of Melville J. Herskovits: Gossip and Scandal," *Current Anthropology* 4.3 (June 1963): 307–316 (311).

70 For a discussion of these autobiographical ties, as well as Wharton's fears about her own racial identity and lineage, see Hoeller, "Invisible Blackness," 57–58.

71 Lee, *Edith Wharton*, 60. Harry, like Mr. Hazeldean, suffered from tuberculosis. And Mrs. Stevens, once widowed, "entertained Oscar Wilde on his visit to New York in 1882" (Lee, *Edith Wharton*, 60).

72 Gluckman, "Papers in Honor," 313.

73 It is noteworthy that Wharton's final, incomplete novel *The Buccaneers* once again envisions a scandal in upper-class society. Re-imagining her early thwarted lovers from her juvenile novella *Fast and Loose*, the synopsis of *The Buccaneers* has two lovers elope, "the scandal of which is to ring through England for years." Yet, just as she refrained from using the more scandalous versions of *The Age of Innocence*, Wharton could not complete the scandalous part of that text. Hoeller, *Edith Wharton's Dialogue*, 197–200.

Chapter 8

1 Edith Wharton, *The Age of Innocence* (New York: D. Appleton & Co., 1920), 42. All subsequent page numbers from the novel will be cited parenthetically and refer to this edition.

Critical Bibliography

Ammons, Elizabeth. "The War." In *Edith Wharton's Argument with America*, 125–126. Athens, GA: University of Georgia Press, 1980.

Asya, Ferda. "Resolutions of Guilt: Cultural Values Reconsidered in *The Custom of the Country* and *The Age of Innocence*." *Edith Wharton Review* 14.2 (1997): 15–20.

Bauer, Dale M. *Edith Wharton's Brave New Politics*. Madison, WI: University of Wisconsin Press, 1995.

Beer, Janet, and Avril Horner. "'The Great Panorama': Edith Wharton as Historical Novelist." *Modern Language Review* 110.1 (January 2015): 69–84.

Bentley, Nancy. *The Ethnography of Manners: Hawthorne, James, and Wharton*. Cambridge: Cambridge University Press, 2007.

Cain, William E. "Edith Wharton and the Second Story." *New England Review* 29.2 (2008): 95–106.

Chow, Sung Gay. "Pollution Control in Old New York: Edith Wharton's 'The Age of Innocence.'" *CEA Critic* 60.3 (1998): 37–49.

Cordasco, Rachel. "Listening to the Narrative Voice in 'The Pit' and 'The Age of Innocence.'" *Studies in American Naturalism* 3.1 (2008): 60–78.

Crowley, John W. "Revaluation: *The Age of Innocence* and the Electronic Revolution." *The Sewanee Review* 121.3 (2013): 427–432.

Daigrepont, Lloyd M. "The Cult of Passion in *The Age of Innocence*." *American Literary Realism* 40.1 (2007): 1–15.

Dawson, Melanie V. *Emotional Reinventions: Realist-Era Representations Beyond Sympathy*. Ann Arbor, MI: University of Michigan Press, 2015.

DiGianvittorio, Lindsay, and Judith P. Saunders. "Janey Archer's Myopia and 'The Age of Innocence.'" *Edith Wharton Review* 21.1 (2005): 15–18.

Dudley, John. "'Beauty Unmans Me': Diminished Manhood and the Leisure Class in Norris and Wharton." In *A Man's Game: Masculinity and the Anti-Aesthetics of American Literary Naturalism* 87–137. Tuscaloosa, AL: University of Alabama Press, 2016.

Evron, Nir. "Realism, Irony and Morality in Edith Wharton's *The Age of Innocence*." *Journal of Modern Literature* 35.2 (2012): 37–51.

Falk, Cynthia G. "'The Intolerable Ugliness of New York': Architecture and Society in Edith Wharton's *The Age of Innocence*." *American Studies* 42.2 (2001): 19–43.

Fracasso, Evelyn E. "The Transparent Eyes of May Welland in Wharton's *The Age of Innocence*." *Modern Language Studies* 21.4 (1991): 43–48.

Fryer, Judith. "Purity and Power in *The Age of Innocence*." *American Literary Realism 1870–1910* 17.2 (1984): 153–168.

Gargano, James W. "Tableaux of Renunciation: Wharton's Use of *The Shaughran* in *The Age of Innocence*." *Studies in American Fiction* 15.1 (1987): 1–11.

Geriguis, Lina L. "Beyond Domestic Grounds: Edith Wharton's Shakespearean Glance in *The Age of Innocence*." *Pacific Coast Philology* 45 (2010): 71–91.

Hadley, Kathy Miller. "Ironic Structure and Untold Stories in *The Age of Innocence*." *Studies in the Novel* 23.2 (Summer 1991): 262–272.

Haytock, Jennifer. *Edith Wharton and the Conversations of Literary Modernism*. New York: Palgrave Macmillan, 2008.

Horne, Philip. "The Age of Innocence: Scorsese, Wharton and James." *Film Studies: An International Review* 3 (2002): 5–17.

Jessee, Margaret Jay. "Trying It On: Narration and Masking in Edith Wharton's *The Age of Innocence*." *Journal of Modern Literature* 36.1 (2012): 37–52.

Killoran, Helen. *Edith Wharton: Art and Allusion*. Tuscaloosa, AL: University of Alabama Press, 1996.

Killoran, Helen. *The Critical Reception of Edith Wharton*. Rochester, NY: Camden House, 2001.

Klimasmith, Betsy. "Salvaging History: Modern Philosophies of Memory and Time in *The Age of Innocence*." *American Literature* 80.3 (2008): 555–581.

Knights, Pamela. "Forms of Disembodiment: The Social Subject in *The Age of Innocence*." In *The Cambridge Companion to Edith Wharton*, edited by Millicent Bell, 20–46. New York: Cambridge University Press, 1995.

Kottaras, Ekaterini. "Metaphors of Deception: Incomplete Speech Acts in Edith Wharton's 'The Age of Innocence.'" *Edith Wharton Review* 26.1 (2010): 10–17.

Kozloff, Sarah. "Complicity in *The Age of Innocence*." *Style* 35.2 (2001): 270–288.

Kress, Jill M. *The Figure of Consciousness: William James, Henry James, and Edith Wharton*. New York: Routledge, 2002.

Lee, A. Robert. "Watching Manners: Martin Scorsese's *The Age of Innocence*, Edith Wharton's *The Age of Innocence*." In *The Classic Novel: From Page to Screen*, edited by Robert Giddings and Erica Sheen 163–178. Manchester and New York: Manchester University Press/St. Martin's, 2000.

Lindberg, Gary. *Edith Wharton and the Novel of Manners*. Charlottesville, VA: University Press of Virginia, 1975.

MacMaster, Anne. "Wharton, Race, and *The Age of Innocence*: Three Historical Contexts." In *A Forward Glance: New Essays on Edith Wharton*, edited by Clare

Colquitt, Susan Goodman, and Candace Waid, 172–187. Newark, DE: University of Delaware Press, 1999.

Mitchell, Lee Clark. "Enamored with an Embodied Style in Edith Wharton's *The Age of Innocence*." *Literary Imagination* 20.2 (2018): 201–214.

Morgan, Gwendolyn. "The Unsung Heroine—A Study of May Welland in *The Age of Innocence*." In *Heroines of Popular Culture*, edited by Pat Browne and Ray B. Browne, 32–40. Bowling Green, OH: Bowling Green State University Popular Press, 1987.

Murphy, John J. "Filters, Portraits, and History's Mixed Bag: A Lost Lady and *The Age of Innocence*." *Twentieth Century Literature* 38.4 (1992): 476–485.

Nicholls, Mark. "Male Melancholia and Martin Scorsese's *The Age of Innocence*." *Film Quarterly* 58.1 (2004): 25–35.

Nowlin, Michael. "Edith Wharton's Higher Provincialism: French Ways for Americans and the Ends of *The Age of Innocence*." *Journal of American Studies* 38.1 (2004): 89–108.

Orlando, Emily J. "Rereading Wharton's 'Poor Archer': A Mr. 'Might-have-been' in 'The Age of Innocence.'" *American Literary Realism 1870–1910* 30.2 (1998): 56–76.

Orlando, Emily J. "'We'll Look, Not at Visions, But at Realities': Women, Art, and Representation in *The Age of Innocence*." In *Edith Wharton and the Visual Arts*, 170–200. Tuscaloosa, AL: University of Alabama Press, 2007.

Peucker, Brigitte. "Rival Arts? Filming *The Age of Innocence*." *Edith Wharton Review* 13.1 (1996): 19–22.

Pizer, Donald. "American Naturalism in its 'Perfected' State: *The Age of Innocence* and an American Tragedy." In *The Theory and Practice of American Literary Naturalism: Selected Essays and Reviews*, 153–166. Carbondale, IL: Southern Illinois University Press, 1993.

Price, Alan. "The Composition of Edith Wharton's *The Age of Innocence*." *Yale University Library Gazette* 55.1 (July 1980): 22–30.

Ridge, Emily. "Workmanship and Wildness: Katherine Mansfield on Edith Wharton's *The Age of Innocence*." In *Katherine Mansfield Studies*, vol. 5. Edited by Janet Wilson, Gerri Kimber, and Delia da Sousa Correa 87–101. Edinburgh: Edinburgh University Press, 2013.

Sakane, Takahiro. "'A Turmoil of Contradictory Feelings': Money, Women, and Body in Edith Wharton's *The Age of Innocence*." *Textual Practice* 29.1 (2015): 71–89.

Saunders, Judith P. "Portrait of the Artist as Anthropologist: Edith Wharton and *The Age of Innocence*." *Interdisciplinary Literary Studies: A Journal of Criticism and Theory* 4.1 (2002): 86–101.

Saunders, Judith P. "Wharton's Borrowing from Crane's Maggie in *The Age of Innocence*." *Edith Wharton Review* 19.1 (2003): 1, 4–8.

Singley, Carol J. *A Historical Guide to Edith Wharton*. New York and Oxford: Oxford University Press, 2003.

Singley, Carol J. "Bourdieu, Wharton and Changing Culture in *The Age of Innocence*." *Cultural Studies* 17.3–4 (2003): 495–519.

Singley, Carol J. "Claire McMillan and Francesca Segal Pay Tribute to Edith Wharton's *The House of Mirth* and *The Age of Innocence*." *Edith Wharton Review* 30.1 (2014): 61–75.

Skaggs, Carmen Trammell. "Looking Through the Opera Glasses: Performance and Artifice in *The Age of Innocence*." *Mosaic: A Journal for the Interdisciplinary Study of Literature* 37.1 (2004): 49–61.

Thomas, J. D. "Tribal Culture, Pantomime, and the Communicative Face in Edith Wharton's *The Age of Innocence*." *Edith Wharton Review* 22.1 (2006): 1–5.

Wahl, Jenny. "Edith Wharton as Economist: An Economic Interpretation of *The House of Mirth* and *The Age of Innocence*." *Edith Wharton Review* 25.1 (2009): 9–15.

Wharton, Edith. *The Age of Innocence: Authoritative Text, Background and Contexts, Sources, Criticism: Norton Critical Edition*, ed. Candace Waid. New York: W.W. Norton, 2003.

Witherow, Jean. "A Dialectic of Deception: Edith Wharton's 'The Age of Innocence.'" *Mosaic: An Interdisciplinary Critical Journal* 36.3 (2003): 165–180.

Wood, Bethany. "Adapting Traditions: Laucane Surrounding the 1934 Film Adaptation of Edith Wharton's *The Age of Innocence*." *Edith Wharton Review* 34.2 (2018): 101–123.

Index